Digital Rights Management

Digital Rights Management

An Introduction

Edited by
D Satish

2010

Icfai Books
The Icfai University Press

DIGITAL RIGHTS MANAGEMENT: AN INTRODUCTION

Editor: D Satish

First Edition: 2010
Printed in India

Published by

The Icfai University Press
52, Nagarjuna Hills, Punjagutta
Hyderabad, India – 500 082
Phone: (+91) (040) 23430–368, 369, 370, 372, 373, 374
Fax: (+91) (040) 23352521, 23435386
E-mail: info@icfaibooks.com, icfaibooks@icfai.org, ssd@icfai.org

ISBN: 9788131407929

Editorial Team: G Vijay and S Madhavan
Quality Support: R Kalyani and B Yagandhar

Contents

Section II

Approaches

Overview

In this internet age one can access most of the information kept in the digital space easily and in most of the cases without paying for it. This has put in doubt the business models which generate revenue out of putting their content online. As most of the content can easily be viewed, copied and distributed by anyone who actually does not have the right to do so, it is increasingly becoming difficult to generate any revenues out of their works. But, thanks to the Digital Rights Management techniques, the owners of such high value content can now look forward to making money out of their hard work.

Digital Rights Management (DRM) is a technology that restricts usage and access to the content to one and all and gives that right to the individual or organization that has been authorized to do so by the owner of the content. In effect, this gives the owner of the content the ability to secure and distribute the content only to the people for whom it is meant.

There have been many battles in the past between the owners and the content and the people who use the media and other means to distribute their content. Some of the popular skirmishes were between the music companies and the radio broadcasting companies and between the film producers and the manufacturers of Video Cassette Recorders. Now the battle is in the digital space – between the content owners and the new and emerging technologies like Digital Video Recorders and file sharing software and networks. The term DRM was coined when IBM and Electronic Publishing Resources launched their first commercial DRM products. The DRM efforts hit the public eye after a researcher Mark Stefik published his paper titled "Letting Loose the Light: Igniting Commerce in Electronic Publication", in which he strongly argued that it should always be possible to define and control who can do what with content, especially, with regard to the devices on which they can be viewed and when they can be viewed and for what price they can be viewed. Building on this premise is a considerable research on DRM solutions. The DRM movement further received a boost by the Highlights of Digital Millennium Copyrights Act, 1998, which makes it a crime to circumvent anti-piracy measures built into most commercial software and also outlaws the manufacture, sale, or distribution of code-cracking devices used to illegally copy software.

There are various forms of DRM solutions. DIVX is a rental form of DVD, where there is a certain time within which the user can view the content for a certain fee after which the access is cut. In A Content Scrambling System (CSS), the user is restricted from copying or redistributing the content meant for him. In a Product Activation form, the user needs to have a specific serial number or code to access the content. Digital watermarking is nowadays popularly used, where the user needs to enter his unique id into the database before accessing the content. Though this technique does not restrict the access to content, it helps to locate the source from where the content has originated and the different distribution routes it has taken. There is also a hash based counter scheme, where there is a function that reads how many times the content is played by the user. But the user has to play it in a DRM system. This is one of the best ways of checking the usage of the digital content in an off-line set up, where monitoring in most cases is impossible. What is also important is that this technology assumes the storage in the user's terminal as non-hostile environment.

There are also many vendors of DRM solutions but it is very important to select the right solution which is specific to the user's requirement. Apart from enquiring about the security features, the purchaser should also ask look for convenience and simplicity of usage. The vendors licensing agreement, the usability in multi-client platforms and compatibility with the existing software and architecture should also be seen. The previous history and the popularity of the product should also be studied. For example, British Library evaluated a lot of DRM systems from various vendors before selecting a vendor who provided a tailor made system for them. Some of the criteria which the British library looked for before selecting the systems were the costs, the simplicity and the way it actually worked. The system chosen offered the following features which best suited the functioning of the British Library: restricting the use of the file to the machine on which it was downloaded, restricting the printing to one copy, saving and viewing of the article for a limited period and disabling forwarding and copying.

While DRM is important to build viable business models, there are also costs involved in it. The costs associated with it include the costs of digital archive system for preserving the content for a long time, the human and personal costs of developing software for preserving digital records and costs involved in te actual storage of digital records. The costs also go up with the scale of the operations.

The primary role of any DRM system is to take care of the stakeholders' requirements. The major stakeholders in the DRM system are the content providers, the license providers and finally the users. The content provider or the content creator requires the DRM technology to support his business model. The role of the license creator is to bind content to license. The license creator negotiates directly with the customers and he can use DRM technology to offer tailor – made access of content to the user. Finally, the user would be drawn by the DRM systems, as they offer a legitimate quality alternative to other dubious sources of content. The basic understanding of these requirements would go a long way in developing a comprehensive DRM solution.

Over the years, DRM has evolved from focusing on copy protection to a technology, which addresses much broader possibilities associated with business opportunities that are built around the general idea of DRM. Even then, the DRM vendors have experienced little success. The reasons may be wrong business models or wrong technology. But the major reason remains the absence of standards. There is a need for a minimal DRM architecture framework that would help guide the development of standards and technologies in DRM. The articles draw from the experiences of the telecom and internet industries early in 1980s, where there were many network technologies and the technology framework was developed which integrated them and also allowed different kinds of services to develop.

For effective implementation of the DRM, the designers of electronic devices like computers and cell phones that play copyrighted content, should play their role. They should not only take into consideration the views of the copyright owners but also study the user requirement and behavior, so that the requirement of both the originator and the user, is met. For this to happen, it is better for the electronic equipment manufacturer to have an interface with them before designing the product.

While DRM techniques have made some headway, there would be a lot more development which the DRM stakeholders have to prepare for. Some of the developments include increase in the virtuality of the DRM objects and distribution systems, systems for tracking and redistribution of digital documents and development of DRM systems for aggregation, protection, anatomization and modernization of personal information.

There are increased calls for DRM usage from advocates who say that the copyrights have to be respected and this is one of the ways of protecting the copyrights. They say that DRM solutions would help the content originator to develop a viable and robust business model. But there are also the opponents of technology, who feel that this would hamper the free flow of information among different users and they might be unduly exploited by the vendors and distributors. Nevertheless, DRM is evolving and it is hoped that all the stakeholders would evolve a common middle path to the satisfaction of the opponents and the advocates of DRM.

This book "**Digital Rights Management: An Introduction**" is an anthology of several articles discussing the history and evolution of DRM covering the legal and regulatory framework, which is now in existence after the coming of the Digital Millennium Copyrights Act (DMCA). The book gives valuable insights into the issues like costs, compatibility and what a customer of DRM should ask for, before buying a DRM package. It is divided into two sections – Concepts and Approaches.

Section I: Concepts

The Digital Rights Management technologies are playing a very important role in allowing conditional access to a copyrighted content, thereby, allowing the content provider to make an economic sense of putting his content online. All this is allowing him to make a viable business model built on his content. The article "**Digital Rights Management: Making Business Sense**" by *D Satish*, discusses the forms of DRM – DIVX, CSS, Product Activation, Digital Water Marking and difference between DRM and Copy Protection Measures. It also, highlights the views of DRM Advocates and Opponents.

The next article "**Contextualizing Digital Rights Management: Past, Present, and Future**" by *Dr Paul Cesarini* discusses the historical context of DRM – right from the 1930s, from the evolution of radio to VCR to present day Internet, DVD and PVR, speaks about how the assumptions behind the DRM evolved. It also highlights Digital Millennium Copyrights Act (DMCA).

The next article "**Free Software and Digital Rights Management – Bitter Enemies or Strange Bedfellows?**" by *Chris J Karr* says, DRM systems are the vertical stack of software components that guard media rights from production to consumption and hence, the DRM systems tend to be a monolithic collection of technology developed and controlled by single vendors. The article presents a hypothetical situation, where a robust free software DRM platform would exist and whether this free software DRM would provide a free software media application to participate in the constant production and distribution process. It also discusses whether free software DRM platform would break the hold of proprietary closed source DRM platform. A free DRM system would make sense, if the motive is to expand the installed base and replace the existing proprietary system.

The succeeding article "**10 Questions to ask any Vendor of Digital Rights Management/Security Software for PDF**" discusses, some of the questions one must ask the vendors of DRM before purchasing any security software.

The next article "**Costs of Digital Preservation**" talks about various costs involved in Digital Rights Management. Costs include – costs of creating a digital repository for long-term preservation of digital records, personal costs, costs of securing software. The article also talks about some other inherent costs like training, maintenance and support costs. Further, it presents a cost model which is prepared in the form of an excel sheet, which would better prepare the company for the costs to come.

The following article "**Core Security Requirements of DRM Systems**" by *H L Jonker* and *S Mauw*, says that DRM systems have many stakeholders like the content providers, the license providers and finally the users. A proper use of the system can only be made, if there is a proper security requirement, which is to be met by all the three parties. The article says that though security of DRM has received some attention, there needs to be a comprehensive look at the core security issues in the DRM. Further, the article develops a simple model after talking to the stakeholders to arrive at the core security requirement.

DRM, apart from preventing illegal piracy, also prevents the "fair use" which the legal system has time and again protected. The next article "**Human Factors in Digital Rights Management for Consumer Products**" by *Marc L Resnick*, calls on human factor practitioners involved in the designing of electronic devices that use copyrighted media, whether it is the computer music player or the cell phones to recognize the effects of DRM on consumer product design. Human factors come into picture while mapping the CRM constraints to the user requirements and designing an interface to make DRM constraints transparent. It is important to take into account the user behavior and user requirements and, therefore, the paper calls for a user interface before manufacturing the product. Finally, the paper says that the interactions with the end users is so important that it would determine the success of the product.

Section II: Approaches

The first article "**The Role of Architecture in DRM Vendor Economics**" by *Pramod A Jamkhedkar* and *Gregory L Heileman*, says that DRM has led to generation of two technologies, the first that focused on copy protection and the second-generation technology, which began to address much broader possibilities associated with business opportunities that are built around the general idea of DRM. But despite this the vendors have not been successful. The paper calls for a well – defined DRM architecture that addresses the business models and gets in standards. The paper says that even a specification of a minimal architectural framework would help guide the development of technologies in DRM, and also help identify the role that standards play while defining the architecture. Further, the paper draws from the experiences of the telecom and Internet industries and calls for a layered framework.

The next article titled "**DRM, Trusted Computing and Operating System Architecture**" by *Jason F Reid* and *William J Caelli*, says that, of late, there are some trusted computing initiatives like

Microsoft's Next Generation Secure Computing Base have tried to address this problem but the protection architecture and the control model of mainstream operating systems makes them inappropriate for DRM because a decrypted content cannot be protected against the privileged process. Further, the paper says that, if a DRM is to be deployed in the open computing platform, the operating system should implement the reference monitor concept, which is built on mandatory access control model.

The paper that follows "**A Trusted key Management Scheme for Digital Rights Management**" by *Yeonjeong Jeong*, *Kisong Yoon*, and *Jaecheol Ryou*, proposes a management scheme that provides delivery of the key used to encrypt a digital content from the package server to digital rights management clients in a secure manner. The system presented in the paper protects a digital content from attacks, as the paper recommends the sending of the encrypted digital content through a package server and only the DRM clients can decrypt the encrypted digital content.

The next article "**Controlled Sharing of Personal Content Using Digital Rights Management**" by *Claudine Conrado*, *Milan Petkovic*, *Michiel van der Veen* and *Wytse van der Velde*, talks about the controlled distribution of personal digital content by users. In typical DRM systems, there are provisions, where the sureness of the content can distribute the content even though it might not be owned. The article proposes a solution, which involves compulsory registration of the user with a trusted authority. The good thing about the proposed system is that, during registration, the association between user identity and content is recorded securely with the authority, while, at the same time, remaining anonymous to others.

A digital watermarking is an imperceptible signal embedded directly into the media content, and it can be detected from the host media for some applications. The paper "**A Novel Water Marking Algorithm for Resistant Geometric Attacks Using Feature Points Matching**" by *Jin Cong*, says that the insertion and detection of digital watermarking can help identify the source or ownership of the media, the legitimacy of its usage, and the type of the content or other accessory information in various applications. The paper aims at reporting a novel method of estimating the geometric manipulation to which present day data hiding is subjected. Further, it finds that the purposed scheme does not require the original image, because reference point information on the original image is contained in the secret key.

The next article "**Hash – based Counter Scheme for Digital Rights Management**" by *Mikko Löytynoja* and *Tapio Seppänen*, proposes a scheme that uses hash function that reads how many times a user is allowed to play that content in a DRM set up. The authors say that such technology is one of the best ways in managing digital rights. This is even more important, when a person is using the digital information in a non-online set up, where monitoring becomes impossible. For checking the number of times used the technology assumes the storage in the user terminal as hostile environment. This is done with the use of operating system and secure hardware.

The last article "**Predicting the Evolution of Digital Rights, Digital Objects, and Digital Rights Management Languages**" by *Jonathan Schull*, talks about anticipating the future of digital rights management and requirements for digital rights languages. The article mentions a few developments which would have an impact on the future of digital rights management like, increase in virtuality of DRM systems and objects, application of digital rights to people who are involved in redistribution, and development of digital rights management for aggregation, protection, anonymization and monetization of personal information. Further, the article calls for tracking the information flow which would eventually give rise to digital life.

SECTION I

CONCEPTS

1

Digital Rights Management: Making Business Sense

D Satish

The Digital Rights Management technologies are playing a very important role in allowing conditional access to a copyrighted content, thereby allowing the content provider to make economic sense of putting his content online. This will allow him make a viable business model built on his content.

There are numerous instances where a high value content posted online is viewed and distributed by others who essentially do not own the content. Eventually, the owner of the content who spent a considerable amount of time and money in generating the content does not make any revenue out of his hard work. Therefore, the economics of putting content online is not working out, making such business models crumble. In fact, this problem is not only experienced by publishers but also by the music, gaming and others in the entertainment industry where the distribution of music, films and games is done by people who do not own the right to do the same. All these have led the industry to call for curbing the access and distribution right of the content to people who do not own any right. These increased calls have led to the incorporation of the copyrights act as well as for Digital Rights Management (DRM).

DRM is a technology that restricts usage and access to the content. This gives the owner of the content the ability to secure and distribute the content only to the people whom it is meant for, thus enabling .them the ability to generate revenues and build a robust business model. Though the term Digital Rights Management (DRM) is relatively new, its purview addresses numerous business challenges that companies and individuals are facing over a long time. The music industry was against playing of their music by the radio stations way back from the 1940s. Later on, the film industry fought against the use of Video Cassette Recorder (VCR) as they felt that it would bring down the number of movie-goers who visit the regular theatres and watch movies on the traditional big screens.

But the advent of the internet and the digital era has drastically challenged their business models. It is now easy and virtually free to transmit the content online. Also the digital media files allow for copying the content a number of times without diluting the quality of the content. Also the drastic fall in the price of the personal computers, digital storage devices and the increasing popularity of the file sharing tools have all contributed to the unabated distribution of content without owning their moral right. The advent of the DRM technology is playing a very important role in curbing this problem.

The DRM vendors started selling their products in the market from the year 2000. But the initial response by the customers was not encouraging. DRM vendors spent most of the time educating their customers about the importance of their products. Slowly the music industry showed some interest in these products but they were worried whether their consumers would accept the change. The next two years were spent on testing these products and evaluating the costs involved. The year 2003 was a landmark year for the Digital Rights Management vendors where some of the vendors experienced success in their implementation. They also started partnering with various content management vendors to evolve a robust product. In the recent years, the revenues of the top DRM vendors stabilized with the standardization of their rights. The weak vendors were acquired by the successful vendors.

Now DRM is very popularly used, not only by the entertainment industry but also by other media such as online music stores like Apple's iTunes stores and also by e-book producers. DRM is built on various technologies either by making changes to the digital media player software by using Cryptography or by Mandatory Access Control System by which restrictions are imposed by software permanently embedded in the hardware.

Basic Forms of DRM

Some of the popular forms of DRM schemes are DIVX, CSS, Product Activation and Digital Water Marking. DIVX stands for Digital Video Express DIVX and is similar to DVD except that it is cheaper as it is a rental format of the DVD. Here, the purchaser of the VIVX disk would only get to view the content for a limited period of time, usually for about 48 hours. Once the time is completed, the user has to pay additional rental charges to use it for some more time. These DIVX disks can only be played by DIVX players who needs to open an account with the DIVX provider and the DIVX player has to be connected by a phone line with DIVX provider. Some of the popular vendors of DIVX are Circuit City, The Good Guys, Ultimate Electronics and Future Shop.

CSS stands for Content Scrambling System where it uses a proprietary algorithm which restricts the use of the content, for example, compilation or reproduction. These CSS sets are licensed to manufacture digital equipments. CSS also prevents encrypted content to be viewed in any platform. It is widely used by the DVD producers nowadays.

Product Activation system validates the license required by the user of the content or the software. Using the Product Activation, the software application hashes the hardware serial number and a specific installation ID is created which is sent to the manufacturer to verify the authenticity of the product key. This is a very important DRM solution which restricts the multiple use of the product or content. Microsoft uses this technique widely for selling its packages in some countries where the user is required to activate the software through the internet. This is also widely used in telecommunication industry.

Digital watermarking takes its name from the water marking of paper money. This technology allows hidden data such as unique id to be placed on the media. Water marking is basically of two types – visible and invisible. In visible watermarking, the signal algorithm is changed so that the signal generated is totally different from the actual signal. Invisible watermarking does not change the signal to a greater extent and only minor changes are made. This creates a database of unique ids for each copy. Though this technique does not prevent copying, it would show a chain of users and one can easily trace the original source of this content distributor.

DRM and Copy Protection Measures

DRM is sometimes mistaken for copyright protection measures. But there is a considerable difference between these. While DRM gives a conditional access to content and copyrighted material, the copy protection technology which is also known as copy prevention technique prevents duplication as well as access to content. There are some others who feel that DRM is a more general term when compared to Copy Protection, as it includes all sorts of management of works which in turn includes copy restriction. But on the other hand, copy protection also includes non-digital measures. While DRM schemes are DIVX, CSS, Product Activation and Digital Water Marking, copy protection techniques include Dongle, Bus Encryption, Key File technique and Code Morphing technique.

Though DRM makes business sense, its advent is not without its share of controversy. There are some who vouch for DRM popularly known as DRM advocates and others who are against DRM known as DRM opponents. While the DRM advocates have played their role in supporting the business models of the online content providers, the role of the DRM opponents is also very crucial, as their views have perhaps resulted in flexible forms of DRM solutions.

View of DRM Advocates

DRM advocates feel that the DRM is highly essential for making business and economic sense to the content provider. They feel that the owner of the digital content should have the sole right to control and distribute his digital works. They say without this power, not many would be willing to post their work in the online digital space. It is also important to note that the DRM solutions have not resulted in damaging the user devices and also have not caused any problem for the users.

The DRM advocates say that the benefits of DRM far outweigh the problems caused to the customers. Digital content would only be available to the person who requires them and who is authorized to view it. In this way, the traffic is reduced and the actual user who is in need would access the content easily. Also the credibility always exists. The advocates also say that the opponents of the DRM always oppose the hardware and media owners but never seriously questioned the creative owners of the digital content who depend on it for their earnings. Hence the DRM opponents should recognize the fact that the hardware vendors and media are providing conditional access in response to the artistic creativity.

DRM Opponents Speak

The opponents of DRM feel that DRM curbs the right to free information. They feel that big media houses charge unreasonably heavy amounts for content. They draw parlances to put a person in prison. They feel that DRM manages right to access the way a prison manages the freedom. They feel that the word 'Rights' in DRM is a misnomer and it should be replaced. They say that it should be replaced by the word 'Restriction', making it Digital Restriction Management.

If DRM technologies permit the reading of information only through a particular machine, then this would seriously create barriers for easy availability of content even after the prescribed copyright period comes to an end. Some of the opponents feel that DRM opposes the right to private property saying that the DRM component may end up controlling the device the user owns by restricting its usage.

Business Proposition

While the debate over DRM gains momentum, considerable efforts are being put in by the DRM vendors, in improving the DRM solutions by enhancing the security as well as providing the user of the content flexible options. While DRM is essential for making a business proposition out of a creative work, the DRM solution vendors should also be careful not to make rigid solutions that would lead to unwanted exploitation and impinge on the ability to view the free information which could turn out to be the trigger or base for some creative noble thought.

(D Satish is a Faculty Member with the IBS, Hyderabad. He can be reached at dsatish2000@yahoo.com).

2

Contextualizing Digital Rights Management: Past, Present, and Future

Dr Paul Cesarini

This article explores the historical context of digital rights management (DRM), and it examines how DRM technologies and the accompanying assumptions that initially arose from them evolved into the host of rights models the educators and others now use, or in most cases, are forced to use. It suggests that the reasoning behind even the earliest forms of DRM remain essentially the same even today; that is, under the guise of protecting existing intellectual property and exploring new market opportunities, DRM cement existing business models and distribution methods, regardless of whether doing so hinders emerging technologies and emerging opportunities in education. This article also includes a brief overview of the Digital Millennium Copyright Act (DMCA), including an analysis of the reasoning behind its initial creation and the resultant unintended consequences it has had on innovation, creativity, and computer-mediated learning.

Source: Journal of Industrial Technology, Volume 20, Number 4, September 2004 - December 2004. www.nait.org

Why Digital Rights Management?

When discussing DRM, what, precisely, am I talking about? Digital Rights Management usually has been broadly defined, with approximate definitions such as "the description, identification, trading, protection, monitoring and tracking of all forms of rights usages over both tangible and intangible assets including management of rights holders" (Planet eBook, 2003). How could such a harmless-sounding term as digital rights management potentially create so much difficulty for teachers and learners? In order to examine how DRM "fits" in terms of teaching and learning with technology, it is necessary to examine how DRM originally evolved.

Hard-fought skirmishes in the past concerning copyright and intellectual property may initially seem far removed from the various measures of digital protection employed today (Cesarini, 2003). Yet, the current state of DRM technologies and policies now exist only because such debate ever occurred. In 1908, for example, the music industry railed against player pianos (Maier, 2002). Decades later in 1931, the music industry waged pitched battles against the latest technology at the time: radios. They unsuccessfully argued that hotels could not play recordings of their copyrighted songs on their in-house hotel radio stations. Additionally, in 1968, the publishing industry fought vigorously against photocopiers, claiming libraries did not have the right to allow researchers to make copies of medical articles and documents. Similar battles went on between content producers and users of new technologies over the next few decades, pitting the television networks against cable television, and Hollywood against the VCR. The battle over the VCR reached such a level of divisiveness that Jack Valenti, the recently retired Chairman of the Motion Picture Association of America (MPAA), compared the VCR to a murderer. Valenti stated "the VCR is to the American film producer and the American public as the Boston strangler is to a woman home alone" (Maier, 2002).

The current policies and technologies of control asserted over new and emerging technologies like Internet radio, digital video recorders (DVRs, also called personal video recorders, or PVRs), and peer-to-peer file sharing networks (P2P) closely resembling similar battles fought over the past century. In each successive case, the technology may be different but the central issue remains: What is the balance between giving content consumers convenience, flexibility, and choice, and giving content producers security and revenue?

Although it is difficult to isolate the historical origins of DRM with any degree of certainty, Rosenblatt, Trippe, and Mooney (2002) generally agree that it came about with the maturation of the Internet. That is, the Internet is the primary arena that duplicates copyrighted digital files that are distributed. Prior to that, the arena was largely one of "sneakernet": duplicate copies of copyrighted digital files were manually distributed either by hand or mail. As such, it could then be argued that before the Internet existed as we have come to know it, DRM was limited to technologically enforcing software copyrights. There was simply no large-scale mechanism in place for the distribution of unauthorized audio and video. Of course, bootleg cassette tapes of concerts were available, but were limited to underground cultures (i.e., face-to-face exchanges at social events). Consequently, there was no equally large-scale effort to squelch such efforts.

All that has changed. Metcalfe, Cerf and others collectively brought together Ethernet, TCP/IP, and a host of other connectivity protocols needed to link together millions of computers worldwide. Web browsers and file transfer protocol (FTP) applications gave users of information technologies convenient, point-and-click interfaces for exchanging content. Search engines such as Google and Metacrawler gave people the means to sift through and isolate the information and content they needed. New compression techniques and cheap hard drives enabled them to condense and store vast amounts of audio, video, and text on devices to the size of keychains. These technological advances grew and continue to grow each year, and our collective capacity to find uses for them also has grown. Unfortunately, the same technologies that educators use to communicate, teach, and learn, can also easily be used to illegally encode and transfer copyrighted digital works. Such a Jekyll-and-Hyde use associated with many of these technologies has led to a barrage of frustration for content producers and content consumers; yet, as Strong suggests, the issues associated with this struggle over the future of digital media and copyright "are never clearly defined and frequently are not known until the end of a lawsuit" (Strong, p.178). Herein lies the problem.

"Letting Loose the Light"

As the proliferation of bandwidth and inexpensive storage media grew, so did rights models, or the "specification of who can do what to or with a file" (Rosenblatt *et al.,* 2002, xi). Rights models first arose out of UNIX-based mainframe environments, and their associated permission settings capable of being imposed on directories and individual files. The methods of imposing rights models manifested in a variety of forms throughout the 1980s and early 1990s, depending on the specific company and product. Quark, for example, was infamous for its widely adopted use of the so-called "hardware dongle". It would be physically attached to a port on a computer, and it was necessary to run authorized copies of their flagship design tool, Quark Xpress. According to Rosenblatt *et al.,* other rights models that were adopted by different companies included "guiltware" or "scareware," which made stern warning messages visible on the media and during installation, and the somewhat offensively named "naziware," whereby combinations of both serial numbers and product activation keys were needed to unlock software. Additional methods included requiring the physical media that the software had been shipped on be inserted into the computer using it, whenever the software was needed. These various methods of imposing rights models proved at best only slightly effective, though, and often resulted in confusion and frustration.

For example, the widespread rollout of Quark Xpress at university computer labs was difficult at best. Quark did not allow their product to use typical site license management tools, such as Sassafras Software's Key Server program. Although most software site licenses could be rolled out remotely then scaled to whatever numbers of computer the license dictated, the widespread adoption of Quark Xpress on campuses necessitated an equally widespread dongle adoption – all manually installed, in a one-to-one ratio per system. Quark has since modified its methods of imposing rights models for Quark, but it is still generally considered one of the more inconvenient and frustrating ones currently in use.

The term "digital rights management" itself was likely first coined in 1994, when IBM and Electronic Publishing Resources launched two of the first well-known, commercially available DRM products (Rosenblatt *et al.,* 2002, xi – xii). Even though these products no longer exist, much of the technology used in them continues in other forms. These and other DRM efforts were then collectively shoved into the public eye by way of a landmark paper by Mark Stefik, titled "Letting Loose the Light: Igniting Commerce in Electronic Publication." Stefik was a researcher at the famed Xerox Palo Alto Research Center, the center responsible for innovations such as the graphic user interface, the mouse, ethernet, postscript printing, and a host of other technology systems that comprise much of modern computing. In this paper, Stefik argued that "it should always be possible to strictly define and control who can do what to a piece of content, when, on what devices, and for how much money or other form of consideration" (Rosen-blatt et al., 2002, xii). Additionally, Stefik coined a term that now carries with it much negative connection: trusted system. Trusted systems were, in Stefik's view, devices that hold data and "implement a precisely defined set of behaviors on that data", with no way of accessing or modifying that data other than by way of the trusted system. Stefik's view of DRM and trusted systems amounted to a rigid, restrictive world where "all content rights are defined and controlled by automated processes" (Rosenblatt, *et al.*, 2002, xii). Luckily for educators, Stefik's views were only partly accepted by business and commercial interests.

Enter the Digital Millennium Copyright Act

Regardless of whether Stefik's notions of near-complete control of media by copyright holders were embraced, or even technically possible, the idea of the trusted system remains very much alive today. This is perhaps where the 1998 Digital Millennium Copyright Act (DMCA) truly comes into play as the enforcement and punitive mechanism of DRM. That is, without the DMCA, it would not matter what rights models are employed by different types of content producers. Trusted systems would exist only if their features were desirable by consumers and institutions. However, this is not the case. The DMCA and proposed legislation such as the so-called "Berman Bill" (a Bill sponsored by Rep. Berman and Sen. Hollings) that would legalize network attacks by content producers essentially call for the universality of trusted systems, in the home, at the workplace, and in the classroom.

If this sounds somewhat far-fetched, it may be because federally mandated trusted systems and federally sanctioned computer cracking seem antithetical not only to higher education, but also to America. It may also seem as though such legislation would not be enacted in the first place or would be technically unfeasible even if enacted. In the case of the Berman Bill, it remains to be seen if it will be passed into law and then whether it will be technically possible to implement it.

However, the lobbying organizations for the content-producing industry, including the Recording Industry Association of America (RIAA) and MPAA, have already initiated similar undertakings using far more questionable tactics. In fact, the RIAA recently attempted to attach a rider to an antiterrorism bill that would have authorized the RIAA to launch Distributed Denial-of-Serve (DoS, or DdoS) attacks to computers suspected of storing copy-righted audio and video files. The end result would be partially or completely disabled systems. The key term in this case is suspected. That is, no actual proof would be necessary to launch such an attack; it would be left up to the discretion of the content producer (McCullagh, 2002). Had this rider passed, it would have effectively meant it was open season on personally or institutionally owned systems. Students working against a paper or presentation deadline could well have been locked-out of the computer they were using. Faculty giving a lecture via distance learning software could well have been knocked offline by a DoS attack if their computer was suspected of storing such infringing content.

Additionally, the rider stipulated that content producers could not be held liable or otherwise responsible for any data loss or corruption resulting from the attack. This particular rider did not pass; however, newer efforts are under way which would not only allow the RIAA or MPAA to partly or completely disable a system, but would also potentially allow the remote deletion of certain file types often associated with piracy. Students or faculty with vast libraries of legally acquired digital audio or video files might unexpectedly find them being deleted by way of virus-like programs. These programs are being quietly financed and stealthily distributed by the content producing industry, all under the shield of the DMCA (Sorkin, 2003).

As for the DMCA itself, it has been used as a legal club to stifle innovative classroom technologies and squelch academic freedom for over fours years and shows little sign of abatement in this regard. The DMCA was enacted as a compromise solution to protect Internet Service Providers (ISPs) from being held liable for the transmission of copy-protected works by their subscribers. Sara Duetsch, associate general council at Verizon, described the DMCA being conceptually started much earlier, though. She states that:

> It started in . . .1994 when the US Patent and Trademark Office came up with their 'green paper' (policy document) on the National Information Infrastructure (NII). It talked about this horrible new device called the Internet that was a giant copying machine. One of the conclusions of the green paper was that the best policy was to hold the service provider liable. That phrase awakened a sleeping giant. The telecom industry never paid attention to the topic before. At the same time, the copyright community introduced a bill called the NII Protection Act that made all temporary copies illegal. (McCullagh, 2001)

In this case, the temporary copies mentioned refers to even cached and buffered copies of copy-protected content. However, caching audio and video files is the primary means by which these files are made available online. Web browser caches hold copies of previously-viewed content, such as web pages, as well as audio and video clips. These cached or buffered copies typically serve as a staging areas of sorts, with only the content that has changed being downloaded from their respective sites with each new request. Caching is a quicker and more efficient way to access frequently needed content than having to download every single image, word, and multimedia file associated with the page(s) each time. (Techencyclopedia, 2004)

Because ISPs understandably did not want to be held legally liable for copyrighted works or even the cached copies of these works, they were forced to negotiate what is now known as the DMCA with lobbyists from content-producing industries. Under the DMCA, distributing or rebroadcasting copyrighted materials in any way was a felony, as was disabling any DRM technical measures wrapping these copyrighted works. Although this may not initially seem nefarious, the scope of the DMCA has since been expanded considerably. Duetsch stresses that,

> The content community would like . . .to have the service provider block infringing sites that are not located on our network and to use digital

> rights management tools to stop peer-to-peer transmissions. . . .Their strategy right now is to use DRM bills as a way to reopen the DMCA and to get remedies through forcing technologies on other industries. (McCullagh, 2002)

This notion of mandating DRM has been a constant refrain from the MPAA, the RIAA, and the Software & Information Industry Association (SIIA). From the late 1990s to the present day, steps are being taken technically and legislatively to turn current and emerging technologies into these rigid, trusted systems – regardless of the desires of students, faculty, and end-users of these technologies. Yet, can we blame the content-producing industry? As audio, video, and text becomes increasingly divorced from the physical wrappers that long contained it, widespread piracy continues on a scale previously unimagined. We have seen this manifest itself more and more over the years, with products like Napster, Gnutella, Kazaa, and the now-defunct Aimster, making it relatively easy to transfer text, audio, and video to anywhere, from anywhere. As a result, lawsuits by embattled content producers and copyright holders are an almost daily subject on the evening news.

Will these lawsuits eventually take care of the problem of illegal file trading, or will a different solution be necessary? How will these lawsuits and the current mindset of DRM and trusted systems at all costs affect computer-mediated learning? In his interview with Royle (2003), Fred Von Lohmann, Senior Intellectual Property lawyer for the Electronic Frontier Foundation, argues that the entertainment industry has "made it clear that they will sue any company that uses or offers general-purpose P2P tools." Lohmann also asserts that copyright law has been built on the premise that you go after the guy who actually breaks the law . . .no one ever suggested that Ford should be liable for every bank robbery committed with one of its cars. Yet the entertainment industries appear to want to let all the bank robbers run free and only punish the car makers. It makes you wonder whether the fight is actually about piracy, or if it is instead about asserting control over new technologies. (Royle, 2003)

The end result, according to Lohmann and others, is total control over "culture, radio, television, literature, music, art, information" (Royle, 2003) and knowledge by content producers, regardless of what we hope to accomplish with students in terms of computer-mediated learning.

Institutionally, this control has been stealthily slipping into the electronic classroom, by way of seemingly benign software that many students have become accustomed to using. Windows Media Player (WMP) is a prime example of this. It is the standard audio/video player that comes bundled with any version of the Windows operating system and, as such, has rapidly become pervasive in higher education. Yet, WMP may well pose serious privacy and security concerns, both individually and institutionally (Festa, 2002). According to computer privacy and security expert Richard Smith and others, WMP 8 had the following capability: Each time a DVD was played on a computer, WMP contacted a central Microsoft server to get information for the DVD. When this contact was made, the server was given an "electronic fingerprint" which identified the DVD being accessed and a cookie which "uniquely identifies a particular WMP player" (Smith, 2002). WMP also built a database on the hard drive of the host system, of all DVDs accessed. Additionally, there did not appear to be any option to stop it from "phoning home" when a DVD movie was viewed, or clearing out the DVD movie database on the hard drive.

The Microsoft privacy policy for WMP did not disclose that the software contacts central servers to get this information, nor did it disclose what kind of tracking Microsoft used, what purpose it served, or how cookies were and are used by WMP in this regard. Although it is difficult to determine if these covert forms of DRM exist in the current versions of WMP, clearly such actions represent a technology of control that has little business being in our classrooms.

Educators also are beginning to see the negative consequences of the DMCA as they affect our pedagogical decisions. These consequences have manifested in a variety of ways, in a variety of disciplines:

- If a computer science instructor wants to demonstrate to students how the Content Scrambling System (CSS) used in commercials DVDs works by writing a relatively simple program to allow these DVDs to play on Linux-based systems, doing so would potentially be a violation of the DMCA, and has been the subject of an on-going series of lawsuits initiated by the MPAA. (Borland, 2004)

- If that same instructor wants to examine how Internet content filtering systems such as Net Nanny or Cybersitter work by reverse engineering the programs to see how and when they under-block and over-block web sites, doing so would potentially be a violation of the DMCA. (Leydon, 2003)
- If an instructor in electronics and computer technology wants to demonstrate how hardware modification chips function, by way of a project involving adding such a chip to a proprietary system such as Microsoft's Xbox (for the purposes of installing open source software on the system), doing so would potentially be a violation of the DMCA. (Fahey, 2004)
- If a specialist in encryption technology were to find gaps in copy protection standards used in commercial electronic books eBooks, and then presented those findings at a research conference here in the United States, doing so would potentially be a violation of the DMCA. This exact scenario occurred with when Russian encryption specialist Dmitri Skylarov presented such findings about DRM technology used to protect Adobe eBook content, a derivative of the PDF format. Skylarov was arrested immediately after his presentation, and was jailed for over two months as the Justice Department attempted to build an ultimately unsuccessful case against him. (Dvorak, 2001)

In short, many seemingly innocuous pedagogical and research activities could now be violations of the DMCA, and could – as in the case of Dmitri Sky larov – result in arrest and prosecution. Fair use and/or educational use would not necessarily be a strong enough shield to protect the academic freedom of the instructor or potentially even the institution itself from a DMCA-based legal assault. Such consequences could have a chilling effect on future research in these and other areas, perhaps even leading to academic conventions and conferences in these areas being held outside the US to avoid potential prosecutorial efforts in the future.

DRM: Classrooms of the Future?

How do technologists deal with a rapidly "wrapperless" society, a society where content is no longer bound by physical media? Kurzweil (1999) and others debated this very issue over a decade ago. He stated:

> We are used to paying for the knowledge content of products so long as it is integrated into something with mass. We recognize that a $300 software product is physically identical to a few $2 floppy disks, and thus we are primarily paying for the information contained therein. We are aware (or should be) that the manufactured cost of a compact disc recording is less than 50¢ (depending on volume), and that again we are paying for the (musical) information. It is, after all, the information we are after. We obtain no pleasure from the discs themselves. (Kurzweil, 1999, p. 300)

Barlow agrees, referring to it as a simple problem with a complex solution. He states, "If our property can be infinitely reproduced and instantaneously distributed all over the planet without cost, without our knowledge, without its even leaving our possession, how can we [content producers] protect it?" (1999, p. 318-319). Unfortunately, the answer is simple: They cannot digitally protect it in the manner in which they have been accustomed. I believe that time is at an end. Existing patent and copyright laws are at best ill-equipped for the nuances associated with emerging technologies. Barlow goes on to assert that most technology "is detaching itself from the physical plane, where property law of all sorts has always found definition. . . Even the physical/digital bottle to which we've become accustomed – floppy disks, CD-ROMs, and other discrete, shrink-wrappable bit-packages – will disappear". (Barlow, 1999, p.319)

Additionally, even Larry Ellison, mercurial CEO of Oracle, agrees. Years ago in Cringely's *Triumph of the Nerds: The Rise of Accidental Empires* documentary about the birth of the personal computer industry in America, Ellison predicted the death – and utter impracticality – of the wrapper. He stated:

> Me going down to the store and buying Windows, I've got to get into my car, drive down to a store buy a cardboard box full of bits you know encoded on a piece of plastic CD-ROM and you bring it home and read a manual to install this thing – you must be kidding you know, put the stuff on the net – it's bits, don't put bits in cardboard, cardboard in trucks, trucks to stores, me go to the store, you know, pick the stuff out, it's insane. (Cringely, 1995)

Ellison espouses the same wrapperless society as Barlow, Kurzweil, and others did before him. This wrapperless society seems not only logical but likely inevitable, particularly with broadband Internet access gradually displacing narrow band analog modems across the country. The distribution mechanism is there. Unfortunately, this distribution mechanism also represents the worst nightmare of our traditional content providers for audio, video, and text.

How, then, do content-producing industries deal with many of their products not having standardized file formats, standardized DRM, or even a standardized distribution method? This is the situation the RIAA has been in for some time now, pre and post-Napster. This is the situation in which the MPAA is currently immersed, battling a host of nimble peer-to-peer services such as Gnutella, Freeway, and others that cannot be easily sued. This is the situation the publishing industry dreads, but cannot avoid. For all three industries, all of which have numerous products and services entwined into the fabric of computer-mediated learning and by default technology literacy, the question remains How do we continue to profit when the distribution mechanisms relied on for so long are becoming less and less relevant to more and more people? There is no easy answer, of course, and it is certainly a monumental issue. Fundamental changes in content distribution will likely be necessary, along with a further consolidation within the respective content-producing industries. Yet, many of these changes – particularly those that involve confusing and restricting DRM rights models – will undoubtedly affect literacy and our students' collective ability to create, innovate, and think critically.

For example, take the hypothetical scenario suggested by Tim O'Reilly at a panel discussion titled The *Near Future of Digital Rights Management.* O'Reilly is the founder and president of The O'Reilly Network, a publishing company focused on technology and software-related texts and course materials. At this panel, O'Reilly posited that the near future of DRM could well be one where piracy prevention is the primary goal, with all other communication, collaboration, and pedagogical considerations falling a distant second. O'Reilly asks:

> What if there was a law that said you couldn't browse the Internet with any device that could be attached to a printer? . . .maybe content providers

> want to make sure they get page hits from people reading their material. If you print (their material) and give it to a friend, (they) wouldn't be able to track it to get credit for that additional reader. (Steinberg, 2003)

O'Reilly suggests that while most publishers would not care about tracking and getting credit for the additional reader (presumably to charge higher advertising rates), in the near future some publishers might care, and their solution to this problem is to lobby Congress to pass additional laws regulating information and communication technologies. He continues, and suggests the following scenarios:

> Imagine a law that says it's illegal to produce a device that can both display content in a browser and connect to a printer. Now there's someone concrete to sue if the law is broken. Imagine the law says more than that. Suppose it said that your device has to check in with some central authority on a regular basis. This is so that if a device can browse the Internet and later finds a way to connect it to a printer, then the web browsing capabilities can be disabled by this central authority. You would be buying a device because it could perform certain functions – but later these functions can be disabled (remotely) by someone without your permission. (Steinberg, 2003)

Admittedly, trying to imagine O'Reilly's hypothetical situation as reality may seem a bit of a stretch. The implications of having a significant amount of online content being essentially locked away from any device capable of generating hardcopy would be antithetical to teaching and learning with technology.

Unfortunately, O'Reilly's scenario is not too far off from proposed legislation such as the Consumer Broadband and Digital Television Protection Act (CBDTPA). If this bill became law, Princeton University professor Ed Felton argues it would "prohibit the manufacture or distribution of 'digital media devices,' unless those devices include government-approved copy restriction technology". (Felton, 2003)

What is a digital media device, according to the CBDTPA? Unless specifically stated as being exempt, a digital media device could be any hardware or software device that reproduces works in digital form; converts copyrighted works in digital form into a form whereby the images and sounds are visible or audible; or retrieves or accesses copyrighted works in digital form and transfers or makes available for transfer such works to hardware or software described in subparagraph (B) (Felton, 2003). Based on this definition, Felton compiled what he refers to as a "hit list" of current devices that would be illegal under the CBDTPA, would necessarily be pulled from the shelves of stores, and removed from computer labs and computer-mediated learning environments, then eventually replaced by "trusted system" versions deemed CBDTPA-compliant. Examples of such prohibited digital media devices could well include:

- *Cockpit Voice Recorders:* Newer versions of these use digital storage, rather than tape;
- *Hearing Aids*: These devices convert copyrighted works in digital form (say, a track played from a CD) into a form whereby the sounds are audible;
- *Scanners*: These peripherals can duplicate copyrighted images and digitally store them; and
- *Zip Drives*: These are capable of digitally transferring and storing copyrighted works.

Felton's list currently details numerous products and devices commonly used in different industries particularly in education institutions that would technically be illegal if the CBDTPA becomes law. While actually confiscating and disposing of every such device would be a logistical impossibility, not to mention a huge drain on federal and state resources, Felton's list demonstrates that O'Reilly's hypothetical scenario could actually represent the near future of DRM.

That is, if the CBDTPA passed, or if newer legislative efforts such as Orrin Hatch's Inducing Infringment of Copyrights (INDUCE, or IICA) Act passed, and if even a smaller-scale crackdown on "digital media devices" (as defined by the CBDTPA) were to occur, the impact on teaching and learning with technology would be felt far and wide. Institutions of Higher education, many of which are already reeling from deep cuts in state funding, would scramble to comply. Existing computer labs would have to be physically and systematically reconfigured, as systems with CD-RW drives, Zip drives, scanners, and related hardware and software deemed illegal would be removed from the lab or uninstalled from the computers, or otherwise rendered inoperable for the sake of compliance. New methods for digital storage and file transfer would have to be created and implemented, to ensure no student is duplicating, sending, or receiving copyrighted materials. DRM-based technologies would have to be incorporated into mail servers, to prevent illegally duplicated email attachments. PowerPoint would have to incorporate some form of DRM, to prevent the insertion of copyrighted images, audio, and video into presentations. The same would apply for web publishing software, such as Dreamweaver. The ability to educate our students in computer-mediated learning environments would open to reinterpretation, based on dictates from the content-producing industry.

Conclusion

Technological change is rarely easy, and the growing pains associated with how digital media is replicated and distributed will almost certainly continue to be hotly contested issues for years to come. The needs of the content producing industry are all too often in direct contradiction with the legitimate, fair use needs of honest consumers of this content. This attempted control of how we use technologies to access information, by Microsoft, by the MPAA, by the RIAA, or by similarly large institutions, files in the face of traditional notions of computer-mediated learning. In the name of fighting piracy, the policies and technologies of control are vying to alter the social and cultural contexts we have come to expect from teaching and learning with technology.

As faculty and working professionals in technological industries, I believe we should collectively have a greater, more prominent voice in determining how the digital media technologies we use to teach and learn evolve. The problem is that we are not currently exercising that voice. Affiliation with digital media advocacy groups such as the Electronic Frontier Foundation (EFF), the Center for Democracy & Technology (CDT), Computer Professionals for Social Responsibility (CPSR), and DigitalConsumer.org should be actively promoted and encouraged within our respective disciplines, at our conferences, and in our institutions. These organizations actively lobby and litigate to protect current digital rights such as space-shifting, time-shifting, and format-shifting digital content, fair use, and first sale that we have all come to rely on for years inside and outside the classroom. I believe our professional organizations should also move to take official stances against pending legislation that seeks to control access to or distribution of digital media, much as how organizations in other disciplines frequently do, such as the American Library Association's stances against the DMCA and USA PATRIOT Act (Clark, 2004). If we opt not to promote stronger ties to these and similar organizations, and if we instead opt to remain passive in the face of far reaching DRM technologies and policies, we may soon be faced with an unfortunate reality. All emerging digital media technologies and tools, however potentially useful to computer-mediated discourse and pedagogy, might one day have to be officially sanctioned by legal departments of the content producing industry prior to be released to us, the technologists that use them.

(Dr Paul Cesarini is an Assistant Professor in the Department of Visual Communication & Technology Education (VC&TE) at Bowling Green State University. His current research and work focuses on digital rights management and the on-going erosion of fair use for audio, video, and text. Prior to teaching in VC&TE, Paul created and managed the BGSU Student Technology Center, Laptop Loan Program, and annual Technology Fair. He reads Wired far too much.)

References

Barlow J, (1999). "The Economy of Ideas: A Framework for Rethinking Patents and Copyrights in the Digital Age". In V Vitanza (Ed.), *Cyber-Reader* (pp. 299 - 319). New York, NY: Allyn and Bacon.

Borland J, (2004, January 22). Hollywood group drops DVD-copying case. Retrieved September 8, 2004, from *http://news.com.com/Hollywood+group+drops+DVD-copying+case/2100-1025_3-5145809.html*

Cesarini, P (2003). "Digital Rights Management: Coming Soon to a Class Near You". National Association of Industrial Technology, 2003 Annual Conference Proceedings.

Clark, L (2004, June 29). "ALA Supports Supreme Court Decision on Child Online Protection Act". Retrieved September 3, 2004, from *http://www.ala.org/ala/pr2004/june2004/COPASupremect.htm*

Cringely, R (1995). Triumph of the Nerds: The Transcripts, part III. Retrieved October 5, 2004, from *http://www.pbs.org/nerds/part3.html*

Dvorak, J (2001, July 23). The Skylarov Gambit. Retrieved September 3, 2004 from *http://www.pcmag.com/article2/0,1759,25446,00.asp*

Fahey, R (2004, September 4). "USA: Jail sentence and fine for mod chip retailer". Retrieved August 20, 2004 from *http://www. gamesindustry. biz/content_page.php?section _name= pub&aid =1 502*

Felton, E (2003, February 9). "Freedom to Tinker". Retrieved January 3, 2004, from *http://www.freedom-to-tinker.com*

The Information Society Project. (2003, November 24). "Introduction: The Transition to Digital". Retrieved January 10, 2004, from *http://www.nyls.edu/pages/1511.asp*

Kurzweil, R. (1999). "The Future of Libraries". in V Vitanza (Ed.), *CyberReader* (pp. 291-303). New York, NY: Allyn and Bacon.

Leydon, J (2003, April 10). "DMCA strikes again in N2H2 filtering list". Retrieved September 2, 2004 from *http://www.theregister.co.uk/2003/04/10/dmca_strikes_again_in_n2h2/*

Maier, M (2002, April). "Technophobia Over the Years". Retrieved July 14, 2002 from *http://www.business2.com/articles/mag/0,1640,39436,FF. html*

McCullagh, D (2001, October 15). "RIAA Wants to Hack your PC". Retrieved December 15, 2003, from *http://wired.com/news/con-.ict/0,2100,47552,00.html*

McCullagh, D. (2002, August 27). "Verizon's Copyright Campaign". Retrieved January 13, 2003, from *http://news.com.com/2102-1082-955417.html*

Planet eBook. Ebooks Glossary. Retrieved Feb 2, 2003, from *http://www.planetebook.com/mainpage.asp?webpageid=70*

Rosenblatt, B, Trippe, B, & Mooney, S (2002). *Digital Rights Management: Business and Technology.* New York: M&T Books.

Royle, B (2003, January 8). "Interview with Fred Von Lohmann". Retrieved November 20, 2003, from *http://techfocus.org*

Smith, R (2002, February 20). "Serious Privacy Problem in Windows Media Player for Windows XP". Retrieved December 3, 2003, from *http://www.computerbytesman.com/privacy/wmp8dvd.htm*

Sorkin, A. (2003, May 4). "Software Bullet Sought to Kill Music Piracy". Retrieved January 4, 2003, from *http://64.225.202.40/mediadefender/press%20about%20MD/nytimes_5_8_03_pg1.htm*

Stefik, M (1996). *Letting Loose the Light: Igniting Commerce in Electronic Publication.* Internet Dreams: Archetypes, Myths, and Metaphors. Cambridge, Massachusetts, MIT Press. 219-253.

Steinberg, D (2003, October 10). The Near Future of Digital Rights Management. Retrieved October 23, 2003, from *http://www.oreillynet.com/pub/a/mac/2002/10/03/drm.html*

Strong, W. (1999). *The Copyright Book: A practical guide.* Cambridge: MIT Press.

"TechEncyclopedia". Retrieved October 3, 2004 from *http://www.techweb.com/encyclopedia/*

Highlights of Digital Millennium Copyrights Act
• Makes it a crime to circumvent anti-piracy measures built into most commercial software. • Outlaws the manufacture, sale, or distribution of code-cracking devices used to illegally copy software. • Does permit the cracking of copyright protection devices, however, to conduct encryption research, assess product interoperability, and test computer security systems. • Provides exemptions from anti-circumvention provisions for nonprofit libraries, archives, and educational institutions under certain circumstances. • In general, limits Internet service providers from copyright infringement liability for simply transmitting information over the Internet. • Service providers, however, are expected to remove material from users' web sites that appears to constitute copyright infringement. • Limits liability of nonprofit institutions of higher education – when they serve as online service providers and under certain circumstances – for copyright infringement by faculty members or graduate students. • Requires that "webcasters" pay licensing fees to record companies. • Requires that the Register of Copyrights, after consultation with relevant parties, submit to Congress recommendations regarding how to promote distance education through digital technologies while "maintaining an appropriate balance between the rights of copyright owners and the needs of users." • States explicitly that "nothing in this section shall affect rights, remedies, limitations, or defenses to copyright infringement, including fair use..."
Source: www.ucla.edu

3

Free Software and Digital Rights Management – Bitter Enemies or Strange Bedfellows?

Chris J Karr

The article presents a hypothetical situation where a robust free software DRM platform would exist and whether this free software DRM provides a free software media applications to particulate in the constant production and distribution process. It also analyzes whether a free software DRM platform breaks the hold of proprietary closed source DRM platform. Further, it says, a free DRM system would make sense if the motive were to expand the installed base and replace existing proprietary system.

In recent years, digital rights management technology (DRM) has become an important issue to free software users and developers. Free software users first experienced this issue when they discovered that they were unable to legally play their DVD discs on their Linux and BSD computers. In recent months, users carefully observed a technological arms race between Apple Computer and hackers working to circumvent the Fair-Play system used to protect digital files purchased

Source: Free Software Magazine Issue 6, July 2005. © Chris J Karr. Reprinted with permission.

from Apple's iTunes Music Store. Finally, when Tivo released its TivoToGo show-sharing technology a few months ago, eager Tivo users discovered that their files were not usable on non-Windows platforms.

DRM is the content industry's response to the additional power that digital playback and distribution technology has granted consumers. In an environment where digital files can be perfectly duplicated in seconds, DRM attempts to disrupt that power by preventing users from modifying and distributing content without the permission of that content's producer. Content producers presently find themselves in an odd situation. Digital technologies have the potential to revolutionize their business by allowing them to directly market and distribute content to their customers. On the other hand, the same power that producers have to streamline their operations also allows unscrupulous users to likewise disrupt that business and act as distributors in the producers' stead. Because of this, content producers have been hesitant to fully embrace networked digital technologies. Rather than risk the possibility that their media may escape their exclusive control, content producers choose to forgo the benefits of online distribution and retain their less efficient traditional business models.

Since DRM systems strive to be a vertical stack of software components that guard media from production to consumption, complete DRM systems tend to be monolithic collections of technology developed and controlled by single vendors. Microsoft backs the Windows Media platform for audio and video. Apple uses a system called FairPlay to encode tracks distributed from its iTunes Music Store. Real Networks attempted to deploy a system called Harmony that was compatible with Real content. Since these systems are constantly under attack by users wishing to strip the DRM from content, these companies have chosen to keep the systems proprietary and the sources closed. Keeping the source closed adds another layer of obscurity that DRM hackers must overcome in order to compromise the system.

While the details of implementing a robust DRM system are best left to network and security gurus, consider the hypothetical situation where a robust free software DRM platform exists. Would free software DRM provide the means for free software media applications to participate in the content production and distribution processes? Could a free software DRM platform break the hold of

A Graphic from Microsoft's "Play for Sure" Campaign for the Windows Media Platform

proprietary closed source DRM platforms? Would content producers and consumers embrace a free solution? Or would a free software DRM platform be an unacceptable ideological compromise that would do little to advance free software's pragmatic goals?

The Players in the Rights Management Game

There are three main actors in any rights management scenario. Media consumers create a demand for content, which content producers likewise attempt to supply. The content producers create a demand for rights management software, which DRM vendors attempt to supply. While the consumers are negatively impacted by DRM, the producers choose to impose DRM upon consumers as an additional cost of obtaining content via electronic means.

Both producers of commercial content and rights management technology have one overriding goal: to exploit to the fullest extent possible their content and technology. Their goal is to maximize profits. For content producers, this is achieved by finding the right balance between their desire to charge high prices and the consumers' desire to purchase at low prices. Selling content to ten people paying five dollars each is more desirable than selling only two copies for twenty-dollars each. Conversely, selling to forty people for one dollar a copy is worse than selling to ten customers for five dollars each. Since production costs are fixed and independent of the size of the market, and distribution costs are negligible, content producers will search for the "sweet spot" where the supply and demand curves intersect.

Rights management technology vendors play a different game. Real, Microsoft, and Apple are all battling to produce a standard and widely adopted DRM platform. If one company's system fails to gain wide acceptance, content producers and device manufacturers will opt to license the competitors' more popular systems. This market is strongly affected by positive feedback loops and tipping points – a more popular system will be adopted by more device manufacturers and software developers, which will encourage more content producers to use the popular system, etc. The spoils of this fight are significant. If one company can gain dominance over the others, it will leverage that success with its DRM platform to become dominant in the other areas of the media industry – production, distribution, and playback.

Finally, consumers are the final actors in the rights management scenario. An ideal outcome for consumers is that there is no DRM at all. Consumers would be free to use the content as they see fit. However, producers are not willing to provide this freedom as it negatively impacts their ability to sell more content. While the record industry is rightfully derided when it provides inflated numbers of decreasing sales due to peer-to-peer technology, some sales are undoubtedly lost to free downloading. Further, when consumers indiscriminately share content in violation of copyright laws, a social effect emerges where people become accustomed to not paying for content. While there is a larger discussion to be had about adapting media business models to reflect modern realities, producers' current refusal to release unencumbered content is perfectly rational.

Rights Management and Free Software

The problems for free software that modern DRM platforms introduce are that proprietary systems are closed source and it is impossible for free software users to obtain and legally play protected media using free applications. Microsoft's

DRM platform is limited to the Windows operating systems and the devices that license Microsoft's media technology. Apple's FairPlay technology is limited to the iTunes media player and the iPod portable device. Since none of these applications are made available on free software platforms, free software users are in same position as they, with respect to DVD content seven years ago, were unable to play their purchased content. While it is possible to play some of these files on free software platforms, the user has to circumvent the DRM and likely violate copyright law.

Since this situation does not serve the interests of software users and developers, does it make sense for the free software community to introduce an open DRM platform of their own? Can a free software DRM platform be used to advance free software projects and principles?

Making the simple assumption that it is possible to create a strong free software DRM platform, how would such a system impact the current struggle between users, content producers, and DRM vendors? Let us presume that this hypothetical free software DRM platform has the following traits:

1. The rights enforcement would be strong and secure enough to inspire confidence among the content producers. Producers would be comfortable releasing media to all users under such a system.
2. The platform would be freely available to all interested developers. Developers wishing to create compatible software would not be required to pay a fee or license any technology.
3. The platform would be available on free and non-free platforms, including portable devices.
4. The platform would be flexible enough to accommodate different locales' individual copyright laws.

If such a system existed, would it be a compelling alternative to existing proprietary rights management packages? Current DRM vendors stand to lose the most with the introduction of a free DRM platform. The availability of an open platform is an enticing offer for content producers and consumers worried about single-vendor lock-in. If content producers release materials with this free

A Screenshot from Tivo's Windows-only Beta Client

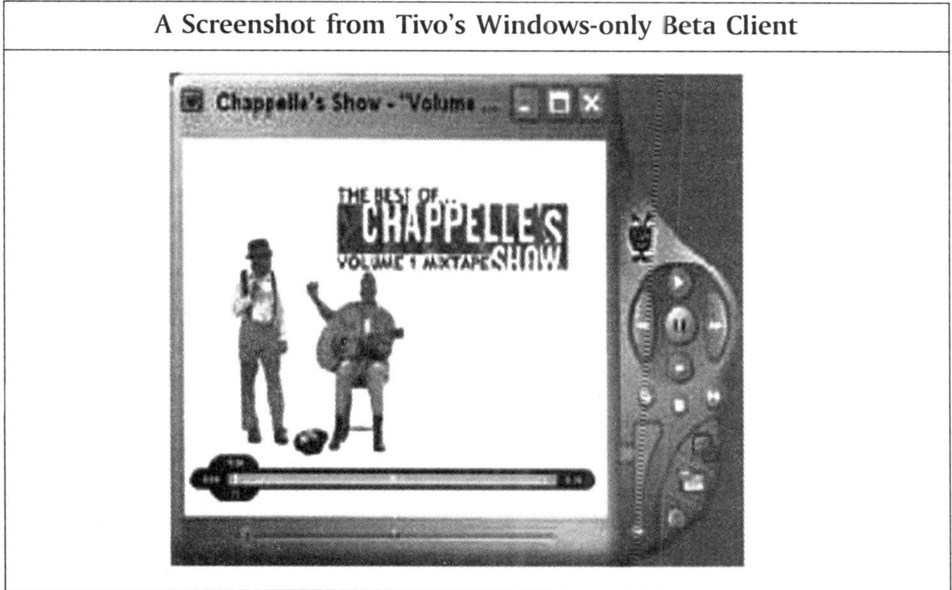

system, there will be additional pressure on software vendors and device manufacturers to include support for the free format. Since the cost of including this technology is limited to implementation and does not include any licensing fees, software and device vendors would not worry about their business being held hostage by a single software vendor.

Consumers gain the most with an introduction of a free DRM platform. Users of traditionally neglected platforms like Linux would finally obtain a measure of parity with Windows and Mac users when dealing with media content. Further, since the code responsible for rights management no longer excludes anyone, creators of applications like media playback and cataloging applications would no longer be shut out of the media marketplace. This would introduce competition and diversity in the media software market.

"Rights Management" versus "Rights Declaration"

In the discussion so far, the focus has been placed on strong DRM platforms – that is, software platforms that attempt to prevent users from exercising some functionality or other, such as playing protected files on unauthenticated machines. An alternative to a strong DRM platform is a robust rights declaration scheme.

A Snapshot of the Hymn Project Website. Hymn is Fairplay Circumvention Software

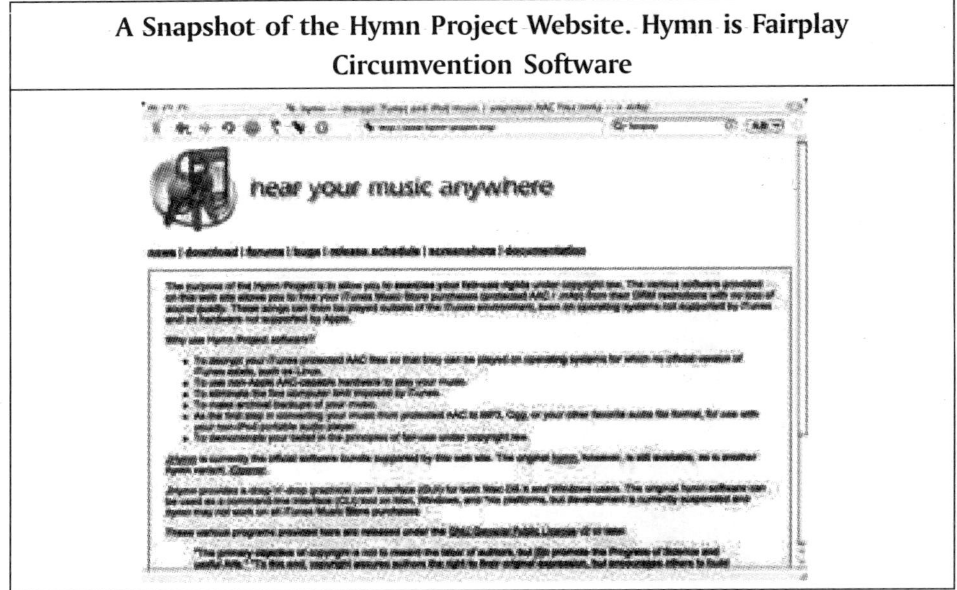

In a rights declaration scheme, the software encodes licensing and rights data, but the software does not attempt to limit users from using the content. Rather than encoding the rights enforcement in software, a rights declaration scheme uses social pressure and shared values to keep users honest. While a strong DRM platform attempts to be an impenetrable system, a rights declaration scheme acknowledges that it is probably impossible to build a perfect DRM system, and developers' time is better spent elsewhere.

There are a number of advantages that rights declaration schemes have over rights management platforms. First of all, by implicitly trusting the media user, rights declarations are simpler to implement than DRM. Rights declaration preserves the notion of fair use, an idea that is anywhere from difficult to impossible to encode in any DRM technology. Further, since the rights declaration encoded media is open and unprotected, its contents can enter the public domain without any outside intervention. Finally, rights declarations help alleviate the problem of orphan works. Since the rights are encoded in the files, it is simple to determine the proper copyright owner. In a DRM system, if the authority providing the content and authorization disappears, users are often left with useless encrypted bits of data as they replace hardware and software components.

Rights declaration is more in sync with the free software movement's philosophical goals than any DRM software. A strong DRM system will be required to prohibit users access to parts of their machines. For example, in a strong DRM system, media would be unable to play without using DRM-aware applications. System software like audio drivers would be required to prohibit the user from being able to digitally extract decoded audio. Video drivers would need to be rights-aware in order to prevent a user from capturing still frames and reconstructing a video's content in an unprotected format. All DRM systems demand hard technical compromises from the users, whereas rights declaration schemes only require new code that is able to display and encode licensing information.

Does a Free Software DRM Platform make any Sense?

In order to answer this question, another question must first be answered: is it better for the free software community to compete with proprietary DRM systems to avoid becoming irrelevant in the media landscape, or should they stay true to their principles and refuse to limit their users rights? If the primary goal of free software is to expand the installed base and to replace existing proprietary systems, a free DRM system makes a lot of sense. The lack of proprietary content on free platforms is a severe competitive disadvantage. Users will not adopt a free software platform where they cannot use their purchased music, videos, or images. If content producers refuse to release accessible versions of their media, users lose when a compatible DRM system is not available. However, if the goal of the free software community is to offer a reasonable and unencumbered alternative to proprietary systems, a decent rights declaration framework would be sufficient to establish an alternative to proprietary media and formats. (This is already happening with the use of open source software licenses and Creative Commons content licenses.) While it is unlikely that Hollywood and the recording industry's big money makers would participate in such a scheme, plenty of smaller content producers could use unencumbered media to promote their work and market it to a group of users who are underserved by the traditional media industries.

Ultimately, free software's users and developers will answer the question about free software and DRM. If a demand for mainstream electronic content materializes, content producers and developers should collaborate to bring that content to free platforms. If users and developers of free platforms decide that they are better off without mainstream content and the compromises it brings, the community will continue to embrace, use, and create free media of their own. As more users are empowered by content creation and distribution technologies, a shift from the traditional monolithic model of content creation and distribution to a more distributed grassroots model may render the question moot.

(Chris is a software developer living in Chicago. He is currently working on web-based educational systems and getting a number of new podcasts off the ground. He can be reached at cjkarr@mac.com).

4

10 Questions to ask any Vendor of Digital Rights Management/Security Software for PDF*

The article points out to some of the questions one must ask the vendors of DRM before purchasing any security software.

1. Does the software provide Standard Security or DRM?
2. How Secure is the Product?

   Security vs. Usability

   The FileOpen Approach

   A few words on cracks and malicious programs
3. Are the secured files native PDF?

   Third-Party PDF Viewers

   Document Wrappers and "Plug-Outs"
4. Does the vendor hold the Integration Key License Agreement (IKLA) with Adobe Systems?

---

* This is an updated version.

---

5. Does the software support multiple client platforms?
6. Will the secured PDFs display in Internet Explorer or other Web browsers?
7. Does it work with past and future versions of Adobe Reader?

   Backward Compatibility

   Forward Compatibility
8. Does the vendor respect the principles of copyright and privacy?
9. Is the software architected for Interoperability?
10. Has the product been proven in the marketplace?

1. Does the Software Provide Standard Security or DRM?

"Standard Security" refers to the basic level of password security offered by the Adobe Acrobat product. Standard Security allows you to place an open/change password on an individual PDF document and control the basic access such as whether or not a document can be printed. There are many third-party tools available that allow you to place Standard Security on batches of PDFs via your server. But the security provided by these tools is still the password-based Standard Security, with all the limitations posed by that system, primarily that passwords are easily transferred from authorized users to non-authorized users.

DRM (Digital Rights Management) in the context of PDF means the ability to control whether or not the Adobe Reader will open or print a PDF depending on the permissions granted to the end-user by the publisher. Adobe Systems has set forth a framework for third parties to provide DRM tools for Adobe Reader via their "Security Handler" plug-in architecture. Security Handler plug-ins are small files that need to be installed only once (in the case of the FileOpen plug-in, with no user interaction necessary), and from then on manage the opening, viewing, and printing of PDFs encrypted with the DRM vendor's product. Since a Security Handler plug-in effectively controls the actions of the Adobe Reader, Adobe Systems do not let just anybody sell them (see Question no. 4).

Thus, the two means to secure PDF files that will open in Adobe Reader are passwords and Security Handler plug-ins. Any vendor who tells you that their product does not use passwords or plug-ins is either displaying PDFs in a third-party viewer, or controlling Adobe Reader from outside the purview of plug-in architecture ("plug-outs"), which places their product outside the Adobe's sanctioned framework. While the PDF file format itself is an open standard and anyone can write a third-party viewer for it, Adobe Reader is a copyrighted, proprietary viewer controlled by Adobe Systems. "Plug-outs," in addition to being inherently insecure (see Question no. 3), may violate the Adobe Reader End-User License Agreement and find their actions blocked by future versions of Adobe Reader. Indeed, it should be assumed that all such programs will be disabled at the level of the operating system, as OS vendors implement code-signing to ensure the integrity of applications and prevent hijacking by malicious programs.

2. How Secure is the Product?

Security vs. Usability

No software can offer absolute security but only a greater or lesser degree of vulnerability. The old saying that "the only secure computer is one that is in a locked room and switched off" illustrates the challenge: the more secure the system, the less useful it must be.

The goal for DRM is to create a system that is as secure as possible without degrading the experience of the authorized user (the publisher's customer). Of course, there are circumstances in which information must be secured at all costs, irrespective of any reduction in its usability. Recently, analysts have begun to describe this product category as "Enterprise Rights Management" (ERM), as distinct from the "Digital Rights Management" category, where products must be usable by consumers. Adobe's Policy Server is an example of an ERM system, whereas FileOpen's tools are, and have always been, designed for DRM.

The FileOpen Approach

So what is the right level of security for a DRM system? We believe that it is a combination of strong encryption, publisher-defined keys stored separately from documents, the transfer of those keys over a secure protocol, and a communicating client plug-in which can respond to changes in permission after the PDF has been delivered. Balanced with the need for broad compatibility with the diversity of Adobe Reader versions and operating system configurations, this approach has been successfully implemented in publishing applications as well as corporate implementations in which the security requirement is paramount.

The FileOpen WebPublisher3 system, of which our Publisher3 product is a turnkey implementation, is composed of an Encryptor module that produces security PDFs according to the Adobe PDF specification, and a Client, which is a Security Handler plug-in to the free Adobe Reader (as well as the paid versions of Adobe Acrobat).

Encryption Key Lengths and Compatibility

WebPublisher3 employs RC4 encryption as dictated by the PDF specification. Publishers have a choice of encryption key length depending on which versions of Adobe Reader they wish to support, 128-bit or 40-bit. 128-bit encryption was not supported in Adobe Reader 4 or earlier, when 40-bit encryption was the maximum level exportable under the law. Adobe has recently introduced support for 256 bit keys; however, use of these keys restricts backward compatibility still further, requiring that the users have Adobe Reader 7. At present, our customers have told us that they prefer backward compatibility to longer key lengths, but we may add support for 256 and AES (Advanced Encryption Standard) in future versions of the software.

Publisher-Defined Keys and Secure Transmission

Importantly, the actual keys used by FileOpen's Encryptor are generated by the publisher, i.e., the document owner. This is significant because it means that only that publisher knows the decryption key, and neither FileOpen Systems nor a third party has a "backdoor" way of opening files encrypted using our software.

The keys to encrypted files are stored by, and known only to, the publisher's PermissionServer, which is also entirely under the control of the publisher. The client/server communication for key transmission is typically routed over SSL, though http can be used if the publisher prefers. If offline permission is granted, the client stores keys in a local file encrypted using RC4 with a 128-bit key.

Communicating Client

Once the key has been delivered to the end-user's machine, the FileOpen Client plug-in passes that key to Adobe Reader in order to permit display of the file. The PDF remains under the control of the FileOpen plug-in running inside the Adobe Reader, and can be set to be viewable only as long as a valid session is open with the publisher's server. The Client plug-in is able to communicate with the server to check permission status every time the end-user attempts to open a PDF and view or print a particular page. These communications occur in the background and no difference is apparent to the end-user in their experience of using the PDF. In the event that a user encounters a limitation in their permissions or a revocation of permissions, the Client plug-in will display a message that is completely customizable by the Publisher and can be localized in the language of their choice (for example, to invite the user to return to the publisher web site to renew their subscription).

Of course, many publishers wish to grant some of their users offline access to a secured document, so that it may be viewed on an airplane, etc. Using WebPublisher, the publisher may grant offline permission to a document, with the option to set an expiration period on offline access after which the user must return to the publisher's site for renewed permission.

A Few Words on Cracks and Malicious Programs

All vendors of security software have a target on their backs from the hacker community. Any vendor who claims that their product is "unbreakable", is hastening the day that a hacker will prove them wrong. The best a vendor can do is to follow the example of Adobe and Microsoft, in releasing patches quickly and reducing vulnerabilities in future versions.

FileOpen systems make available fully-functional evaluation versions of our products available for publishers to put through rigorous testing before they license the software.

3. Are the Secured Files Native PDF?

Look carefully at the filename extension of a document secured with a vendor's security software. If it does not end in .pdf, the files are no longer native PDF and will not open in Adobe Reader. They will require the end-user to download and install either as a third-party viewer or un-wrapper program in order to open your secured PDF.

Third-Party PDF Viewers

Why does it matter if the secured documents require a proprietary viewer to display? It depends on your goals for distributing your documents. If you are trying to control your documents in a corporate setting, it means installing this new viewer on every end-user machine, probably requiring administrator privileges to do so. If you are trying to perform this installation over the Internet, this will inevitably result in frustrated calls to your tech support line. Otherwise, you will have to ask your end-user to get their IT department to physically install the viewer on their machine. On the other hand, you would be hard pressed to find a computer in any corporate environment that does not have the Adobe Reader pre-installed, or a corporate employee who is not familiar with opening normal PDFs.

If you are in the publishing business, it is hard to imagine why you would eschew the installed base of hundreds of millions of Adobe Readers around the world. Adobe System has put over ten years and untold dollars into establishing PDF as a standard and Reader as its default viewer. It is free, it is trusted, and everyone has it already.

Document Wrappers and "Plug-Outs"

The intermediate approach of creating an application that wraps around the Adobe viewer, adding security from the outside, has been tried by several third-party vendors over the years. This approach suffers from severe limitations.

First, while it is possible to re-encrypt a PDF file with some cipher and/or key length that is stronger than those chosen by Adobe, this provides an advantage only while the file is in transit or being stored. Once the file is opened in Acrobat, it is necessarily subject to all the risks of a PDF file in Adobe Acrobat.

Some vendors have attempted to enhance the security of the Adobe applications by running an external program ("plug-out"), to protect Acrobat, as it were from its own limitations. Besides being extremely questionable from a legal and ethical standpoint and burdensome to end-users, this approach has been demonstrated to be insecure.

The method depends on the parasite (the plug-out) not being detached from the host (Adobe Reader). Such systems work by having the external program decrypt the outer layer of the file and passing the resulting PDF (now protected only with Standard Security or no security whatsoever) to Adobe Reader for display. The problem is that the external program must now oversee the Reader to prevent malfeasance and must also prevent itself from being closed and the Reader left running, as this would leave the PDF file exposed in the now-unprotected Adobe Reader.

It should be apparent that no application vendor would condone this approach, which amounts to ceding control over that vendor's own program and user interface to an untrusted third party. As noted above, this technique closely resembles to that employed by the writers of trojans and cracking software, and thus can be expected to be outlawed by future operating systems.

The wrapper approach also degrades the seamlessness of the user experience, by adding another layer of software during the opening and usage of files. This typically disables some of the more attractive features of the PDF experience – for example: browser integration, Fast Web View and fill-in forms.

4. Does the Vendor hold the Integration Key License Agreement (IKLA) with Adobe Systems?

Any vendor of a DRM/Security plug-in for Adobe Reader must hold an Integration Key License Agreement (IKLA) with Adobe Systems. This agreement sets forth strict guidelines for those actions a security plug-in to Adobe Reader can and cannot perform. The prohibitions include:

- Interfering with the document permissions originally set by the copyright holder.
- Introducing viruses, worms, Trojan Horses or similar malicious codes.
- Degrading or interrupting the Reader user experience.

- Implementing a commercially non-viable Security Feature which reflects poorly on the Reader brand.
- Displaying a PDF document in the window of an application other than the Reader.
- Providing access or displaying content secured using Security Features other than through the use of the Plug-in.

The IKLA carries with it a substantial annual fee which signifies the commitment on the part of the vendor to the Adobe Reader platform.

As mentioned above, any vendor of a PDF DRM product who does not hold the IKLA either has their own PDF viewer, or is controlling the Adobe Reader from the outside as a "plug-out." Such vendors have not agreed to the restrictions of the IKLA listed above, which set the standard for the actions of DRM client software for PDF.

5. Does the Software Support Multiple Client Platforms?

Cross-platform operability is PDF's very reason for existence. But if a Security Handler's client plug-in only works on Windows, then only the end-users on Windows will be able to open the PDF, regardless of whether they have permission. This problem is particularly important to the publishing market, for which Macintosh and Linux users make up a significant portion of end-users.

6. Will the Secured PDFs display in Internet Explorer or other Web Browsers?

One of the most appealing features of PDF is Adobe's integration of the viewer with other applications, principally web browsers. PDF files delivered over the internet will open in the main window of most common browsers, and by now most end users are familiar with this experience.

DRM systems that re-encode PDF files typically break this interaction, forcing files to be opened outside the browser. And even when they permit opening in the browser, they cannot support the rapid-download feature, known as "Fast Web View," which makes large PDF files appear to load instantaneously.

Acrobat and Reader also work in other environments, e.g. with e-mail, from CD-ROM or within Groupware programs, and any DRM system that does not operate within the Adobe applications is unlikely to work seamlessly in all these places.

7. Does it work with Past and Future Versions of Adobe Reader?

Backward Compatibility

Lack of backward compatibility is a drawback of many security and DRM offerings, and there is an inverse correlation between backward compatibility and encryption key length. To the consternation of Adobe partners everywhere, old versions of Adobe Reader occupy the majority of end-user desktops and persist even in corporate environments. Security vendors must take advantage of the security improvements of each new release of Adobe Reader, while continuing to work in older versions, all in the same client plug-in. As the publisher, you may have to compromise between the level of security you desire and how far back you wish to go in Reader-compatibility. For example, 128-bit encryption was not supported in Adobe Reader 4 or earlier. FileOpen WebPublisher and Publisher products give you a choice between 128-bit (requiring Reader 5 or later) and 40-bit encryption (supporting Reader 4 or later).

Forward Compatibility

Whether a DRM vendor's client software will function in future versions of Adobe Reader should be of great concern to publishers. Neither security vendors nor publishers have any control over whether or when an end-user will upgrade their version of Adobe Reader. An end-user will continue to attempt to open the secure PDFs you have delivered to them after they upgrade their Acrobat Reader. Forward compatibility depends on a number of factors – are the PDFs produced by the DRM software native PDF according to the PDF specification? Does the DRM software conform to Adobe's IKLA? Does the vendor have a positive relationship with Adobe Systems such that future versions of Adobe Reader will not explicitly block the actions of their client software?

8. Does the Vendor respect the Principles of Copyright and Privacy?

DRM is about protecting the intellectual property of publishers, corporations, and individuals. As the owner of your content, you should choose your DRM vendor carefully – after all, their product will literally have a "lock" on your content in the marketplace. Vendors of DRM products should "walk the walk" of copyright protection in their business practices. Do they respect the rules set forth by Adobe Systems governing how DRM tools should interact with Adobe Reader? Or do they ally themselves with the hackers who seek to undermine PDF security?

Security and DRM software vendors must also be good citizens on the desktop of the end-user. This means respecting the privacy of the end-user (not relaying information to the publisher or themselves about anything other than their use of the secured file), and not seizing control of important processes of the operating system in the name of better security.

9. Is the Software Architected for Interoperability?

DRM is only one part of a publishing or document management system – in order to create a viable solution, the DRM subsystem must be integrated with databases, web servers, browsers, other desktop software, etc. The FileOpen offering is designed to be as open and interoperable as it is possible to be while still providing DRM functionality.

The interoperability of FileOpen WebPublisher enables publishers to use it as an additional layer of security on top of existing firewalls, extending the same business logic in use on their Web servers to their PDF documents out in the field with minimal programming. WebPublisher is also designed to interface seamlessly with any e-commerce system, playing the critical role of making sure that only users who have paid for documents can open, view, or print them.

To succeed on the Web, or in the corporate environment, software must be designed from the ground-up for interoperability. We know that Acrobat itself is a "good citizen" in the Web ecosystem, and that PDF has become one of the foundation technologies of online publishing because it embodies the perfect mix of openness and managed development. And while it may seem contradictory to speak of openness and DRM in the same sentence, the same guiding principles that apply to Acrobat and other web applications must also apply to DRM systems – a software package designed to operate as a closed system – will always present unacceptable choices to integrators and developers.

10. Has the Product been proven in the Marketplace?

As a publisher, the last thing you want is to have your legitimate end-users unable to open your secured documents. Any DRM tool has to place software on the end-user's machine, whether it is a plug-in, wrapper, or proprietary viewer. And any DRM vendor who has been around for more than a year or so will tell you from experience that it takes time and testing and constantly fixing to develop client software that will work smoothly on the majority of end-user desktops. There is no substitute for years of experience in the real world of PDF users – not millions in venture capital, or the strongest encryption in the world.

FileOpen Systems has been developing DRM software for PDF since 1997, and the FileOpen WebPublisher plug-in has been distributed to millions of desktops around the world since its release in 2002. Our customers benefit from the peace of mind of knowing that our software has withstood the test of time, and that as a licensed Adobe Security Partner, will continue to innovate and meet the challenges of the future.

5

Costs of Digital Preservation

The article examines various costs involved in Digital Rights Management. Costs include – costs of creating a digital repository for long-term preservation of digital records, personal costs, costs of securing software. It also discusses some other inherent costs like training, maintenance and support costs. Further, the article presents a cost model which is prepared in the form of an excel sheet which would better prepare the company for future costs.

Cost Indicators and the Cost Model

Testbed has studied the costs involved in the long-term preservation of digital records, drawn up a list of indicators which exert an influence on the total cost of preservation, designed a computational model for the calculation of these costs, and compared the costs involved in the various methods for the creation of digital records and in the various preservation strategies.

These costs are estimates based on Testbed's studies and experience, published information, and information others have supplied to Testbed. These detailed estimates are intended to encourage others to submit their comments on these figures, and to report the costs incurred in practice.

This discussion is, in the first instance, focused on the larger archives; however, it is also applicable to the local storage needs of ministries and other (government) agencies. The costs identified will always be incurred, irrespective of whether the relevant records need to be stored for no more than 10 or 20 years or come into consideration for permanent preservation. Although the scale of the storage system or repository and the relative sizes of the different components of the installation may vary, the following cost factors will in any case need to be taken into consideration.

Although the following list might initially appear to be extremely detailed, it is nevertheless important not to overlook any of these factors. It will, in particular, be necessary to calculate capital and personnel costs. Digital preservation will continue to develop and change. Consequently, the functionality for sustainable preservation of digital records will also need to change. The costs incurred in making future changes need to be incorporated in the computational model right from the very beginning.

Summary of the Cost Indicators

The costs involved in the long-term preservation of digital records are influenced by a number of factors. These are summarised below. In the following discussion, a digital archive is included as an element of the costs, as is the storage of the digital records, for example, in an RMA (Records Management Application) or a DMS (a Document Management System). It is often difficult to specify the demarcations between the actual use of the records, their local storage, local preservation, archiving, and long-term preservation. The concept of the 'records continuum', which is ideally suited to use in this context, can be defined as: 'a consistent and coherent regime of management processes from the time of the creation of records (and before creation, in the design of record keeping systems), through to the preservation and use of records as archives.'

Consequently, digital preservation is not just a necessity for archival repositories, but also for every organisation. Each organisation will need to specify its own requirements, determine its own demarcations, and tailor the cost model discussed in this chapter to its specific situation.

Testbed makes a distinction between the following cost indicators:

1. The cost of the digital archival system (a digital depot or repository) and functionality for the long-term preservation of digital records[1]
2. Personnel costs.
3. The cost of the development (or procurement) of software and methods for the preservation of digital records.
4. The cost of the actual storage of digital records.
5. Other factors that exert an influence on the total cost.

1. The cost of a digital repository and functionality for the long-term preservation of digital records.

The cost of a digital archival repository and functionality for long-term preservation is comprised of various components. The cost model indicates the major factors and the minor factors. It also explains which indicators are influenced by the different ways in which records can be created and by the different preservation strategies, and which indicators are not sensitive to (strategic) choices of this nature.

1.1 The Physical Space

1.1.1 Server room, with air-conditioning

1.1.2 Sufficient office space

1.1.3 Conference room

1.1.4 Toilets and kitchen

1.1.5 Security.

Physical space is required for systems for storage and long-term preservation. Servers will be required for the storage of digital records and for the management of long-term preservation. It may be advisable to set up separate development, test and production facilities for long-term preservation. This can reduce the risks and increase productivity. There will also be a need for offices and conference rooms, for both the staff and visitors.

---

1 See: Functional specifications for a preservation system.

1.2 Hardware for the Digital Archival Repository

1.2.1 Servers for the storage of digital records

1.2.2 Disks, tapes, or other storage media

1.2.3 Backup equipment

1.2.4 Network communications.

Hardware is required for the storage of records (in a file system, archival repository, or RMA). It will also be necessary to configure the storage equipment once an impression has been gained of the number of records that will need to be stored.

Appreciable costs can be incurred in the purchase of storage media (tapes, CDs). Make sure an adequate amount is budgeted for effective storage and backup media.

Network facilities may also be important. Archival repositories that receive large numbers of digital records from diverse locations may require a high-speed connection or a flexible connection capable of accommodating varying loads.

1.3 Software for the Digital Archival Repository

1.3.1 Operating system

1.3.2 Security

1.3.3 Specific software for archives management

1.3.4 Old software applications

1.3.5 New (current) software applications

1.3.6 Display programs

1.3.7 Communications software

1.3.8 Database licences.

This section covers issues such as the purchase of operating systems and the standard software for databases. There will also be a need for protection software (against viruses, unauthorised access, and tampering with the archives by unauthorised persons), besides a need for specific software for the receipt and storage of authentic digital archival records, such as Depot 2000 or the Digital

Archive System of the United Kingdom National Archives[2]. Every organisation which works with digital records will, irrespective of its size, have a need for a DMS (Document Management System) or an RMA (Records Management Application).

The following discussion assumes that the archival repository possesses functionality to provide access to the stored records. Consequently, in addition to the customary storage software, there will also be a need for specific applications or display software which enable users to display (or use) the stored records.

Communications software and network and database licences are two other issues that are often overlooked when preparing the budget.

1.4 Hardware for the Preservation System

1.4.1 Servers for the preparation of software

1.4.1 Servers for the testing of software

1.4.3 Servers for the storage of records before preservation action

1.4.3 Servers for the storage of records subsequent to preservation action

1.4.5 Work stations for programming work

1.4.6 Disks and tapes

1.2.3 Backup equipment

1.2.4 Network communications

1.4.9 Reading equipment for tapes and disks.

The preservation system may require computer systems (servers and storage) of the same type and size as the archival repository. This is necessary so that the preservation system can receive groups of records with a total size in excess of several terabytes. The system will need to store these records in a safe manner ready for, for example, performing preservation operations (such as migration or emulation), assessing the results of preservation actions, and returning the preserved records to the archival repository (digital depot).

---

2 *http://www.pro.gov.uk/about/preservation/digital/archive/default.htm*

In addition, more servers and storage equipment may be required for the development and testing of:

- Preservation methods,
- Software to evaluate the results of preservation operations,
- Other tools.

When automated tools are to be developed and tested, the test system may need to test large datasets so as to collect sufficient statistical proof of the tools' success.

The preservation system may need a variety of different types of reading equipment to read the various formats of tapes and/or disks.

1.5 Software Preservation System

1.5.1 Operating systems

1.5.2 Program environments

1.5.3 Security

1.5.4 Old software applications

1.5.5 New (current) software applications

1.5.6 Software for the preservation of documents

1.5.7 Test and evaluation software

1.5.8 Communications software

1.5.9 Database licences.

Extremely comprehensive software may be required for the sustainable preservation of records. The preservation system may require more than one operating system, since it may be necessary to transfer records from their original operating system to another operating system capable of an improved preservation performance. In addition, there may also be a need for more than one programming environment if the organisation plans to develop in-house software tools or modify third-party tools.

The preservation system will also need to cater for a comprehensive package of software applications. This will allow for research into the different options for preservation and experimentation with a range of records and record-batches.

Automation is a significant factor in controlling the costs of large-scale digital preservation. Manual processing is one of the largest cost items for digital preservation. Consequently, automated preservation actions and automated evaluation (tests) are significant factors in controlling the costs of digital preservation.

2. Personnel Costs

This Section reviews the staff duties involved in the operation of a preservation system. The discussion reviews the numbers and types of staff that will be required. The cost model discussed later in this chapter is based on the time that will be needed from such staff, who have various qualifications and skills.

Personnel costs always form a major factor. The necessary staff could be selected or recruited specifically to work upon the digital archive and preservation system. However, in some instances, it may be preferable to second staff from other disciplines (such as the records-management department or the ICT department). In yet other situations, preference might be given to the use of temporary employees, or to the use of the services of a specialised company.

2.1 Duties of Digital Archives Personnel

2.1.1 Compile requirements

2.1.2 Obtain funds and support

2.1.3 Design and construct the digital archives.

The staff will need to begin by designing and constructing the digital archive. This will require a budget for between one and two man-years; cost calculations should not underestimate this.

Even designs obtained from other organisations or purchased from a commercial supplier will still require modification to meet the needs of the specific organisation.

2.1.4 Stocking the digital archive

2.1.5 Process management

2.1.6 Managing the digital repository

2.1.7 Security management

2.1.8 Quality control system and documents

2.1.9 Standard Operating Procedures (SOPs)

2.1.10 User manuals.

Once the digital archive has been constructed, the next step will be to develop the procedures and commence the management of the digital archive. The internal management encompasses the security and access procedures, a comprehensive quality system (to ensure the authenticity of the records stored in the digital repository), everyday SOPs (Standard Operating Procedures), and user manuals.

Management can also incorporate external activities, such as the identification of records, the arrangement of records, acquisitions, and cataloguing.

2.2 Duties of Preservation System Personnel

2.2.1 Compile requirements

2.2.2 Obtain funds and support

2.2.3 Design the preservation system

2.2.4 Construct the preservation system

2.2.5 Process management

2.2.6 Management of the preservation system

2.2.7 Ongoing security management

2.2.8 Quality control and documents

2.2.9 SOPs

2.2.10 User manuals.

The staff responsible for the preservation system will also first need to design and construct the system. They will then need to establish the quality control system, the SOPs, and the procedures. Finally, they will need to begin the development of the preservation methods and evaluation tests, and start work on the sustainable preservation of the records.

Once again, the costs incurred in the development and construction phase are easily underestimated.

2.3 Duties of Public-services Staff

2.3.1 Access management

2.3.2 Training and schooling.

3. The cost of the development (or procurement) of software and methods for the preservation of records

3.1 Determine Authenticity Requirements

3.2 Analyse Authenticity Requirements

One important Testbed conclusion was that digital preservation is not a question of all or nothing. In many instances, the characteristics of records that are essential to the records' integrity and authenticity can be separated from other less important characteristics. Digital preservation activities can then focus on those aspects of essential importance to the integrity and authenticity of the record.

The aforementioned tasks can be carried out solely by the organisation that created the records. The initial costs incurred in digital preservation relate to issues such as determining the authenticity requirements for each batch of records. In an ideal situation, these requirements will be specified by the records managers. However, in some situations, it may be necessary for the (authenticity) requirements to be determined by a multidisciplinary team comprised of specialists such as archives-management and IT specialists, whereby every member of the team has some experience in the other specialists' fields.

The cost model assumes that (authenticity) requirements will need to be determined for each batch of records. A batch contains records all made with the same application, the acquisition or preservation of which all takes place at the same time. It will later be shown that the size of the batch is a critical factor in the cost.

3.3 Design Preservation Approach

3.4 Develop Preservation Approach

3.5 Preservation Software (parser, etc.)

3.6 Viewing Software

Once the authenticity specifications have been determined, the next step is to design and develop a suitable preservation approach. Since this is a lengthy process that requires a large number of skills, it is assumed that an international collection of shared preservation strategies will gradually be developed. However, even then it will still be necessary to evaluate these strategies in terms of the specific requirements of the batch of records in question. In some instances, it will ultimately be necessary to modify the approach.

3.7 Test the Approach

3.8 If Approved, Continue

3.9 If not Approved, Return to 3.1, 3.2, or 3.3

3.10 Document the Approach

Finally, each strategy or approach will need to be tested and documented. All the IT operations involved in each preservation system will need to comply with the most stringent quality standards. A high level of quality is of essential importance to the authenticity, since the quality systems and the documentation are needed to prove that the preservation actions have achieved the intended results, and that they have had no influence on other records. A high level of quality also increases the probability that the approach will be re-used in this or other preservation systems.

4. Cost of the Performance of Preservation Actions

This Section reviews the costs incurred in the performance of preservation actions on digital records. Within this context, the 'performance of preservation actions' can relate to diverse activities:

- The migration of records (transformation).
- The performance of a migration on request.
- The use of emulation to retain the accessibility of records.

These can be specified with OAIS terminology[3]. A migration or other form of transformation of the records results in changes to the Archival Information Package (AIP) stored in the archives. AIP1 is changed into AIP2. AIP2 serves as the basis for the DIP (Dissemination Information Package) issued to applicants. Migration is one of the preservation strategies examined by Testbed.

The performance of a 'migration on request'[4] has no influence on the AIP. It is possible to produce a DIP which differs from the last DIP produced by the same AIP. It will in any case be necessary to produce a DIP that is both authentic and accessible. Migration on request will require the preparation, testing and issue of an appropriate software tool before the migration (or another form of transformation) is carried out. If a user requests a record, the correct tool is retrieved and the record subsequently transformed. The user receives the transformed copy in the form of a DIP. The transformed copy can be stored, or deleted once the user has finished with it.

Another form of transformation which Testbed examined as a possible approach to the sustainable preservation of records is conversion to XML. The costs for this are included in the migration. The possible cost benefits of XML (because it is an open standard, is expected to have a long and useful life, and can be interpreted by a variety of applications) are explained below. Conversion to XML changes the AIP from AIP1 to AIPX, whereby AIPX is in XML.

Retaining access to digital records through the use of emulation has no influence on the record contained in the AIP. In principle, the DIP will also remain unchanged in the future, although in practice, it may be necessary to implement a number of small modifications to the DIP to accommodate future technology. In this respect, Testbed has examined the UVC approach formulated by IBM. This approach is based in part on emulation, and in part on migration.

---

3 *http://ssdoo.gsfc.nasa.gov/nost/isoas/ref_model.html*

4 'Cedars Guide to Digital Preservation Strategies', Clare Jenkins, April 2002.

In fact, and as will be revealed by our cost model, the cost of digital preservation activity is only a small fraction of the total cost of the digital archive. The cost of digital preservation also depends on the size of the batch: the cost model will reveal that grouping records in larger batches is a particularly cost-effective approach.

4.1 Determine which Digital Records will need to be Preserved

4.2 Construct the Interface with the Archives-management System

4.3 Incorporate Systems for Electronic Records Management, DMS, RMA

4.4 Receive Digital Records

4.5 Select the Preservation Strategy and Approach

Records which will need transformation, or which require the development and testing of an emulator, can be identified by an automated process (a technology watch, or a process within an RMA or DMS) or by means of manual identification. Records requiring transformation will first need to be selected and transferred to the preservation system, after which a preservation strategy can be assigned to them.

4.6 Preparing Records for Transformation

4.7 Supply Metadata

4.8 Repair or Modify Records

In specific circumstances, it will be necessary to prepare records for transformation. Records will be in need of 'repair' if metadata are missing, or when the records possess properties that could pose risks with the selected preservation strategy. This can be a slow and labour-intensive process that accounts for the majority of the costs.

Automated methods for the assignment of metadata or the repair of records can greatly reduce the associated costs.

4.9 The Transformation of Records using the Selected Method

4.10 Evaluation of the Transformation

4.11 The Records are Accessible

4.12 The Records are Authentic

4.13 If NO, Return to 4.9 or to an Earlier Step.

4.14 Storage of Preserved Records in the Digital Archives

The final step is to transform the records. Every transformation will need to be evaluated to demonstrate that the records are still accessible and to ensure their authenticity and integrity after the transformation. Within the context of this discussion, 'transformation' refers both to migration and conversion to XML.

Transformed records shall need to be transmitted to the digital archive, where they will be stored until further preservation actions are required and where access to the records can be managed.

Note: it is assumed that hardware emulation is not employed. When hardware emulation is used, there will be (virtually) no transformation costs, and no recurrent costs for the preparation of records. The cost model reviews the long-term cost benefits offered by emulation.

5. Other Factors that exert an Influence on the Total Costs

Other factors not mentioned in the above summary are also of relevance. These indirect factors can, however, account for a substantial proportion of the total costs. In addition, they can also have an influence on the impact of a number of the aforementioned factors.

5.1 Public Services

5.1.1 Number of users

5.1.2 Required training and support tools

5.1.3 Required maintenance and support.

The degree to which users draw upon the services of the archive and preservation systems will have a great influence on the costs; however, the provision of services also offers an opportunity for the generation of income. Kevin Ashley has drawn up a summary of the costs incurred in providing public services[5].

---

[5] Digital Archive Costs: Facts and Fallacies, Kevin Ashley, DLM Forum 1999. *http://www.europa.eu.int/ISPO/dlm/fulltext/full_ashl_en.htm*

5.2 The time between Preservation Actions

The time between preservation actions is a critical cost factor. The more preservation actions, the higher the costs. In addition, more preservation actions increases the risk of affecting the authenticity and integrity of the records, and there may also be a need for additional tests.

The costs can be reduced with longer periods of time between the preservation actions. However, preservation actions carried out at excessively great intervals of time can increase the risk of problems with digital preservation and the cost of preservation.

5.3 Technology Watch – Assessing when the Hazards Increase

A technology watch requires the monitoring of the hardware, software and systems used for the current records. The threatened obsolescence of components on which the digital records are dependent will give cause to the need for an evaluation and implementation of the necessary measures.

5.4 Supplementary Storage Requirements

Testbed recommends that the original files of the preserved records also be stored. We advise that text document records are stored in both PDF and XML. These recommendations increase the storage space required for each record. In some instances, the space can be increased by a factor of between three and five. Although storage is relatively cheap, this will result in additional costs.

5.5 Links to the Management Systems for Electronic Records

Testbed has not examined links in DMSs or RMAs. However, it is to be expected that these links will be desirable at some point in the future. Extra costs will be incurred in the construction and maintenance of these links.

5.6 Volume of Records

The expected volume of the records to be stored and managed will have substantial consequences for the costs. The storage costs increase linearly with the volume. Moreover, the required space will increase even more rapidly when the records need to be stored in a variety of formats (for example, the original file format and two migrated formats).

More expensive servers and storage systems may be required for large volumes of records (more than 500 Terabytes), in particular when there is a need for rapid access to the records. It should be noted, however, that the cost of digital preservation is influenced more by the variety (diversity) of the records than by the volume of the records. Records that make use of various functions of an application or different application software will generally require different preservation strategies, or at least a variety of tests for the preservation strategies. For this reason, it will cost less to preserve a few large batches of records which all use the same application (maybe also the same template) and have the same authenticity requirements, than it will a large number of small but diverse batches that take up the same amount of storage space.

5.7 Requirements for Authenticity and Reliability

The authenticity requirements for a specific type of records constitute a significant cost factor. Consider, for example, a text document. Preservation of this will be a relatively simple task when only the plain text (the content) needs to be preserved. Highlights can also be preserved, at a slightly increased cost. However, the costs will increase if the exact position of each character on the page and the exact colour must to be preserved. This will also complicate the preservation tests for the approach.

For this reason, it is important that the authenticity requirements are determined in as comprehensive and realistic manner as possible.

5.8 Preservation of the Systems themselves

5.8.1 Preservation of the archival system

5.8.2 Preservation of the preservation system.

Finally, it will also be necessary to preserve the systems themselves. These costs will in part be covered by depreciation, as a result of which, funds are made available for a three to five-year replacement cycle. However, it is also possible that specific elements of the preservation system form part of the digital record or preservation object[6], as a result of which, these will need to be preserved separately.

6 See Chapter 5 of the Database recommendations for a further explanation of what is referred to as the 'preservation object'.

One example of such an element is the preservation log file, the logbook of earlier preservation operations, which will also need to be preserved. Another example is the emulator, which will need to be preserved to ensure for the continued accessibility of the records and for their possible reuse.

Cost Model: Results

A cost model has been prepared in the form of an Excel spreadsheet. This computational model (version 1.0; 20 April 2005) is available from the Testbed website: (*http://www.digitaleduurzaamheid.nl/index.cfm?paginakeuze=185&categorie=6*). The following sections review a number of the most important conclusions, and relate these to other general information about the costs of preservation and of archiving records. The sections are arranged in the lifecycle of a record, i.e., its creation, acquisition (by the archive), transformation and, where applicable, emulation.

1. Assumptions made for the Computational Model

It is assumed that there are six categories of staff, who are paid four different hourly salaries. It is also assumed that each category of staff works 1620 hours per annum. A cost category is assigned to each category of staff and will be used in later parts of the spreadsheet:

- Administrative Support (1), hourly wage EUR14
- Archivist/Records Manager (2), hourly wage EUR25
- Supervisor (3), hourly wage EUR32
- Data-management Assistant (4), hourly wage EUR18
- Programmer (5), hourly wage EUR25
- Senior IT Assistant (6), hourly wage EUR32.

The above salaries have been assumed for the purpose of calculations with the computational model; they are, of course, open to discussion and/or amendment. Amendments can be made to all calculations in the computational model that make use of the relevant salary.

It is assumed that the archive and preservation system will need four types of space. An estimate has been made of the cost of furnishing each type. A proposal has also been made for the number of staff, based on full-time equivalents (FTEs), to be based in each category of space. Once again, amendments can be made to the computational model that will influence the results from the calculations.

- *Space for the digital archive system*: 1 FTE, categories 2 and 4; costs EUR1,897,400 in the first year and EUR632,403 in every successive year; storage capacity 100 Tb.
- *Office space*: 1.4 FTE, categories 1 and 3; costs EUR7,400 in the first year and EUR2,466 in every successive year. Standard office equipment and furnishings.
- *Development and test area*: 3FTEs, categories 4, 5 and 6; costs EUR50,200 in the first year and EUR16,731 in every successive year. This room will be equipped with additional software (program environments) and hardware (inclusive of older systems and newer systems). These facilities will be used for the development of digital preservation tools.
- *Space for the digital preservation system*: 3FTEs, categories 2, 4 and 5; costs EUR279,600 in the first year and EUR93,190 in every successive year. This room is intended for the acceptance, transformation and testing of digital records. The equipment will be capable of storing 10 Terabytes of records each time. If so required, this room can be combined with the space for the digital archive.

The facility specified here should be able to manage a total of 100 Tb of records, and could readily be expanded to 1000 Terabyte (1 Petabyte) or more. This facility would be able to cater for the annual acquisition and transformation of 40 batches of e-mails (2000 e-mails in each batch), 20 batches of text documents (200 documents in each batch), 20 batches of spreadsheets (20 in each batch), and 20 databases. A batch of 4000 e-mails costs about the same as a batch of 2000 e-mails, provided that they have been created in a durable manner. Every year, this facility would be able to develop 55 ‘preservation approaches’, each for a different batch of records. It would be possible to carry out more work at the same cost in the event that different batches resemble each other. For example, it would be possible to use the same preservation approach for two batches of text documents which differ only with respect to the process in which they were used, but that were created by the same application, possess the same properties, and are governed by the same authenticity requirements. The use of the same preservation approach would result in substantial cost savings.

The aforementioned batches would require a total storage capacity of 5 Gb (on the basis of 50 kb per e-mail, 100 kb per text document, 250 kb per spreadsheet, and 2 Mb per database). The discrepancy between these figures and the total storage capacity of the model facility compared, on the one hand, with the NARA figures for electronic records or on the other hand, with the Amsterdam Municipal Archives, indicates two things:

- the estimated number of digital records that can be processed by a team is probably a conservative estimate;
- the automation of the procedures used for the acquisition, inspection, and transformation of digital records will result in tangible benefits.

2. The Creation of Documents

From the recommendations that Testbed has made for four types of records, it will be clear that digital preservation begins at source, i.e., at the time of the creation of the records. The creation of records in an appropriate manner is a quicker, cheaper and less risky manner of obtaining suitable durable records, compared to the 'repair' of those records at a later date.

Testbed has estimated the costs incurred in the creation of durable documents with the appropriate metadata, the addition of metadata and performance of repairs after 2 years or less, and the addition of metadata and performance of repairs after 10 years or less.

The differences in cost per record become substantial when they are applied to batches of 1000 records.

Approximately, EUR333 must be paid for the creation of a batch of 1000 records in an appropriate manner (the first bar in the graph). This calculation is based on a cost of EUR0.33 for the creation of a well-constructed record.

Graph 1: Cost of the 'repair' of Records

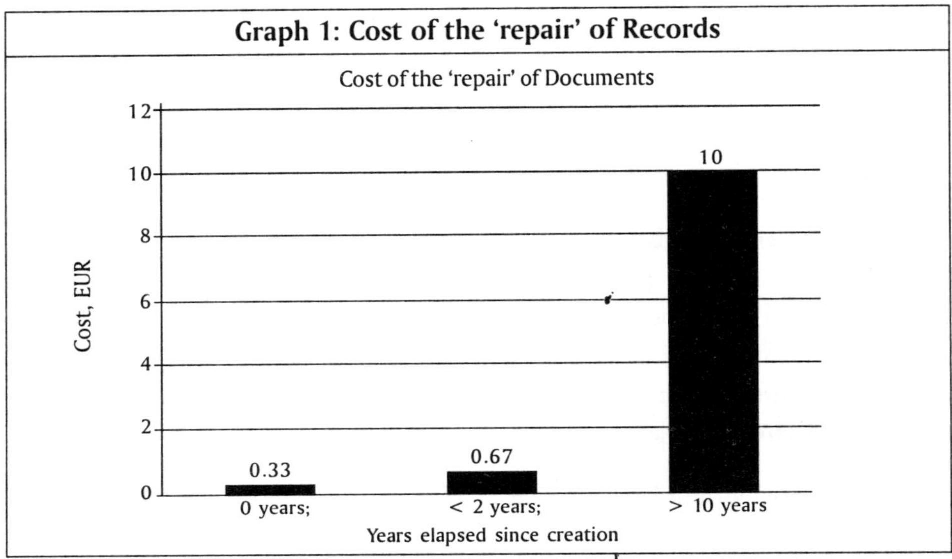

Conversely, it will cost EUR10,000 (the third bar in the graph) to 'repair' a batch of 1000 badly created records.

Another good example of this effect is the cost difference of emails that have been preserved from a standard email application (such as Outlook), compared to e-mails preserved using a system focused on durability, such as Testbed's XML/e-mail application. The usual cost incurred in the acquisition and input of metadata amounts to EUR1.41 per normal e-mail, whilst the cost is no more than EUR0.06 per XML e-mail. The difference is that the XML emails are already equipped with the appropriate metadata and structure.

Accession to an Archive

The accession phase shows the effect of batch size on costs. This effect continues into the sustainable preservation phase. At every stage, larger batches of records cost less to manage. The reason for this is that metadata and processes can be added to 10,000 similar records as quickly as they can be added to one record. The time required to process a batch of records does not depend greatly on the size of the batch. For this reason the cost per record is much lower for large batches. How can records be grouped into batches? A group of records from the same application (such as an e-mail or a word-processing program) that all contain

Graph 2: Cost of Acquistion and Preservation of Existing e-mail Messages

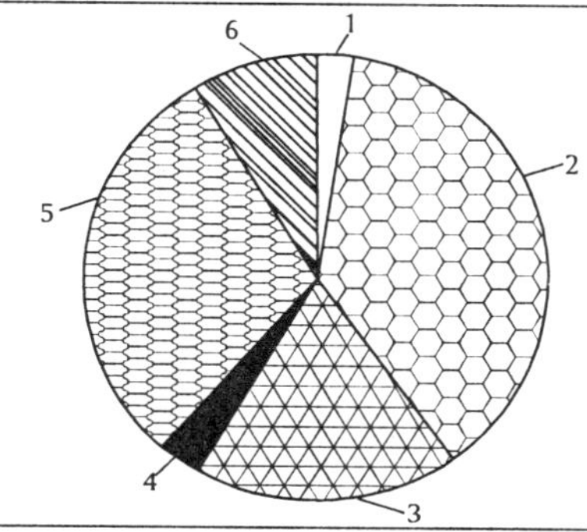

Legend:

1 = Acquire and appraise batch of e-mail,

2 = Necessary metadata,

3 = Repair digital records,

4 = Determine authenticity requirements for batch,

5 = Develop and test the preservation approach,

6 = Perform preservation and assess of e-mails.

The above legend relates to both graphs. In the below graph items 2, 3 and 5 are all 0.

Graph 3: Cost of Acquisition and Preservation of Existing XML e-mail Messages

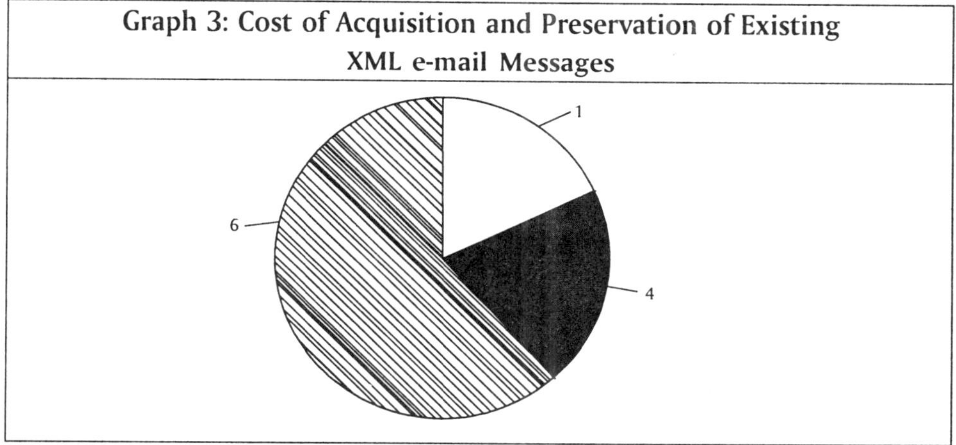

explicit and correct metadata and which can all be processed in the same manner, can be processed together in a batch.

The graph reveals that the total cost for acquiring and preserving the e-mails decreases from EUR 102 per e-mail to EUR 2.35 per e-mail when the batch size is increased from 20 to 2000 e-mails. Acquiring and preserving e-mails already created in XML (for example, using the application developed by Testbed) costs even less (EUR 0.34 per e-mail for a batch of 2000 e-mails). The development of the approach is the most costly element of the process. If the approach can be used by several batches of records, through careful process design, then a significant saving can be made.

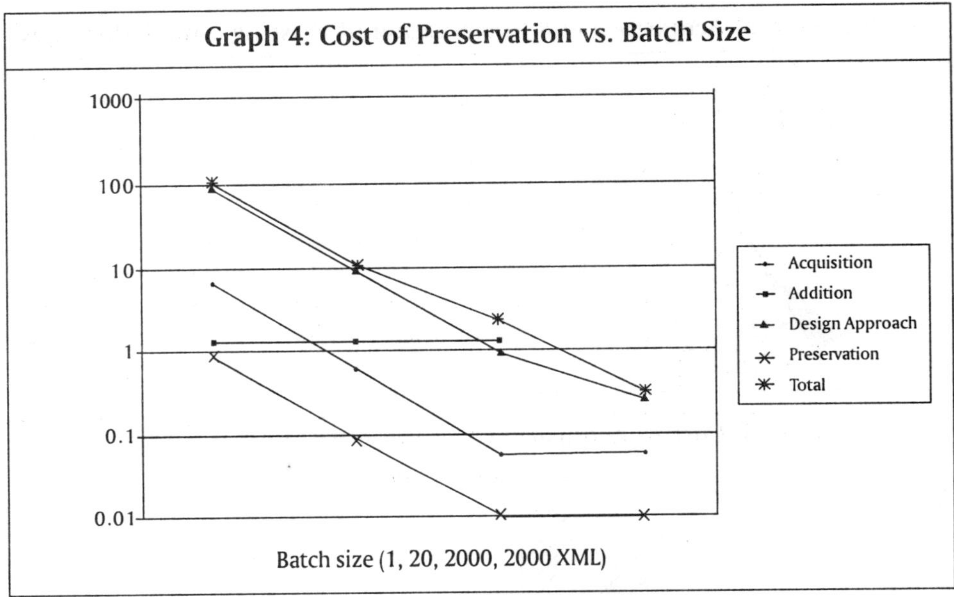

3. Transformation of Different Types of Records

It is difficult to compare the costs of different preservation methods because they depend on so many different factors, the specific values of which will vary between different organisations. The migration costs have been calculated for each of the four record types investigated by Testbed. The costs for transformation do not differ substantially. The majority of the costs relate to the development and testing of the approach, and testing the transformed records. These costs remain constant for the migration from one application (version) to another, or for transformation to a standard format.

As discussed above, the size of the batch is one of the most significant variables for the transformation. For the purposes of this comparison, it is assumed that e-mails are supplied in batches of 2000, text documents in batches of 200 and spreadsheets in batches of 20, and that databases are received and managed on an individual basis.

Testbed's experience has also revealed that the amount of work involved in adding metadata to each type of record, and in developing and testing the requisite transformation, varies with the type of record. The following graphs show the costs for existing and new records (such as records created in XML, whereby the correct metadata can be added at the point of creation).

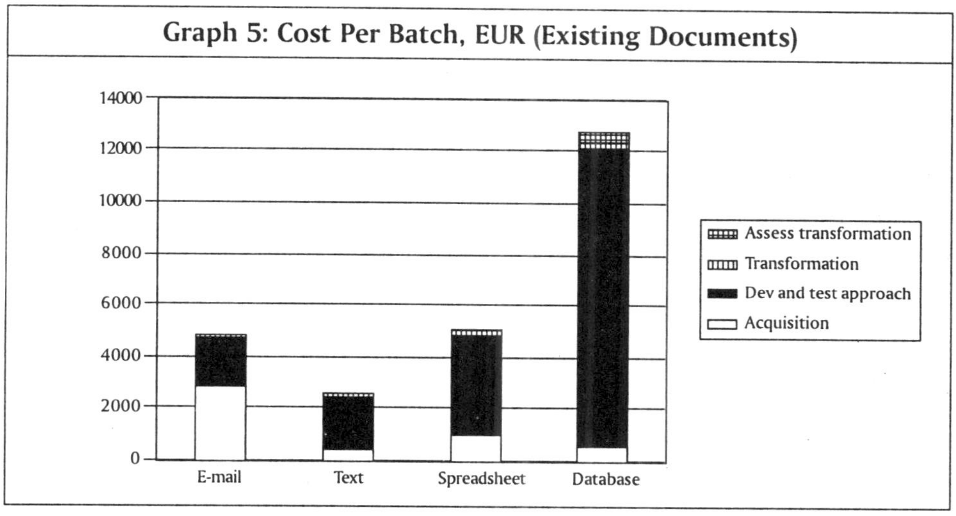

Graph 5: Cost Per Batch, EUR (Existing Documents)

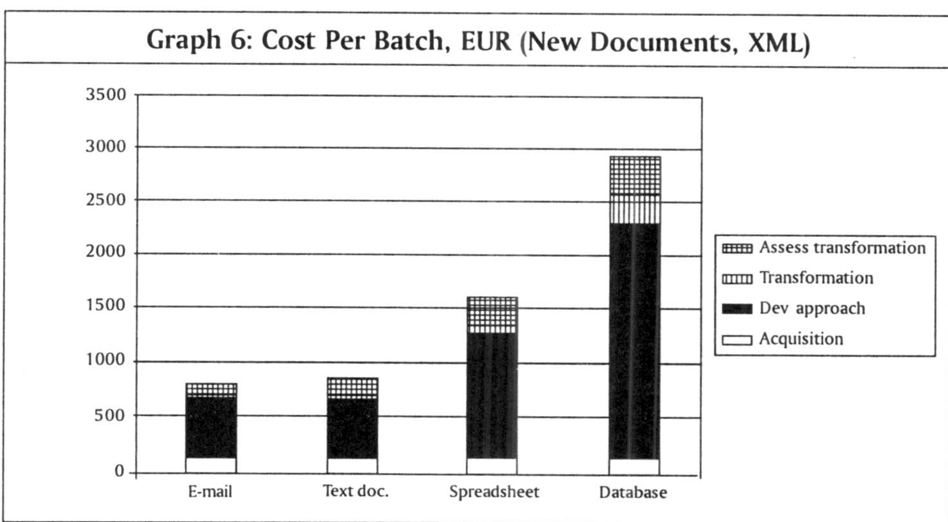

Graph 6: Cost Per Batch, EUR (New Documents, XML)

The total acquisition and preservation costs for batches of well-formed records are much lower than the costs for batches of badly created records. Acquisition (which here encompasses the repair of records and the metadata) is a significant cost item for badly formed records. Substantial costs will also be incurred when developing the approach. The development costs per batch can be substantially reduced if the approach can be shared by several batches.

4. Emulation (Inclusive of the UVC Approach)

Hardware emulation, the only form of emulation included in this review of the costs, offers two benefits when compared to migration as a preservation strategy. The first advantage is that the records themselves do not need to be modified. The second is that one emulator can be used for a variety of record types. Consequently, one Pentium-PC emulator would cover text documents (whether prepared in Word, Open Office or Lotus SmartSuite), spreadsheets, and desktop databases.

The following graph compares the costs for the maintenance of a collection of records, including e-mails, text documents, spreadsheets and databases, over a 100-year period. This collection resembles a shopping basket: arbitrary, but nevertheless illustrative. It is assumed that:

- The records need to be migrated every 5 or 10 years.
- New emulators are needed every 7 or 15 years.
- Once the authenticity requirements for a batch of records have been identified, they do not have to be re-assessed.
- Once added, metadata do not need further modification (other than the automatic addition of new preservation metadata about each preservation operation).
- This cost calculation uses a 'basket' of records containing one batch of each type of records, together with a mixture of existing and newly-created (durably-created) records.
- It is estimated that the development of an emulator will require 1.75 years of work by a team of three persons.

In this second graph, it is also assumed that ten batches of each type of records must be preserved and that each type can make use of the same emulator, but that different migration operations are required for each batch, for example, as a result of different authenticity requirements.

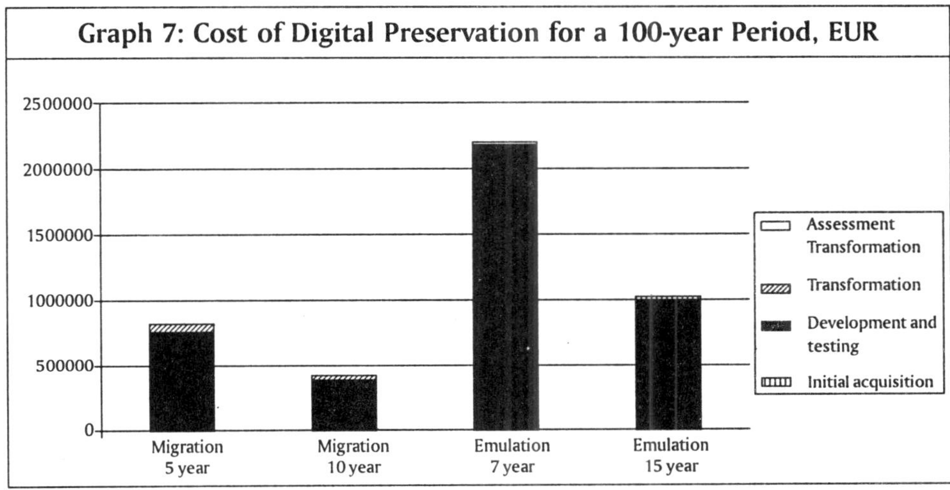

Graph 7: Cost of Digital Preservation for a 100-year Period, EUR

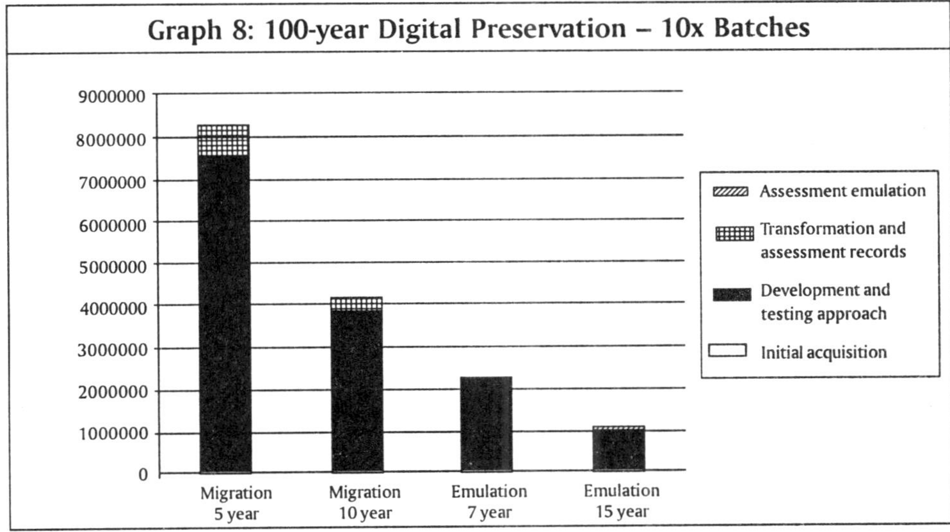

Graph 8: 100-year Digital Preservation – 10x Batches

The advantage of emulation in this example is that only one emulator need be developed for all records created by application software that used to run on the old emulated platform. In contrast, records from different software applications will require different migration approaches, and differences in authenticity requirements between batches from the same application can require different approaches.

5. Cost Information from other Sources

Testbed has obtained information about the cost issue of digital preservation from a number of other sources. This information can be used for an independent check of the calculations and the cost model. For the purposes of these cost comparisons, it may prove useful to consider the following equivalences:

- 1 metre of records (linear, on a shelf) is approximately equal to
  - 0,09 cubic metre (based on A4 pages), which is about
  - 3 cubic feet, with about
  - 6,500 pages that, in digital form, would occupy about
  - 65 Mb of storage space (as flat text).

Delft University of Technology, Utrecht University

The team in Delft and Utrecht has published a cost estimate for medium-term digital preservation that is one of the most detailed and carefully-considered estimates published to date. Dekker, Durr *et. al.*[7] have analysed the costs for the maintenance of records over twenty years.

National Archives of Canada

The National Archives of Canada employs about 661 FTEs and has an annual expenditure of about CAD 49,000,000. This excludes certain services supplied by other agencies, such as accommodation. The total costs of the National Archives amount to about CAD 90,000,000 per annum.

Of the main expenditure, EUR30,460,000 (at CAD 1 = EUR0.6217), about 30%, was destined for the acquisition and management of records, 18% for the management of government information, and 26% for services, awareness, and assistance.

The Annual Report of the National Archives of Canada (see www.archives.ca) notes that during his 15-year period of office, the then Prime Minister Mr. Pierre

[7] An electronic archive for academic communities, November 2001.

Trudeau created some 1.3 Mb of electronic information. The offices of the current Prime Minister, Mr. Jean Chretien, create about 1.3 Mb of digital records every day.

The current records stored by the National Archives comprise 111 km of paper government text records, 45 km of paper text documents from private individuals, 3.2 Gb of digital records, 2,500,000 maps and architectural drawings, 345,000 hours of audio, video or film, and 22,734,000 other items. The cost of managing government records amounts to about CAD 80 per meter shelf, equivalent to about EUR50 per shelf meter.

The UK National Archives (formerly the Public Record Office)

The UK National Archives (formerly the Public Record Office) looks after about 176 km of records at a cost of about GBP97 per metre (EUR135) for the selection and preservation of the records.

Providing access to the records results in additional costs for each visit, namely GBP5.59 (EUR7.80) for on-site access and GBP0.13 (EUR0.18) for online access.

The UK National Archives has a workforce of 451 FTEs and an annual budget of about GBP35,600,000 (= EUR49,662,000). The annual reports are published on *www.nationalarchives.gov.uk and www.pro.gov.uk.*

National Archives of Australia

The National Archives of Australia (www.naa.gov.au) has a workforce of about 435, of whom 322 work full-time. The annual budget is about AUD148,000,000 (EUR83,428,000 at an exchange rate of AUD1 = EUR0.5637) of which AUD38,274,000 (EUR21,575,000) is destined for personnel and operational costs. (The remaining costs relate to depreciation, which in Australia also includes changes in the value of the collection itself.)

US National Archives and Records Administration (NARA)

The NARA Performance Report 2002[8] indicates that the budget for 'space and preservation' amounted to USD128,000,000 (EUR109,000,000 at

---

8 *http://www.archives.gov/about_us/strategic_planning_and_reporting/2002_performance _report.html#goal3*

USD1 = EUR0.8524), with 338 FTEs. This also includes digital preservation, which is not stated separately in the accounts. NARA reported that in the preceding year, the volume of 'logical records' (digital records) increased by 60% and that the volume of digital records during the presidency of President Clinton increased by 1500% (a factor of 15) in comparison with the preceding presidency.

Of these significant electronic holdings, 98% records are accessible, irrespective of their original format. NARA now manages about 4×10^9 'logical records'.

It should be noted that the total NARA budget amounted to USD286,000,000 (EUR244,000,000), and that in 2002 it had a workforce of 2829 FTEs.

NARA's digital preservation programme has 48.5 FTEs. Of these, 42.5% are active in ingest, i.e., maintaining relations with records producers, receiving records, generating Archival Information Packages (AIPs). A further 20 work on digital archival storage: receiving the AIPs, managing the storage hierarchy, monitoring quality, and generating access copies. 8% are engaged in data management, 7.5% in accounting, and 14% in user services and access. Preservation planning takes up 8% of staff time.

Amsterdam Municipal Archives

In 2001, the Amsterdam Municipal Archives acquired 350 metres (and 16,435 objects) of new archives. The digital archives were also expanded by 185 Gb. The Archives have a workforce of about 160. The reports are available from *http://gemeentearchief.amsterdam.nl.*

6

Core Security Requirements of DRM Systems

H L Jonker and S Mauw

The use of Digital Rights Management (DRM) systems involve several stakeholders, such as the content provider, the license provider and the user, each having their own incentives to use the system. Proper use of the system implies that these incentives can only be met if certain security requirements are fulfilled. Although security of DRM systems has received quite some attention, a systematic overview of the core security requirements for DRM is missing. In this paper, we will conduct a stakeholder analysis and develop a simple, generic conceptual model to arrive at such a set of core security requirements.

1. Introduction

There has been a long and ongoing struggle to secure content (a term used to indicate works of art, such as music, literature, movies, etc.) against unlimited copying. Computers have had a strong impact on this struggle, as creating a copy on a computer is almost effortless. This has traditionally been seen as a threat to content creators. However, with the recent rise of broadband Internet connections, this also means that selling and delivering content online is becoming a viable business venue. The main obstacle for this is to prevent unsanctioned redistribution of the delivered content.

Digital Rights Management (DRM) systems have been created for this goal. The purpose of a DRM system is to protect (digital versions of) content. Content is bound to a license, and the content is only accessible under the terms stated by the license.

In recent years, there has been a strong push into the research and development of DRM systems. There has been work on various related security aspects such as secure storage [19], traitor-tracing [11, 17], watermarking [2], fingerprinting [4, 15] and tamper resistant code [6, 1]. There have also been various proposals for models of DRM systems with specific properties [3, 13, 12, 18].

These proposals incorporate various security requirements. Some of these requirements assure core DRM functionality, whereas other requirements realise the specific properties for which that architecture was constructed (e.g., in the case of MOSES [18], interoperability). The emphasis of such proposals is usually on the latter type of requirements. It is not uncommon that the requirements assuring core DRM functionality receive a lesser treatment. These requirements are often not all made explicit, nor is a justification for them provided. Which of these requirements are made explicit varies from proposal to proposal, which means that the set of requirements that assure core DRM functionality is scattered.

There are several reasons to make this core explicit. The first and foremost reason is that security is an enabling factor for DRM systems. DRM systems are designed to provide a solution for a security problem. An understanding of (the justification for) the core security requirements is crucial for fundamental comprehension of the security of DRM systems.

Moreover, knowledge of the core security requirements is instrumental in the construction and verification of DRM systems. Such knowledge enables developers to better understand the consequences of security trade-offs. In practical systems, such trade-offs between desired features and security requirements are not uncommon.

For example, Apple's iTunes allows the user to create a CD of protected music. Naturally, Apple realised that such a CD could be used to "rip" the music. Nevertheless, this feature was deemed more important than the costs in terms of loss of security. In this case, an informed decision has been made. In other respects, some of the design decisions of iTunes seem less well-informed and have a negative impact on the overall security of the system. A more detailed examination of iTunes follows in Section 4.2.

There seem to be several reasons why the core requirements of DRM systems have not yet been made explicit in a systematic way. Digital rights management as a research topic is still a young and developing field. As mentioned before, research into digital rights management has been focused on specific architectures that solve particular problems and on security techniques which are used in DRM systems.

This paper is a continuation of the work started in 2004 [10]. That work was based on practical observations, which led to a practically oriented overview of security aspects of DRM systems. This paper uses a more structured approach to identify core security requirements and provide a justification for them.

The goal of this paper is thus focused on a particular aspect of the design of DRM systems, viz. security. Our aim is to systematically derive the core security requirements. Although there is a wealth of methodologies supporting system analysis and design, the methodologies for deriving security requirements are only at their infancy. Therefore, our research will start by identifying some useful methodologies and combining their strengths.

In order to provide a base for the found security requirements, we describe a model which limits itself to the core processes of a DRM system. The generic nature of this core model of DRM functionality implies that requirements found for it are applicable to most DRM systems. The extensibility of this core model indicates that it can be augmented to accommodate additional functionality, and therefore, that this model suffices for our needs.

The rest of this document is organised as follows: Section 2 details the approach we used to arrive at our security requirements, resulting in a list of security properties and a generic process model of DRM systems. These form the basis of the security requirements in Section 3. Section 4 examines the practical application of this research. And finally, we present some conclusions in Section 5.

We would like to acknowledge the assistance of several persons. The comments and commentary of ir. Lex Schoonen and ir. Jan Verschuren were invaluable during our research, and we are grateful for their constructive commentary. We would also like to thank Paco van der Linden and Jilles Tjoelker for sharing their investigations of security risks of Apple iTunes and Microsoft Windows Media DRM, respectively. Finally, we thank Yan Liu for proofreading this paper.

2. Problem Analysis

To establish the core security requirements of DRM systems, we performed a problem analysis. The analysis led to a terminology and a description of the desires of the various involved parties. These desires are used in Section 3 as the foundations for the security requirements of the system.

The problem analysis consisted of three steps. The first step established core stakeholders, their incentives and relevant terminology of DRM systems. The second step consisted of deriving the desired security properties from the incentives and the terminology. The third step consisted of deriving a process model. The process model is to capture the core operations occurring in DRM systems.

2.1 Establishing Terminology, Stakeholders and their Incentives

The first step in deriving the security requirements is a stakeholder analysis. The purpose of this step is to determine the individuals (or roles) who have an interest in using a DRM system, and their incentives for participating. This understanding of their incentives is important, as these incentives lead to security requirements.

To establish the stakeholders and their incentives, a method similar to and inspired by several existing methodologies from the field of Information Systems has been used. We based our research on a variety of methodologies, such as domain analysis (see e.g. [16]), stakeholder analysis (for an overview see [14]), system decomposition (see e.g. [20]). Normally, these methods assist in designing a system. However, our goal was not to design a system, but to focus upon a system's security aspects. Parts of these methods were accordingly adapted to capture the security aspects of DRM systems.

Our problem analysis resulted in a description of DRM systems, including the various incentives for parties to participate in the use of a DRM system. Using this description, the terminology involved was established. We then focused on establishing the main stakeholders to concentrate on the core of DRM systems, which allowed us to establish the more important terms of the terminology. The list of stakeholders contained such parties as: media company, developer, user, network provider, reseller. Each of these parties can play at least one role in a DRM system.

The analysis distinguished three types of core[1] participating roles: the content creator, who creates content; the license creator, who binds the content to a license; and the user[2], who wants access to content. This list of core roles emphasised the following terms of the terminology: (acquisition of) content, (acquisition of a) license, renderer, access.

Each of these roles has various reasons for taking part in a DRM system, and thus related security concerns. The following outlines their incentives:

> The content creator is a role filled by stakeholders that create content, such as media companies. They can use DRM technology to support new business models. For instance, they can create a bundle of desired content and other content. Such a bundle could increase the content's value for users (e.g. by including the 'making of' footage), or it could increase revenue for the content creator (e.g. by including commercials). Besides that, using DRM technology, it is possible to offer a revenue-generating alternative for traditional downloading. This means that DRM technology can open a new market. Finally, offering content online in a digital version means that the per-content overhead costs are low – there is no need for plastic casing, a colourful cover, etc.
>
> The license creator binds content to a license. This role saves content creators the overhead of negotiating directly with their customers. The license creator can use DRM technology to offer tailor-made access to content to users.

1 They each play a crucial role they must all be present for a DRM system to function.

2 We prefer the computer science term 'user' over terms originating from other fields, such as 'client', 'customer' and 'consumer'.

On top of that, overhead compared to selling physical media is substantially reduced, because digital content takes up little physical space and the presentation of the content can also be done digitally. By offering a clearly legitimate and known-quality alternative for downloading, license creator can open up a new market. And lastly, as the content is bound to a license created by the license creator, most content distributed in this way will not spread beyond the license creator's control.

Users will mainly be drawn to DRM systems since they offer a legitimate, known-quality alternative to more dubious sources of content. Ease of use is an important consideration in this regard: if use of the system or acquisition of content becomes bothersome, a user might turn back to other sources. Another advantage that DRM systems could offer users, is the possibility to restrict the access to (and thus the cost of) content to precisely what the user wishes.

The considerations and reservations mentioned in the descriptions above indicate desired security properties. These considerations are translated using the terminology to establish desired security properties in Section 2.2.

2.2 Desired Security Properties Per Role

The second step of the problem analysis consists of deriving the desired core security properties of each relevant stakeholder, by combining the stakeholder analysis and the established terminology.

The high-level properties of this section are then made precise as concrete security requirements in Section 3.

For each core role of DRM systems, a translation of the incentives into desired properties is provided. There are various security solutions that come into play in this process (e.g. a payment infrastructure). We confine our examination to the core of a DRM system, i.e., those processes modelled by the conceptual process model of Figure 1.

As the intent of this section is to establish which security properties are desired for DRM systems, properties outside the scope of DRM systems (such as those governing negotiations between parties, those ensuring that all parties uphold their end of contracts, those governing the privacy of the business operations of license creators, etc.) are not considered below. Properties of DRM systems that are not security related (e.g. functional properties) are also not examined. Lastly, we confine our examination to the core of a DRM system, i.e., the protective measures a DRM system provides for digital content.

In Table 1, the incentives for each stakeholder are expressed using the established terminology. Together, these properties form a solid foundation for the core functionality of DRM systems and therefore, they also provide sound underpinnings for the security properties of DRM systems. These properties are necessary for DRM systems. They would be sufficient, if the descriptions in Section 2.1 of the incentives are complete, and if the translation is correct and complete.

Table 1: Security Properties as Desired Per Role	
Content Creator	
m.1	Content is only accessible by untampered components created by the official system developers, under the conditions of a valid license issued by a bonafide license creator for those components.
License Creator	
r.1	Content is only accessible by a renderer with a valid license issued to that renderer, originating from the license creator, under the terms stated in that license.
r.2	Precisely deliver what has been requested, in a consumable form, at the desired time for the licensee.
r.3	The impact of breaking the system must be constrained.
User	
u.1	Precisely acquire a consumable form of the content that the user desires, at the moment the user desires it.
u.2	To order licenses or content on the user's behalf requires the intensional participation of the user.
u.3	Neither content nor licenses can be linked to the user.
u.4	The user is aware of all negotiations resulting in an agreement between her and the license creator, and consents to the terms of any such agreement.

2.3 Conceptual Process Model

The second step of the problem analysis consists of the development of a conceptual process model. This model relates the basic processes in the DRM system to each other, and can be refined to provide a basis for identifying security requirements. This process model is then combined in Section 3 with the list of security properties to establish core security requirements of DRM systems.

To ensure that the model is applicable to as many DRM systems as possible, it must be as generic as possible. In order to derive such a generic model, we started with one component for the three core roles in a DRM system: the content creator, the license creator and the user. The content creator's component is linked to the license creator's, and the license creator's to the user's. Components for other roles were left out as they can be introduced when necessary – such additions would merely constitute refinements of the model. The resulting model was subsequently refined to incorporate various specifics of DRM systems.

The first refinement was motivated by distinguishing two types of content: digital content (which the system is to protect), and analogue content (which a user can consume). This results in splitting the user's component in two: one to convert digital content to analogue content (the content renderer), and one to communicate with the license creator's component (the content processor).

The second refinement was instigated by a design decision common to all DRM protected content: access to the protected content is bounded to a license. This results in splitting the license creator's component in two parts: one providing the bounded content (content binding), and one providing accompanying licenses for said content (license creation).

This leads us to the conceptual model depicted in Figure 1:

Figure 1: A Generic Model of the Core Processes in a DRM System

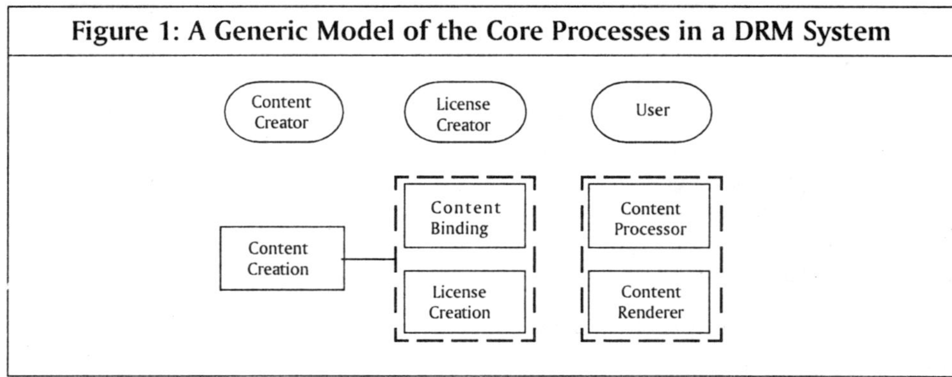

The processes modeled in Figure 1 operate as follows: The content creator creates the content, which is bound to a license by a license creator. The user can acquire the bound content and the appropriate license, which the content processor uses to access the content (if and when allowed). The content is then rendered by the content renderer.

As Figure 1 models the core roles and processes in DRM systems, it can be refined to comply with almost all existing DRM architectures. For example, to comply with the functional architecture of the Open Mobile Alliance [12], the model can be refined to incorporate the roles of content issuer and license issuer.

2.4 Conclusions of the Problem Analysis

The problem analysis has provided two results: a list of security properties desired by the core stakeholders, and a conceptual process model of the processes taking place in a DRM system. Taken together, these results elucidate security requirements of the core functionality of a DRM system.

Completeness of these descriptions can have a large impact on which security requirements are found. After all, the more complete the given descriptions are, the more complete the derived security requirements will be. The methods we adapted to arrive at the given descriptions support a systematic derivation of security requirements, but do not guarantee completeness of the results. Despite this, we believe that, due to the systematic approach, the descriptions are sufficiently exhaustive for our goals.

3. Core Security Requirements

In this section, the incentives as described in Section 2.1 are used as a basis for establishing the security requirements per stakeholder upon the model shown in Figure 1. In Section 2.2, they were reworded to describe the precise desires of the stakeholders. In this section, that rewording is translated into security requirements upon the model.

Below, each requirement of the previous section is refined into security properties for the model depicted in Figure 1. To describe a specific DRM system in greater detail, both that model and these requirements could be refined.

m.1 – Content is only accessible by untampered components created by the official system developers, under the conditions of a valid license issued by a bonafide license creator for those components.

Concretely, this leads to the following points:

1. (Authorisation) Only license creators can acquire content from the content creator.
2. (Secrecy) The content is protected from eavesdropping when it is communicated to another component of the system.
3. The points discussed below at r.1 for content accessibility.

r.1 –Content is only accessible by a renderer with a valid license issued to that renderer, originating from the license creator, under the terms stated in that license.

Concretely, this leads to the following points:

1. (Secrecy) The content is only accessible by the manager/renderer components specified in the license on the user side and remains secret until it has been converted into an analogue form.
2. (Trust) The manager/renderer pair on the user side will only render the content if all terms of any one valid license governing this content are met.
3. (Robustness) The internal workings of the manager/renderer pair cannot be influenced or disrupted by the license creator, the user nor any third party.
4. (Secrecy) No secret information necessary for the operation of the components or pertaining to content (e.g. cryptographic keys, content) can be discerned from the manager/renderer pair, nor from the communication channel between them.
5. (Constraint) The domain in which the DRM system offers protection ends at the renderer.
6. (Authentication) No component sends the content to another component, unless the receiving component is authenticated as an official component (i.e., created by the DRM developer) and if the receiving component is allowed to receive content from the sending component.

r.2 – Precisely deliver what has been requested, in a consumable form, at the desired time for the licensee.

Concretely, this leads to the following points:

1. (Integrity) The request should be received correctly.
2. (Availability) The user should be able to contact the license creator, without undue delay.
3. (Availability) The user should be able to receive content and license at any desired time.
4. (Integrity) The content/license should be received correctly.
5. (Authentication) Only authenticated users with whom an agreement has been reached will receive licenses for the content for which that agreement was reached.

r.3 – The impact of breaking the system must be constrained.

Concretely, this leads to the following points:

1. Prevent "Break Once, Run Everywhere".
2. (Updatability) The components of the system can be updated to implement and deal with new or altered protective measures used by the system.

u.1 – Precisely acquire a consumable form of the content that the user desires, at the moment the user desires it.

Concretely, this leads to the following points:

1. (Availability) The services of the license creator are at any time available for the user.
2. (Integrity) Communication between the content binder component and the content processor component cannot be disrupted.
3. (Trust) The license creator sends what has been agreed upon.
4. (Authentication) The license creator must authenticate itself to the user.

u.2 – To order licenses or content on the user's behalf requires the intensional participation of the user.

Concretely, this leads to the following points:

1. (Authentication) To obtain content or a license, the user must authenticate to prove its identity (or pseudonym).
2. (Secrecy) The user's authentication data is only available to the user.

u.3 – Neither content nor licenses can be linked to the user.

Concretely, this leads to the following points:

1. (Trust, privacy, secrecy) The license creator only saves those personal data, for which the user has given permission.
2. (Trust, privacy, secrecy) The license creator only uses those saved data for purposes for which the user has given permission.
3. (Privacy, secrecy) No information concerning the user that the user desires to keep private can be learned from the communication between the user and the license creator (in particular from license/content requests and retrievals).
4. (Trust, privacy, integrity) No third party can acquire personal data concerning the user from the content processor, the renderer or communications between these two components.

u.4 – The user is aware of all negotiations resulting in an agreement between her and the license creator, and consents to the terms of any such agreement.

Concretely, this leads to the following points:

1. Payment only occurs with the user's knowledge and consent.
2. (Integrity) No third party can alter or disrupt the message containing the terms as sent by the license creator to the user.
3. (Trust) The license creator must abide by the terms the user agrees to (and pays for).
4. (Availability) The (financial) consent of the user to the terms set by the license creator must become known in a timely fashion to the license creator.

5. (Non-repudiation) the license creator cannot deny having received payment, nor having received confirmation of consent to the terms.

It follows from the requirements derived from the license creator's desired security properties (r.1, r.2 and r.3) that the components on the user's side should function as a trusted computing base. The points following from property u.3 indicate that the license creator should provide a privacy statement. Requirement u.1.3 implies that the license creator provides a security policy.

4. Illustration of Applicability

In this section, we will illustrate the use of the constructed model and derived security requirements to practical DRM systems. It is not our intention to provide a complete analysis of actual DRM systems, but to indicate the implications of using our results.

Our first case study was performed on a system from a Dutch company which develops DRM systems. This case study was based on our work, previously on reported in 2004 [9]. The system matched our model very well, and our security analysis pointed out a missed requirement in the system (requirement u.4.5). They took into consideration implementing a mechanism to assure the user non-repudiation.

The remainder of this section will describe a comparison of the found requirements to two popular DRM systems, Windows Media DRM from Microsoft and iTunes from Apple. These systems are interesting for a number of reasons: these systems are the most successfully deployed DRM systems in the current market, and both have been successfully attacked. Observe that both systems are refinements of the model depicted in Figure 1.

4.1 Microsoft Windows Media DRM

Microsoft has developed a DRM system compatible with their Windows Media Player. Microsoft has created two file formats that can be enhanced with DRM protection: Windows Media Audio (.WMA, for audio content) and Windows Media Video (.WMV, for mixed video and audio content).

Microsoft's DRM system has a role delivering protected content to the user. This content can only be accessed with a legitimate license. This manner of operating conforms to the process model depicted in Figure 1.

There have been two well-known successful attacks on Microsoft's DRM system (described more fully in [5]). The first attack consisted of replacing part of the renderer that is responsible for rendering audio (the audio driver). Protected music could now be captured after it had been converted to a form understandable by the audio driver, and saved to disc.

In our proposed security requirements, this attack would have been prevented by satisfying requirements r.1.1 and r.1.6. The part of the DRM system on which this attack worked, was the same for each installation. This means that the attack was possible on all installed systems, which violates requirement r.3.1.

Microsoft has released a new version of Windows DRM that was not vulnerable to this attack. Naturally, content packaged under the new system was not accessible with the old system.

A tool called 'FreeMe' is available that attacks content protected for the new version. The creator of the tool has included a detailed analysis of the protection of protected files. The tool is able to determine the keys used to encrypt the content. This is a violation of requirement r.1.4. The manner in which the key could be retrieved was the same for each installed system, which again violates requirement r.3.1.

Microsoft has released a patch for their DRM system. The patch implements measures that support requirement r.3.1 and uses another method to hide the used keys. Patched systems are no longer vulnerable to this particular attack.

4.2 Apple iTunes

iTunes[3] is Apple's online music store. Music is sold in the Advanced Audio Coding format (AAC, see [8, 7]). The audio data inside the AAC file is protected by encryption. The default license allows protected files to be played on up to five different computers, and to burn them to CD.

The manner in which iTunes operates, conforms to the model of Figure 1. Content is delivered to a license creator, which binds the content to a license. The user can then acquire the bound content and an appropriate license.

---

3 *http://www.apple.com/itunes/*

iTunes has suffered from two well-known attacks. The first is by Jon Lech Johansen and captures the decrypted, digital contents before it is converted into analogue form. This attack is similar to the first attack upon Microsoft's Windows DRM system, and the remarks made then apply in this case as well – this attack exploits the lack of compliance to requirements r.1.1, r.1.6 and r.3.1.

The second attack on iTunes bears a resemblance to the second attack on Windows DRM: keys can be learned by outsiders, which enables an attacker to compromise the encryption of protected content. The keys used by iTunes (to protect the key to the encrypted audio) are stored encrypted with a system key. It is known how to reconstruct this key[4] for the Windows platform and for Apple's portable MP3 player. This means that it is possible to remove the encryption from the audio data for these platforms. The remarks made for the second attack on MS DRM apply here as well – this attack exploits the lack of compliance to requirements r.1.4 and r.3.1.

Recently, a third attack on the system was crafted by Johanson. He created a tool (called PyMusique) that replaces the iTunes tool to acquire songs. According to the description of the method[5], the main difference with the official tool is that it skips applying DRM to the downloaded file.

The attack thus consists of replacing a component of the system by an attacker-supplied component. However, no component should send the content to another component, unless the other component identifies itself as a legitimate component. Allowing this constitutes a violation of requirement r.1.6.

4.3 Verifying DRM Design

The list of security requirements can be used as a checklist when verifying security aspects of a design for a DRM system. The generic nature of the process model implies that it is applicable to most designs for a DRM system. Therefore, the requirements derived from it should be met by any matching system.

Additionally, the process model can be refined to model a specific DRM system in more detail. This refined model could be combined with the stated requirements in order to derive more detailed requirements for this specific DRM system.

4 e.g., see *http://www.hymn-project.org/docs/hymn-manual.html#how-hymn-works*

5 *http://www.daeken.com/2004/08/24/itunes/*

5. Conclusions

Digital Rights Management systems offer a method for content creators to allow their work to be spread digitally, without loss of recompensation. Security is the foremost enabling factor of DRM systems.

This paper used a methodical way to derive security requirements from the incentives of the parties involved with a DRM system. A stakeholder analysis identified the key roles taking part in a DRM system, and the main incentives related to these roles. A domain analysis captured the core terminology of DRM systems, from which a process model was derived.

The key roles, their incentives and the core terminology together led to a description of each role's desired security properties for a DRM system. Taken together with the process model, these security properties allowed us to establish the core security requirements of DRM systems.

The method used was justified by validation of the result of each step to known literature and comparison to a DRM system in development by a Dutch company.

The applicability of our findings was justified by comparison to three existing DRM systems. Exploited weaknesses of both Microsoft Media DRM and Apple's iTunes could have been identified in an early state using the requirements we presented. In the case of the system in development at a Dutch company, we were able to point out requirements that had been overlooked.

By using a methodical way to derive security requirements for DRM systems, this paper leads to an improved understanding of the security aspects of DRM systems.

This paper takes a practical stance towards security: it presents a list of requirements to be fulfilled. Compliance with these requirements may not be straightforward – see for example the second attack on Microsoft's Media DRM, which attacked a part that at first might have seem to comply to the relevant requirements presented here. This problem can be prevented using formal verification. Compliance of the used protocols with secrecy and authentication can already be formally verified. There is ongoing research into formally expressing other requirements (e.g. privacy) for protocols. Further developments can lead to establishing a theoretical basis in which it is possible to verify that a trusted computing base complies to the requirements upon it.

The process model used for establishing the requirements can be refined to include more details for a more thorough analysis of a particular system. This would then lead to further refinement in the requirements. Such a refinement requires a loss of the generic nature and therefore, would result in confining the applicability of the resulting findings to systems exhibiting specific characteristics.

(H L Jonker and S. Mauw are with Department of Mathematics and Computer Science, Eindhoven University of Technology, Netherlands. They can be reached at h.l.jonker, s.mavw@tue.nl respectively.)

References

1. H Chang and M J Atallah. "Protecting software code by guards". In *Security and privacy in digital rights management,* volume 2320 of LNCS, pages 150–175. Springer-Verlag GmbH, January 2002.
2. I Cox, J Bloom, and M Miller. *Digital watermarking: principles & practice.* The Morgan Kaufmann Series in multimedia and information systems. Morgan Kaufmann, October 2001.
3. S Guth. "A sample DRM system". In *Digital Rights Management,* volume 2320 of LNCS, pages 32–50. Springer-Verlag GmbH, November 2003.
4. J Haitsma and T Kalker. "A highly robust audio fingerprinting system". In *Proceedings of the 3rd international conference on music information retrieval,* October 2002.
5. T Hauser and C Wenz. "DRM under attack: weaknesses in existing systems". In *Digital Rights Management: Technological, Economic, Legal and Political Aspects,* volume 2770 of LNCS, pages 206 – 223. Springer-Verlag GmbH, November 2003.
6. B Horne, L Matheson, C. Sheehan, and R.E. Tarjan. "Dynamic self-checking techniques for improved tamper resistance". In *Security and privacy in digital rights management,* volume 2320 of LNCS, pages 141–159. Springer-Verlag GmbH, January 2002.
7. International Organization for Standardization (ISO). ISO/IEC 13818-7:2004 – Information technology – Generic coding of moving pictures and associated audio information – Part 7: Advanced Audio Coding (AAC).
8. International Organization for Standardization (ISO). ISO/IEC TR 13818-5:1997/Amd 1:1999 – Advanced Audio Coding (AAC).

9. H L Jonker. "Security of Digital Rights Management systems". Master's thesis, Technische Universiteit Eindhoven, August 2004.

10. H L Jonker, S Mauw, J H S Verschuren, and A.T.S.C. Schoonen. "Security aspects of DRM systems". In R. Pellikaan, editor, *25th Symposium on information theory in the Benelux, 25th Symposium on information theory in the Benelux*, pages 169{176, Kerkrade, The Netherlands, June 2004.

11. A Kiayias and M Yung. "Breaking and repairing asymmetric public-key traitor tracing". In *Digital Rights Management*, volume 2320 of LNCS, pages 32 – 50. Springer-Verlag GmbH, November 2003.

12. Open Mobile Alliance (OMA). OMA-DRM-ARCH-V2_0-20040715-C – DRM architecture.

13. B C Popescu, F.L.A.J. Kamperman, B. Crispo, and A. S. Tanenbaum. "A DRM security architecture for home networks". In DRM '04: *Proceedings of the 4th ACM workshop on Digital rights management*, pages 1 – 10. ACM Press, 2004.

14. A Pouloudi. "Aspects of the stakeholder concept and their impliciations for information systems development". In R.H. Sprague, editor, *Proceedings of the 32nd Hawaii International Conference on System Sciences (HICSS-32),* Los Alamitos, CA, 1999. IEEE Computer Society Press.

15. L Prechelt and R Typke. "An interface for melody input". *ACM transactions on computer – human interaction (TOCHI)*, 8(2):133–149, June 2001.

16. R Prieto-Diaz. "Domain analysis: An introduction". *Software Engineering Notes, 15(2):47–54,* 1990.

17. R Safavi-Naini and Y Wang. "Traitor tracing for shortened and corrupted fingerprints". In *Digital Rights Management*, volume 2320 of LNCS, pages 32 – 50. Springer-Verlag GmbH, November 2003.

18. C Serrao, D Naves, T Barker, M Balestri and P Kudumakis. "Open SDRM – An open and secure digital rights management solution". June 2003.

19. W Shapiro and R. Vingralek. "How to manage persistent state in DRM systems". In *Security and privacy in digital rights management, volume 2320 of LNCS*, pages 176 – 191. Springer-Verlag GmbH, January 2002.

20. I Sommerville. *Software Engineering*. Pearson, 2004.

7

Human Factors in Digital Rights Management for Consumer Products

Marc L Resnick

Digital Rights Management (DRM) is a means through which copyrights can be protected using technology rather than the legal system. It is controversial because it allows content creators to control the level of access that users have to content they have purchased, to a much greater degree than ever before. In addition to preventing illegal piracy, DRM allows content creators to prohibit the "Fair Uses" that the legal system has consistently protected. Human factors practitioners involved in the design of electronic devices that use copyrighted media, including computers, music players, gaming systems, cell phones, digital video recorders, and others, must recognize the effects of DRM on consumer product design. When analyzing user requirements, the interaction between DRM software and user behaviors must be considered. User interfaces should be designed to make the constraints imposed by DRM and the access that is supported easily visible. Including a consideration of DRM and its interactions with interface design will increase the likelihood that consumer electronics are successful.

Introduction

Traditionally, the premise of intellectual property rights has been to create a balance between the private rewards of innovation and the public goods that result from repeated innovation. When intellectual property protection was written into the US Constitution, the purpose was to "Promote the Progress of Science and Useful Arts . . ." Providing income for innovators was a means to that end rather than an objective in itself. The heated debates between Thomas Jefferson and James Madison over how to regulate intellectual property highlight the great challenge of establishing this balance to maximize progress while protecting the rights of both intellectual property owners and users. Companies will not invest the vast research and development resources to bring new products to market if they would not reap the rewards of their innovations. But if protection becomes too strong, the incentive for further innovation is lost and the public good is sacrificed. Companies can continue to sell old products with no fear of competition and innovation will stagnate. Balancing these opposing extremes is crucial.

Copyrights

In the case of copyrights, this balance is achieved in two ways. First, copyrights are given specific lifetimes. Originally, copyrights had lifetimes of 28 years. Over time, this has been extended and currently sits at 70 years after the death of the author for individuals and 95 years for corporations. Second, certain uses that bestow large benefits to society are allowed notwithstanding the existence of an active copyright. These "Fair Uses" include quoting, parodying, using copyrighted materials for teaching or research, and news reporting.

However, just because these uses are allowed, it does not mean that users have a right to them. For example, an educator cannot be sued for excerpting small amounts of a copyrighted work in his or her class. But a company cannot be sued for making this excerpting technologically impossible using their electronic product.

The advent of digital media has created a huge challenge for copyright regulation. It is now technologically possible to make unlimited copies of copyrighted material with a quality as good as the original and distribute them around the world instantly. This is now more common than other kinds of IP theft because it seems to violators that no one is hurt. Many of the file sharing networks are not directly making money on illegal copying. It is easy to rationalize that copyright owners in the movie and music industry are powerful corporations that are not losing money. Copyright piracy thus remains prevalent despite the recent success of legal music downloading services. Ninety-five percent of music file sharing is still done on illegal networks (Woffenden, 2005).

In an attempt to slow down illegal music sharing, the music industry, represented by the Recording Industry Association of America (RIAA), has sued individuals identified as facilitating large quantities of illegal music sharing. The $150,000 fine for each shared music file is a strong deterrent for the typical file sharing college student. But the prevalence of illegal sharing continues.

Another factor that has impacted copyright protection is the nature of the Internet. The technological effects of the Internet on copyright law are more widespread than even its designers realized. A physical book can be read and shared unlimited times without triggering copyright laws because no copies are made during the reading process. But whenever the owner of an eBook reads it, a temporary copy is made and displayed on the screen (Lessig, 2004). Thus, the copyright owner has the legal right under copyright law to govern how many times or how frequently the book is accessed and what can be done with these "copies." Similarly, any time a page is printed or a file is transferred from one device to another, copies are made and the content owner has the right to control access.

Digital Rights Management

Digital Rights Management (DRM) is software that controls access to intellectual property and then controls or monitors copying (May, 2003). This allows copyright owners to use technology to achieve what law enforcement has been unable to accomplish, preventing the illegal copying and sharing of copyrighted material. The type and amount of copying is controlled exclusively by the DRM software, which is fixed by the content owners. For example, the Adobe eBook Reader supports limitations on how many pages can be printed, if the book can be read aloud, and whether text selections can be copied and pasted into other files. DRM can be effective for protecting copyrights in a variety of consumer products, including e-books, music players, mobile phones, PDAs, digital video recorders (i.e., TiVo), personal computers, gaming consoles, satellite radios, and many other media.

However, DRM can over enforce copyright protection by preventing Fair Use (May, 2003). If the DRM system prevents all copying, it may not be able to discriminate between an attempt to send illegal copies of a song to a friend and an attempt to send excerpts of a research article to a student. In the eBook example above, copying is prevented regardless of whether the reader intends to use the material for a Fair Use (Lessig, 2004).

So as the Internet disrupted the balance between copyright owners and users in favor of the users by allowing mass copying, DRM systems disrupt the balance in favor of content publishers by preventing Fair Use copying. Technology has, therefore, created somewhat of an arms race to see which interests can dominate the use of copyrighted material. Whereas in the past, the balance was determined through public debate, it is now set through hardware and software that is largely opaque to the average consumer.

Most consumers are unaware of which uses are illegal and which are allowed under Fair Use. They use the functionality of the hardware as a guide. If the hardware allows a function, it must be legal. This contributed to the problem of music sharing initially because users assumed that if the copying was possible, it must be OK. Once sharing became a common practice, publicizing the illegality was no longer effective. Similarly, consumers can become accustomed to strict constraints that prevent Fair Use and assume that these uses are prohibited.

Where Does Human Factors Come In?

Human factors plays a huge role in the development of consumer products, particularly consumer electronic systems that can support a variety of functionality. As DRM systems are incorporated into consumer products, it is critical for human factors practitioners to be familiar with the constraints they impart. Specifically, human factors are essential in two areas:

Mapping DRM Constraints to User Requirements

The origins of DRM stem from using technology to protect copyrighted content from illegal copying. But, of course, the primary objective is to protect the profits that the content owner earns from legal sale and use. It would be counter-productive for DRM to overconstrain users and not allow them to achieve the variety of tasks for which they purchase these products. Although current implementations of DRM do not seem to take user requirements into account, the future success of consumer electronics dictates that they must (Mello, 2002). Value mapping to compare how much users value certain kinds of legal copying with the expected costs of providing it can be expanded to include the expected costs of illegal sharing that may result. Products that support user requirements in the diverse contexts in which consumer electronics are used will have a distinct competitive advantage.

Browne and Ramesh (2002) describe several areas where current user requirements methods can overlook key needs. Companies often use the requirements of a current version and adjust conservatively from there for future versions. In the rapidly evolving consumer electronics sector, this could be detrimental. Enhanced mobility and new connectivity among devices create many opportunities that will be lost if DRM prevents transportability within an individual's network. Companies also can fail to survey representative users because they feel competent to predict users' needs. Unfortunately, even users themselves often cannot predict how they will use a product (Mello, 2002). This is particularly true for technological products because consumers cannot envision the vast possibilities that technology engenders.

Garmer, Ylven, and Karlsson, (2004) found that different methods of user requirements gather identified different requirements. Usability testing was able to identify quantitative and detailed requirements, whereas focus groups identified contextual requirements. They found little overlap between the methods. DRM must consider both the detailed user requirements as well as the contexts in which users use these products. Garmer, Ylven, and Karlsson (2004) also found significant differences in requirements measured at different locations. Media companies need to take this into account when setting DRM constraints. They must be flexible to accommodate the varying needs of different customer groups.

Designing the Interface to make DRM Constraints Transparent

Even when the constraints imposed by DRM software allow users to accomplish what they want, this ability must be transparent. Function visibility is one of the key usability attributes for any consumer product (Norman, 1998). Companies often have specific language or jargon to refer to particular functions that may not be clear to the consumer. An example provided in Lessig (2004) would be amusing if it were not true. Early versions of the Adobe eBook reader listed the following limitation for *Alice's Adventures in Wonderland*: "This book cannot be read aloud." Some customers did not realize that this indicated that the <read aloud> control on the device was disabled for this book. Instead, parents assumed that the device restricted their right to read the book aloud to their children. The text was changed to "You may not use the Read Aloud button to listen to this book." But the interim public relations mess could have been avoided with some contextual user testing.

Visibility is also a way to engender trust (Karvonen and Parkkinen, 2001). Constraints that are deemed unreasonable by consumers may lead to reduced trust and lower levels of customer satisfaction. Resnick and Montania (2003) found that semiotic factors such as clear paths to redress concerns can lead to higher levels of trust and increased likelihood of purchase. Consumer electronics companies that include DRM systems need to establish this trust to justify the constraints imposed by the system.

Because of the prevalence of children as consumers of electronic products, companies should take special care in the development of user testing protocols. Hanna, Risden, and Alexander (1997) describe several guidelines for usability testing for children. They describe methods for interacting with groups of children of all ages from preschool to high school. Each age group has different cognitive abilities and behavioral characteristics that must be accommodated in any user testing studies.

Conceptual Illustration – Google Print

This example is an over-simplified case to illustrate the importance of applying human factors to DRM systems. Google is developing a new service that would allow users to search through millions of books that have been digitized by Google

(Helm, 2005). The original plan was to partner with book publishers. In this case, a query would return a limited number of pages from the book. There would be a link to the publisher's web site so the user could buy the book if more information was needed. A second plan involves working with libraries to scan books in the public domain as well as copyrighted books. Because books in the public domain have no copyrights, a link to the entire book could be presented to the user in the results. But with the copyrighted books, only a small excerpt would be available as determined by Fair Use principles.

This combination creates a large number of possible situations for each result that appears from a search query. The result could be a public domain book, for which the entire book is accessible. It could also be a copyrighted book made available from a library, for which only an excerpt determined by Fair Use principles is available. It could also be a copyrighted book made available from the publisher, for which the permissions would be set by the publisher. Various amounts of printing, copying, sharing with other users, and transferring between devices could be permitted. For a query with ten books listed on the first page of results, each one could have a different set of permitted uses.

The user does not care which of these sources provided the book, the contractual obligations of Google, or the details of copyright law. The user simply wants access to information. He or she is more concerned with whether the listed books have the information for which he or she is searching, and permit the uses for which he or she intends to use the material. A new level of complexity is added because a book may have the required information, but because of the copyright restrictions, it is not available. Another book may have less information, but be available in total or support a more extensive set of uses.

The first step is to understand how users may want to access and use content from the book. They may want to print the excerpts to which they have access. They may want to copy and paste the excerpts into other documents. They may want to transfer the excerpt between media, such as to portable devices or eBooks. They may want to share the excerpt with others. Companies creating DRM systems need to understand these requirements before deciding which uses to support.

As the interface for this service is developed, it must be transparent and intuitive in the way that these restrictions are presented. A user may only be interested in selecting pages that can be copied into other files and printed. Others may be interested in reading long passages. The search process must support filters that find books meeting these requirements. And users are not interested in a lesson in copyright law. Rather than filtering by copyright status (public domain, etc.), for which many users will not know the associated permissions, the filters should be in the terminology of the user.

Figure 1 illustrates some of the challenges of an interface to convey this information. The interface begins with the notion that users need to know the size of the excerpt provided and whether they will have the ability to copy, print, transfer, or share text from the book. While a web-based system can use additional colors and icons, the basic functionality must be conveyed in a salient and comprehensible manner. This interface uses simple text in the results list with salience for DRM limitations using bold and italics. It also provides the user with the ability to pre-select DRM permissions before submitting the query so that only links that support his or her needs are returned. But because of the many possibilities, it may still be confusing to non-expert users.

Figure 1: Screen Shot of a Possible Interface to provide DRM Functionality

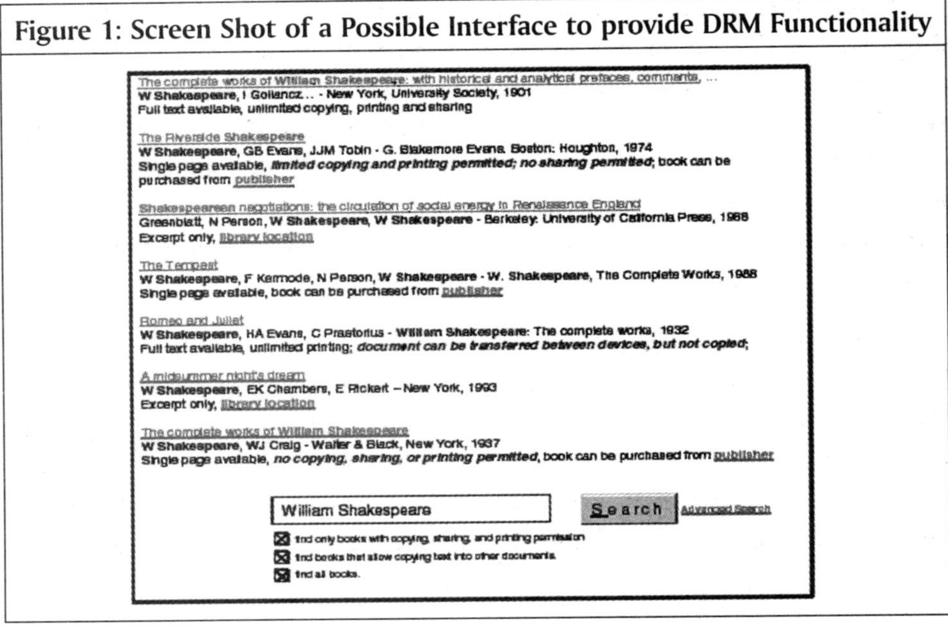

The Problem of Fair Use

This example illustrates some of the difficulty of DRM interfaces, but additional complexity is required when Fair Uses are considered. Even if the content owner does not wish to allow copying, users have traditionally been allowed to copy material for the Fair Uses listed earlier. However, the DRM system cannot determine whether a copy is for a Fair Use or not. It would be nice if users could be allowed to override DRM protection when they engage in a Fair Use, but unfortunately, this right would be abused. The Digital Millennium Copyright Act of 1998 actually makes it illegal to override DRM systems, even to accomplish a Fair Use. Identifying a method to permit Fair Uses while preventing illegal copying remains a challenge for these systems.

One can imagine a password-protected authorization system for which journalists, educators, students, researchers and comedians could be allowed additional privileges specific to their professions. Of course, this trivializes the actual requirements of such a system and would be a nightmare to enforce.

Conclusion

Digital Rights Management systems will become extremely prevalent as more consumer products become electronic. Content publishers are very sensitive to the protection of their intellectual property and prefer to err on the side of overprotection of copyrighted material. It is therefore essential for human factors practitioners in the consumer products domain to facilitate the usability of consumer electronics by considering DRM constraints and interfaces in the design of products.

(Marc L Resnick is from Industrial and Systems Engineering, Florida International University Miami. He can be reached at resnickrn@fiv.edu)..

References

Browne G J and Ramesh V (2002). "Improving information requirements determination: A cognitive perspective". *Information & Management*, 39, 625-645.

Garmer K, Ylven J, and Karlsson I C M (2004). "User participation in requirements elicitation comparing focus group interviews and usability tests for eliciting usability requirements for medical equipment: A case study". *International Journal of Industrial Ergonomics*, 33, 85-98.

Hanna L, Risden K, and Alexander K (1997). "Guidelines for usability testing with children". *Interactions*, Sept-Oct, 9-14.

Helm B (2005). "A Google Project Pains Publishers". *Business Week Online*, Retrieved on 5/24/05 at *www.businessweek.com/technology/content/may200 5/tc20050523_9472_tc024.htm*

Karvonen K and Parkkinen J (2001). "Signs of trust: A semiotic study of trust formation in the web". In *Usability Evaluation and Interface Design* Volume 1. M J Smith, G Salvendy, D Harris, and R J Koubek (eds). Lawrence Erlbaum Associates: Mahwah, NJ.

Lessig L (2004). *Free Culture*. Penguin Press: New York, NY.

May C (2003) "Digital rights management and the breakdown of social norms". *First Monday*, 8, 11, Retrieved on 11/14/03 at *http://firstmonday.org/ issues/issue8_11/may/index.html*

Mello S (2002). *Customer-centric product definition*. AMACOM: New York, NY.

Norman D (1998) *The Design of Everyday Things*. Doubleday: New York, NY.

Resnick M L and Montania R, "Perceptions of Customer Service, Information Privacy and Product Quality from Semiotic Design Features in an On-line Web Store". (2003). *International Journal of Human-Computer Interaction*, 16, 2, 211-234.

Woffenden C (2005). "Millions download music online". Web user news. January, 19, Retrieved on 01/25/05 at *www.webuser.co.uk/news/60797.html*

Section II

Approaches

8

The Role of Architecture in DRM Vendor Economics

Pramod A Jamkhedkar and Gregory L Heileman

The advent of digital rights management (DRM) has led to the creation of two generations of DRM technologies. First generation technologies largely focused on copy protection, and because of this, many erroneously equate copy protection and DRM. Second generation technologies, however, have begun to address a much broader scope of possibilities associated with the myriad of business opportunities that can be built around the more general idea of managing rights. Nevertheless, to date, DRM vendors have experienced very little success in the marketplace. This, in spite of the fact that respected analysts had predicted the growth of a multi-billion dollar DRM market by the year 2004. Experts have postulated a number of reasons for the failure of this market to appear, some related to the business models, others to the technologies themselves, and still others related to the lack of standards in this area. In this paper, we consider the role that the definition of a well-defined DRM architecture will have in addressing these problems. In particular, we consider how the specification of a minimal architectural framework can help

to guide the development of technologies in DRM, as well as help to identify the role that standards should play and where in the architecture they should be defined. It is important to note that a similar architectural framework was instrumental in the development of Internet technologies and standards. Furthermore, the issues faced by the telecommunications industry in the early eighties are quite similar to those currently faced by the DRM industry. Various networking technologies were available, and what was needed was a technological framework that could integrate them and still allow different kinds of services to the applications that involve communication. It was the layered architecture of the OSI model and the hourglass shape of the TCP/IP protocol suite that provided the necessary framework. It is also important to recognize that, in general, layered architectures act as a buffer against rapidly changing technologies. The hourglass-shaped structure of TCP/IP has helped to make the Internet universal. Subsequently, the integration of the Internet into the telecommunications industry was supported by a standardization process. Further, the development of standards promoted the integration of independently developed solutions. This paper makes use of the Internet analogy in order to consider how a layered architectural framework can also promote and guide the development of the DRM industry.

1. Introduction

The digital rights management (DRM) industry is relatively young, emerging over the past fifteen years. In its initial stages, the DRM industry modeled itself along the lines of the prevalent rights management business models in the non-digital world. However, the emergence of digital technology made it possible to create perfect copies of on-line content. Later, the development of the Internet facilitated the dissemination of this content. Hence, most of the DRM technologies developed during the late eighties and early nineties concentrated on copy protection. These are referred to as first generation DRM systems.

Subsequently, those in the DRM industry became explicit in recognizing that DRM is, in fact, much more than copy protection alone. For example, research and development of rights expression languages (RELs) provided a means to express rights in a machine readable form, something that now appears as a basis for DRM. In addition, companies started to use the Internet as a cost-effective means for content distribution. The growth of the Internet also made it possible to create new business models for content distribution, which gave rise to second generation DRM systems. Second generation DRM systems shifted their focus from copy protection to rights expression. This can be seen as a shift of technologies from being content-distributor-centric to that of being user-centric. A slew of technologies emerged in the late nineties which provided solutions ranging from kernel-level rights enforcement to sophisticated facilities such as superdistribution in a single package. What we have witnessed, however, is the failure of most of these technologies [3], as well as a general reluctance towards the prominent use of DRM in commercial applications. There are a number of reasons for these failures, some related to technology, and others to the economics of DRM. In this paper, we consider how these two are related. In particular, we consider the role that technology must play in the specification of a minimal architectural framework for DRM. Such a framework provides the scaffolding upon which multi-vendor DRM solutions can be built, which we believe is a necessity in order for viable DRM markets to emerge. Without such a framework, monolithic one-vendor solutions will continue to be the norm, and these markets will continue to progress slowly.

It is instructive to compare the progress of DRM technology markets to other successful and more mature technology markets. In doing so, a number of important lessons come to light. First, let us consider the general notion of how such markets develop. It has been noted that any technology driven market goes through three different phases [6]. The first phase is simply the raw adaptation of technology in the market space. The second phase involves the development of customized end-to-end solutions in order to solve business problems. The third phase is the integration of the technology in end-to-end solutions that can offer services to a generic customer base. In the DRM industry, the first phase appears to be the development of rudimentary DRM solutions which relied solely on copy protection. These solutions were content-provider-centric and were promptly rejected by the users because they failed to address their needs. The rise of second generation DRM systems can be seen as the transition to the second phase of the DRM market lifecycle. At present, some have noted that the DRM industry appears to be in this second phase [7]. In particular, DRM vendors are busy developing customized end-to-end solutions for users. Due to the difficulty of the transition from the second to the third phase, the "distance" between them has been referred to as a "chasm"; many vendors are not able to make this transition [6]. In the third phase, vendors are able to provide stable solutions, and they can successfully embed their technologies into business solutions which can address the needs of generic customers. In this phase, stable solutions evolve which address the "tussle" between the vendors and the customers, and a de facto agreement is reached between them. In particular, vendors are incentivized to provide solutions that will maximize the usage and visibility of their technologies, while users demand a transparent experience that does not necessarily favor particular vendors. Thus, successful solutions involve a compromise that addresses the needs of the customer on the one hand, and are profitable to the vendor on the other. The third phase also allows the vendors to market their products competitively [7]. As we have mentioned, it appears that the DRM industry is currently locked in the second phase. Transition to the third phase will be greatly facilitated by the development of a framework containing appropriately defined standard that can guide the development of vendor strategies. Indeed, from the vendor's perspective, the determination of where standards should not be defined is just as important as determining where they should be specified. As we will see, a layered architectural framework is useful in helping to decide these issues.

One of the most crucial requirements in the third phase is to provide stable solutions. DRM systems need to incorporate a range of services that can be offered to customers. These services will vary in their nature and complexity depending upon type of content and its usage model. Many DRM vendors tried to incorporate a range of services in their products; however, they failed in trying to achieve this. For example, the IBM Cryptolopes project tried to incorporate complex services into its solutions offering a range of services to customers; however, from a commercial perspective, this project was a failure [5]. Most of the early DRM products collapsed under their own weight in trying to achieve everything. The biggest hurdles in developing stable DRM solutions are trust and security. No matter how user-centric a DRM solution is, its success will eventually depends upon the ability to enforce rights. That is, DRM is largely dependent on security solutions. There is, however, a major difference between security and rights enforcement. Rights enforcement is much difficult to achieve as it is concerned with controlling the usage of the content after delivering it to the user. This gives rise to trust. In many cases, the content provider must establish trust in the user before content can be delivered. It is possible that one security breach involving sensitive data can defeat the whole purpose of a DRM system. DVD encryption provides a good example of how inflexible security soltuions can cause problems. When DVD encryption was "cracked", the security system was inflexible and therefore, it could not recover from the attack. However, this does not mean that DRM systems should not be employed. A requirement is that a system should be able to recover from security breaches in order to stop further exploitations. The system should, therefore, have excellent trust management capabilities which would allow dynamic trust establishment between the content owner and the user. Another problem faced by content distributors are the rapid technological changes in rendering platforms. A DRM system should also be able to adapt to these changes. To provide stable solutions, it is necessary to develop DRM services which will withstand rapid changes in platforms. These are the challenges faced by DRM vendors in developing stable solutions.

In the third phase of the market, the tussle between the customer and vendor should achieve an equilibrium. The solutions should be profitable to the vendor and simultaneously provide enough benefits to the customers. Only when such an equilibrium is reached, can the product survive in the market. If a DRM product overly favors one of the parties, then it will be rejected by the other. We have already seen in first generation DRM systems solutions which involve too much control over the user (in favor of the content provider), but these were rejected by users. On the other hand, content providers are reluctant to use systems which provide too much freedom to the users. In order to achieve an equilibrium, it is necessary to discuss the needs of both vendors and customers and more closely consider where conflicts of interest arise.

In the area of services, customers demand choices. A customer does not want to be overloaded with heavyweight solutions when a lightweight solution is all that is required. In many first generation systems, all the services were bundled in a single product and provided to the customer, who was forced to download the heavyweight product. Since most DRM vendors provide complete DRM solutions, customers are locked into specific DRM vendors. What customers demand is independence of DRM vendors. The customer should be able to switch the DRM vendors with minimal overload. In this sense, DRM now has a reputation of getting in the way of using content. A customer will be reluctant to use the DRM solution if he can get access to the content cheaper through illegal means. Customers are generally not interested in buying the rights to a piece of content which is be restricted to use over a single device. DRM vendors need to address these needs and develop solutions which will allow enforcement of rights over multiple devices.

Vendors want solutions that will be profitable, which requires reaching a wide customer base. It is, therefore, necessary that DRM solutions should be able to use different content distribution models, and also allow the vendor to adapt the product to different business models. It is also necessary that new entrants in the industry are able to integrate their products with existing ones to provide generic DRM solutions.

In this paper, we consider how an agreed upon architectural framework for DRM can facilitate the growth of DRM markets. In DRM as layered system [4], we proposed a layered DRM framework for DRM technologies. In this paper, we consider how such a framework can help to guide the development of technology along with the assist in the establishment of helpful standards.

2. Rationale for a Layered Framework

Consider the client-server model associated with a typical DRM system, where the user of the client machine wishes to purchase a piece of content, and the server side is responsible for delivering the content along with its associated rights. The rights are then enforced on the client machine. There are three basic processes that must be supported within this framework. At the highest level are the dealings of the client system with the server. An intermediate level is concerned with how exactly the rights are specified as well as how they should be interpreted in particular environments. At the lowest level the concern is how the rights are

Figure 1: A Breakdown of the OSI Data Communications Layers and the Proposed DRM Layers into Upper, Middle, and Lower Layers

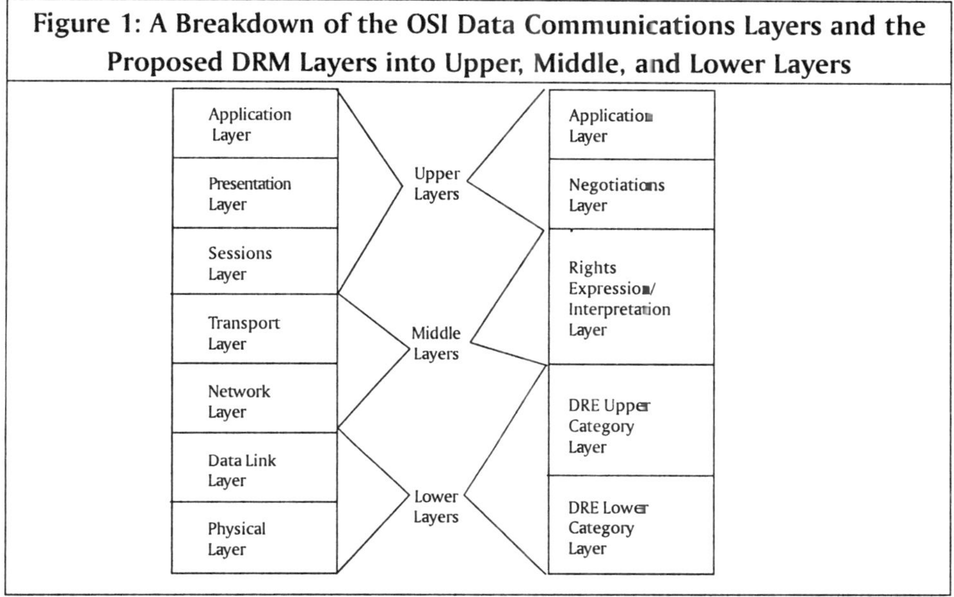

enforced on the client side. The client server dealings will be a part of upper layers. Rights enforcement technologies will be present in the middle layers. Figure 1 gives a detailed breakdown of the DRM layers.

Rights expression and interpretation (REI) form the minimal requirement of any DRM system. Since they constitute the minimal requirement of DRM systems, they are placed in the core of the framework. The REI Layer would provide a common denominator over which various DRM services can be built. Every DRM system would require the REI layer service. New services can be created using the REI service. Just as TCP, HTTP and UDP, etc., are various services created out of IP, REI can provide a common ground for creation of new services.

There are a wide range of services demanded by the users. These services can be created independent of the underlying rights enforcement technologies. The functionalities of these DRM services would be determined by the end-to-end arguments necessary in the DRM system design. The service layers would help the DRM solutions adapt themselves to different business models. The service layers are divided into two parts – Application Layer and Negotiations Layer. Functions which are more central to DRM like trust establishment, interoperability, content tracking, access control, security and watermarking will be implemented in the Negotiations Layer. Application – specific functions like money transactions, personal trust establishment, pricing models, preview facilities and content search facilities will be implemented in the Application Layer. The service layers would represent the upper dome of the hourglass shaped structure as shown in Figure 2.

Figure 2: DRM as a layered system with an hourglass structure. In this case Rights Expression and Interpretation provides the minimal service, and this service is therefore located at the notch of the hourglass.

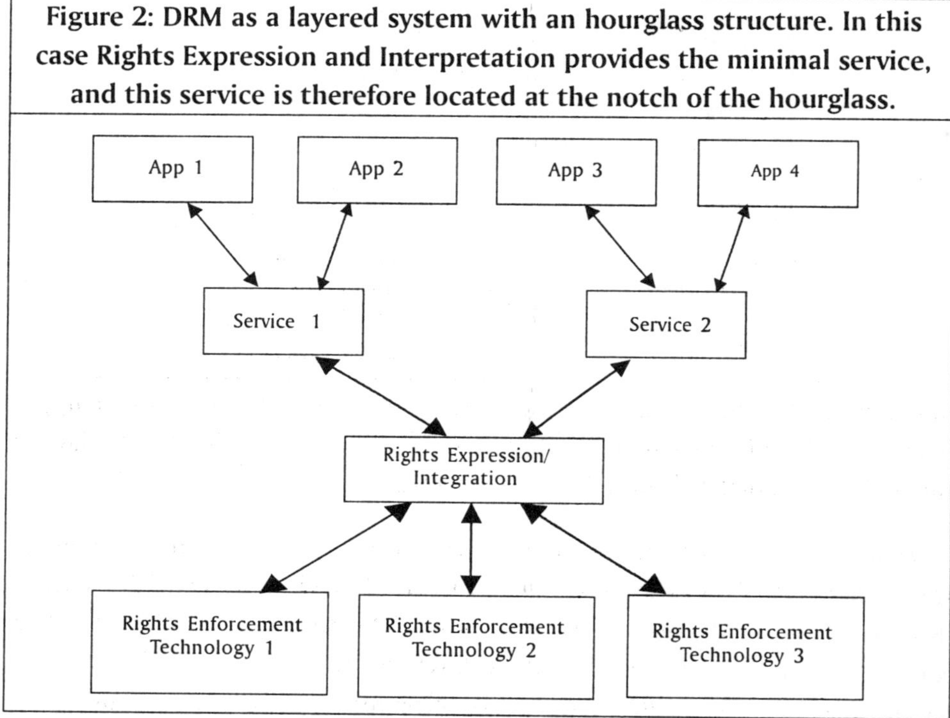

The REI layer would be implemented over the Rights enforcement technologies (RET). Similar to the underlying networks that serve the purpose of actually transmitting the data, RETs attempt to enforce the specific rights associated with particular content items and users. RETs represent technologies that enable rights enforcement. Technologies such as secure containers, authorized domains, watermarking, and trusted platforms will be implemented in the RET layers. These rights enforcement technologies are bound to change with advances in computer science and electronics, though their role would always remain the same. Thus, if the core of the framework is limited to rights expression and interpretation, then the framework will be flexible enough to change with the changing requirements of DRM environments, without invalidating useful applications that have been previously built on top of the minimal DRM services.

2.1 Technologies Independent of Services

In most of the current DRM systems, the services provided by the system are bound to the technologies used for the enforcement of rights. DRM vendors generally have their rights enforcement software running on client devices. Thus the range of services provided to the users is heavily dependent on the rights enforcement solutions available in the DRM systems. In DRM as layered system [4], we proposed breaking down the DRM process into layers. Layered systems help to buffer the services against the rapidly changing technologies. Our work is inspired by the highly successful OSI framework and the TCP/IP protocol architecture. The central idea behind the proposed DRM framework is identification of the minimal requirement of the DRM processes using this service as a separator of rights enforcement technologies and DRM services.

From the server's perspective, it does not matter exactly how rights are enforced on client system. What the server needs is an assurance that the rights will be correctly enforced on the client system. The server should also be assured that the client system understands the expressed rights and can interpret them correctly in order to enforce the rights. If these two goals can be achieved, then the process of rights enforcement can be separated from the DRM services. The glue that holds together the rights enforcement and DRM services is the rights expression and interpretation process. This role is very similar to that of IP in telecommunication networks which holds together the networking services and the networking infrastructure. If we place the rights expression and interpretation layer in the middle, then it is possible to think of the DRM services in the form of an hourglass shape. Rights expression and interpretation (REI) provides the minimal DRM service and should be situated at the notch of the hourglass. Figure 2 shows how DRM can be structured in order to form an hourglass shape. The lower dome consist of the rights enforcement technologies and the upper dome consist of the DRM services. The REI and the upper dome would deal with the end-to-end arguments and lower dome will be implemented on the client side. The REI layer shields the intricacies of digital rights enforcement from the service layers above. It provides a lowest common denominator over which new services would be created according to needs of the DRM environment, leading to specific applications in the upper layer of the DRM architecture. Such a framework would be flexible to the changing demands of DRM going forward.

Ideally, the DRM services can be truly independent of the rights enforcement technologies (RETs) only if it is possible to achieve trust between the server and the RET running on the client machines. We term the trust placed by the server in the client system as system level trust. Negotiations Layer plays a crucial role in establishing system level trust. The REI Layer provides the service of rights expression and interpretation to the Negotiations Layer operating above the REI Layer. The Application Layer operates on the top of the Negotiations Layer. Let us look at the range of services available to the Application Layer.

- System level trust in the rights enforcement technology running on the rendering device.
- Service of rights expression and interpretation.
- Rights enforcement.

These three services provided to the Application Layer separate the services provided by the Application Layer from the rights enforcement technologies on the user systems. The Application Layer services can be developed independent of the underlying technologies running on client systems. Any change in the RETs only affects the system level trust in the Negotiations Layer and leaves the Application Layer unaffected. The Application Layer services are more business specific and play a major role in helping DRM systems adapt to different business models.

2.2 Tussle Spaces

The design of the Internet was inspired by technological challenges. As more people began using the Internet, naturally business models started developing around the Internet. The integration of business into the Internet led to the creation of tussles between Internet players. These tussles started to dominate the development of the Internet. The influence of these tussles, started threatening some of the basic tenets on which the Internet was built. Clarke *et al.* [2] emphasize the need for new design strategies to accommodate different tussles in the Internet players. It is important that these tussles do not affect the stability and flexibility of the Internet. Thus, they propose the following design principles that should be followed in order to deal with tussles:

- Do not design to dictate the outcome. Rigid designs will be broken; designs that permit variations will flex under pressure and survive.
- Modularize the design along the tussle boundaries, so that one tussle does not spill over and distort unrelated issues.
- Design for choice to permit different players to express their preferences.

In DRM as layered system [4], we point out that the challenges currently faced by the DRM industry are similar to those faced by the telecommunications industry in the early eighties. There are, however, some sharp differences in the challenges faced by the DRM industry and the Internet. In the networking world, the technology came first and the business models later. The business models were developed to adapt themselves to the available technology. The design of the Internet and its flexibility later adapted to the changes in the business models and supported the emerging ones. In rights management industry, there are well established rights management business models in place. These models were proved and tested in the non-digital rights management world. Companies are generally reluctant to change their existing business models for newer ones. Any DRM technology should, therefore, be flexible enough to adapt itself to different business models. It should also be able to support any changes in the business models and should work for the new emerging business models.

With regards to tussles, DRM faces more severe challenges than those currently faced by the Internet. DRM is all about business and tussles are an integral part of business. There are three main players in the DRM industry: Content owner, content distributor and user. Each of these players have their own goals. The goal of the content provider is to have a choice in selection of employing a content distributor for his work. The goals of the content distributor include market success, ability to target a large user base, high control over user activity, and keeping out new entrants. The goals of the user include service provider independence, high rights expressive power and choice of services. It can be observed that these goals are conflicting and thus, there exists different kinds of tussles among these players over different issues. Next, we consider some of the important tussles developing in the DRM industry.

Usage Control Tussle – This is one of the biggest tussles in the DRM industry. The content distributor wants to have maximum control over the way the content is being used by the user. On the other hand, the user wishes to have maximum flexibility in the way the content is used. By its very nature, DRM is different than most of the industries. In DRM, the user is generally looked upon as the exploiter and the content distributor or the content owner is considered to be the one who is exploited. This is one of the reasons why the first generation DRM systems were content-distributor-centric and heavily emphasized copy protection. The copy-protection-oriented first generation DRM systems were rejected by users. The users demanded more expressive power and usage flexibility when it came to using digital data. The lack of choice of service and usage flexibility were some of the main reasons for the failure of first generation DRM systems. There is a tussle here. Any DRM system which do not provide the users enough flexibility to use the content are going to be rejected by the users. The content providers will eventually lose out if the DRM system does not work out. DRM systems which provide greater flexibility to the users for using the digital content are more susceptible to security breaches than the DRM systems which exercise a greater control on content usage. The content owners and content distributors will be wary of introducing any sensitive digital content in DRM systems which are susceptible to security breaches. In this case, the user will eventually lose out by paying more money as a result of failure of implementation of DRM system. This is a deadlock. Technology can help to solve the deadlock here.

The layered DRM framework solves this deadlock. The layered framework separates the RETs from DRM services. The DRM user is thus free to use his choice of RET. In a layered framework, usage flexibility allowed by the content provider totally depends on the system level trust that the content provider has in the client RET software. The usage flexibility is high if the the content provider has a high trust in the user RET, whereas it is low if the the trust level is low. Thus the flexibility of the structure is modulated by the trust level between the user and content provider. The user now has a choice of level of usage flexibility he wants to enjoy. A user with sophisticated RET will enjoy a greater flexibility as compared to the one with a rudimentary RET. Usage flexibility is also dependent on personal trust. A user with better trust history will be able to use the content with more freedom than the one with a worse trust history. By implementing these policies, a space is provided for the tussle where the involved parties can compete.

Service Provider Independence – Most of DRM systems built today have the services dependent on the rights enforcement technologies. This forces the users to use a complete solution provided by a single content provider. There is a tussle between the user and the content provider here. The content provider wants to keep the user whereas the user wants to have a choice in selecting his own content provider. In the current DRM setup if a user has to quit one content provider and use a different one, then he has to download the RET software from the other content provider. This acts as a deterrent for changing the content provider. What is needed is a mechanism where a user has the freedom to change the content provider with minimal overhead on hidden part.

Since the layered DRM framework separates the services from the RETs, a user having a single RET on his machine can change the content provider. Independence of services from RETs makes it possible to employ the services of different content providers over a single RET.

2.3 Tussles by Layer

Taking into consideration the different tussles in the DRM industry, each can be identified as being present in a specific layer in the proposed DRM framework. As mentioned in 'Tussle in Cyberspace: Defining tomorrow's Internet' [2], such an identification and separation of the tussles is necessary so that one tussle does not spill over and distort other parts of the system. The separation of these tussles will also make it easier to study and manage these tussles independently.

- **Application Layer:** This layer deals with the business models that would be adopted by the different DRM vendors. Application Layer will experience tussle among the existing DRM vendors and the potential entrants in the DRM industry. The existing vendors will try to keep out the potential new entrants. On the other hand, the new entrants will demand for a space in the existing market.
- **Negotiations Layer:** This layer will experience a tussle between the customers and DRM vendors. Negotiations Layer is a service layer. Users will demand

flexibility of services. The users will demand a range of services from the DRM vendors. The users will want to have the freedom of changing the DRM vendor based on the services provided. The user will, therefore, expect minimal overhead while changing the DRM vendor service. The DRM vendors on the other hand will want to keep the customers and prevent them from going to a different vendor. The process of standardization will play a crucial role in addressing this issue [1]. A similar tussle is faced in the networking industry where users want the freedom to choose the ISPs whereas service providers want to take away that freedom [2].

- *REI Layer*: The REI Layer separates the services from the RETs. The tussle in this layer will be around the choice of RET. The users will want to use the RET of their choice. On the other hand, the DRM vendors will want the users to use the RET developed by the DRM vendors. Currently most of the RETs are heavyweights and require an onerous download on the part of user.
- *Digital Rights Enforcement Upper Layer*: A tussle in the Digital Rights Enforcement (DRE) upper layer will be access control. The DRM vendors will want to have compete control over which softwares get the access to the content. The user on the other hand will want to use the rendering device of his choice to view the content. The tussle can be solved by implementation of appropriate protocols in the Negotiations Layer.
- *Digital Rights Enforcement Lower Layer*: Tussles in this layer will be over the freedom to use the content over multiple devices. This is one of the major tussles in the DRM industry. The users want to have complete freedom over the way the content is being used. The users demand to use the content over multiple devices of their choice. On the other hand, the DRM vendors wish to have a strict control over which devices get access to the content. This tussle can be resolved by having sophisticated trust establishment mechanisms by which the DRM vendor will have a guarantee that the rights are not violated, when the content passes from one device to the other. SealedMedia technologies implement this functionality by using the concept of roaming licenses to emulate a physical license [8].

2.4 Innovation versus Standards

We discussed the tussles emerging in the DRM industry in the different layers of the DRM framework. As noted in Clarke *et al.* [2], the outcome of the tussles need not be defined by technologists. Any attempt to bias these tussles in favor of a particular party will be rejected by the other one. It is necessary to create a right environment where an equilibrium can be reached among the players with conflicting interests. The creation of the right environment is actually defining the standards. Standards should be carefully defined so as to control the impact of tussles on the system architecture on one hand and allow a well controlled evolution of the technologies on the other hand by providing enough space for innovation. A layered architecture for DRM will help to achieve this equilibrium. As seen before, it is possible to identify and separate the tussles in the DRM industry according the different layers. Effective management of these tussles will depend upon how standards are defined in such a system. The definition of the standards will depend on the interests of each of parties involved in the tussle and the impact of their interests on the layered framework.

2.5 e-Content Business Models

Most of the DRM systems are modeled on the rights management systems which existed in the non-digital world. One of the biggest challenges faced by the DRM industry is that the DRM systems should be flexible enough to adapt themselves to the existing business models and also the emerging ones. Some of the DRM business models discussed in [7] are:

Paid Downloads – In paid downloads, the user pays to the content provider every time he buys content. Paid downloads emulate the physical world business model where one goes to a store and buys a book and has to pay every time a purchase is made. It has been pointed out that paid downloads work for high valued products. The issues with paid downloads are as follows [7]:

1. Complex to use content
2. Complex to use DRM technology
3. Device independence necessary.

Subscriptions – Subscription is service based and hence, is a more sophisticated business model than paid downloads. Subscriptions are advantageous to the content providers as well as the users. The subscription model helps the content providers to estimate the revenues well in advance. To the users, subscription is beneficial because it is easy to use content under subscription. One of the biggest hurdles in deploying subscription is the inefficiency of the rights enforcement technologies [7].

Pay-per-view and pay-per-listen – Pay-per-view and pay-per-listen business models are service based. Every time the service is utilized by the user, the user is supposed to pay to the content provider. This business model has been successful in video content. Video on Demand service is provided by many content providers with decent success in hotels and flights. The pay-per-view business model has been successful in time sensitive content, where the content has a little value after a specified period of time [7].

Usage metering – Usage metering is service based. The total charge put on the user is determined by the metered usage of the service. Usage metering works well with the low income group because they can control the usage and expect to be billed accordingly. In case of DRM usage, metering can be well implemented because DRM is capable of recording the usage of the content and correspondingly report it to the content provider. Usage metering has more of market value than being helpful in collecting revenues. Usage metering can help in collecting usage patterns and customer preferences.

Peer-to-peer and Superdistribution – Peer-to-peer and superdistribution have started gaining importance in the DRM industry. Technologies like Napster and Kazaa have helped in sharing files over the network. Peer-to-peer networks can transfer data along the chain of users in the network. Superdistribution is a process where the content is distributed through a chain of users. Each user in the chain acts as a distributor himself and the payments propagate back along the distribution chain with each distributor getting his share of payment. It is desirable for the DRM industry to use the peer-to-peer technology to achieve superdistribution. If implemented, this can provide a very sophisticated and fast content distribution model which will help both the content provider and the user. The content provider will be able to reach a wide range of users with little investments on his part. The user will benefit with cheaper rates and access to a huge content database.

All these business models are suited best for a selective content and a selective group of customers. A business model which is profitable in a particular environment may prove to be disastrous in another one. It is, therefore, necessary that the DRM vendors are able to adopt to any of these business models with ease. These business models offer various services depending on the need of the customer. These services are implemented differently in each of these business models. These services are payments, monetary transactions, establishment of personal trust and risk assessment etc. The DRM vendors will desire that making changes to these services to change over to a different business model should not require to make changes to the complete DRM solutions. It should be possible to make the changes by having least impact on the other parts of the system. The DRM layered system addresses these issues by identifying and placing these functions in a separate layer so that changes can be made to them by not affecting the other layers of the system. The functions influenced by the business models are placed in the upper layers. Most of the functions mentioned can be separately implemented in the Application Layer while some of them will require support from the functions in the Negotiations Layer.

The same is true for content distribution models. If a DRM vendor wants to switch over to a different content distribution model than the existing one, then it should be possible to do so with minimal overhead. The protocols implemented in the Negotiations Layer and the REI Layer will decide the type of distribution model adopted by a DRM vendor. Let us consider the case of superdistribution where the customer also assumes the role of a content distributor. In this case, protocols can be implemented in the Negotiations Layer to check the capabilities of the customer to act as a content distributor. The propagation of payments along the distribution chain can be handled in the Application Layer. A layered DRM framework separates functions deciding the distribution methods from the rest of the system, making it possible for the vendor to adopt a different distribution strategy with minimal changes in the remaining system.

3. Vendor Economics

One of the major tussles in any industry is the space for new entrants, which is normally blocked by the established parties already active in the industry. This is essential for a healthy competition within the industry. Competition leads to better services and innovation. It is, therefore, the responsibility of the designers to provide enough space for the new entrants and the smaller players. The standards in the framework should also be defined so that it gives enough space for the vendors to provide attractive services to the users that will give them a edge over their competitors. It is essential for the existing DRM vendors to meet the changing needs of the users and ability to respond to the changes in the business models. DRM solutions are useless if there are security breaches in the DRM solutions. Technology should, therefore, provide means for the DRM solutions to detect security breaches and recover from them in order to keep the confidence of content owners. Let us look at each of these aspects to see what role technology can play to provide solutions for these challenges.

3.1 Space for New Entrants

Currently, DRM vendors provide complete solutions to DRM. Interoperability of DRM is still in its initial stages. Thus, the DRM vendors are expected to provide services as well as their own rights enforcement technologies. Rights enforcement technologies are sophisticated high technology solutions. A huge amount of investment is necessary to develop near foolproof rights enforcement technologies. This deters new entrants who do not have enough capital to invest in DRM. Also since services are not independent of the RETs, operating system and rendering device manufacturers do not get enough incentive to incorporate DRM in their products unless they decide to provide complete DRM solutions. As a result of this, we have DRM vendors who try to provide complete solutions including rights enforcement, with little support from operating system and rendering-device vendors. These rights enforcement technologies have overlay architectures and thus are susceptible to security breaches at kernel levels. This would not have been the case if enough support is provided by the operating system and rendering device manufacturers. It is also the case that these vendors try to meet every DRM requirement. The size of their solutions, changes in DRM requirements and rapidly changing rendering devices often make these DRM solutions obsolete.

The layered DRM framework divides the process of DRM in layers and essentially separates the services from rights enforcement technologies. As pointed out earlier, the range of services provided by the DRM vendors would depend on the amount of system level trust the DRM server has in the RETs running on user platforms. It is, therefore, the responsibility of the user to buy sophisticated RETs to enjoy a wider range of services. To enjoy wide range of services, the users would demand sophisticated RETs from the device manufacturers and operating system vendors. This is a justifiable incentive for the device manufacturers and operating system vendors to include sophisticated DRM solutions in their products. This provide a boost for investment of significant capital in the research and development of sophisticated RETs. This is possible because there is no obligation on the rendering device and operating system manufacturers to provide complete DRM solutions.

The separation of DRM services from the RETs makes it possible to provide DRM services independent of RETs. This makes it possible for the potential entrants in the DRM industry to provide DRM services. The potential entrants can provide attractive DRM services to the users without making large investments in the RETs. Since it is possible to provide a choice of service at the Application Layer and the Negotiations Layer, the new entrants can choose the choice of service they intend to provide without invading the market of other DRM vendors.

3.2 Space for Competition

As discussed earlier, the DRM vendors provide complete DRM solutions. Most of the times, users have to download the rights enforcement software to use the DRM services. This process locks the users in using the services of a certain DRM vendor. The separation of DRM services from the RETs, addresses this issue and makes DRM vendor as independent as possible. Given this, DRM should provide space for the DRM vendors to implement services with added value so that they have an edge over their competitors in providing DRM services to the users.

The Application Layer and the Negotiations Layer, both of which are service layers, address this issue. DRM vendors can provide attractive DRM services to the users, by providing different kinds of services in these layers. Different kinds of attractive pricing models can be implemented in the Application Layer. Range of system level services can be implemented in the Negotiations Layer. Lightweight DRM services implemented in the Negotiations Layer will address the needs of naive DRM users, while heavyweight DRM services will address the needs of sophisticated users. It is essential that standards are carefully defined so that they provide enough space for the DRM vendors to provide competitive offerings.

3.3 Survival

The requirements of the DRM industry are rapidly changing. It is necessary for the DRM vendors to adapt themselves to the new emerging business models. The technology should, therefore, provide the ability to employ different business models without making major changes in the already installed technology. Security breaches in the DRM systems are a major deterrent for the content owners to introduce their products in the DRM market. To survive the competition, the DRM vendors should be able to recover from the security breaches in their solutions. This is essential to maintain the confidence of the content owners and also prevent losing the market share. It is, therefore, necessary for the DRM technologies to provide protection against security breaches.

Complex services can be created in the Application Layer to adapt the DRM solution to different business models, to cater the needs of different users and stay alive in the competition. Here are some of the services can that be implemented in the Application Layer:

- **Money Transactions:** This service would include facilities for the payment of the purchase. This service can be very simple which would include means of payment by the user to the service provider, in case of normal distribution of content. This service will be very complex in case of superdistribution where the payments propagate along the distribution chain. Complex money transactions can be built for B-to-B applications.
- **Content Tracking and Usage:** The information on content usage and tracking of content can be provided to the user by means of the Application Layer. This information will be passed on to the Application Layer by the Negotiations Layer.
- **Risk Assessment:** Risk assessment means calculating the total risk associated with the transaction. Risk assessment calculation depends upon a number of factors like personal trust, system level trust, nature of data, importance of data, nature of rights demanded by the user and vulnerabilities in the

transmission medium etc. Application Layer can provide the service of risk assessment. Application Layer would need the services of Negotiations Layer to calculate the system level risk.

- **Pricing Models:** Dynamic price calculation can be implemented in the Application Layer. Dynamic price calculation is calculating the price of the rights for some content on-the-fly. *Corbis.com* implements this functionality for calculating the price for the images sold under "rights managed" category. The price of an image is calculated depending on the nature of rights demanded by the user. Complex algorithms can be used to determine the price of an image by using the transaction risk calculation. If implemented in this manner, this service will require support from the Negotiations Layer.

Content tracking and usage information gathering can be implemented in the Negotiations Layer. To survive in the industry, the DRM solution must have facilities for detection of violation of rights so that corrective actions can be taken to recover from the security breaches. In order to recover from the security breaches, it is essential to first detect security breaches. The service of detecting content usage and rights violations will be implemented in the Negotiations Layer. Client systems can provide audits on the usage of the content on the their systems. Sealed media technology uses this method to track the usage of content on the client systems [8]. Negotiations Layer can have standard protocols for maintaining and reporting the usage audits. Once the audits are obtained from the clients, a system can be implemented at the server part of the Negotiations Layer to detect any violations of rights. If it is found that unprecedented rights violations are taking place on certain systems, corrective actions can be taken to recover from the security breaches on those systems.

4. Conclusions

In this paper, we point out how a layered DRM framework will facilitate the development of stable DRM solutions which will help to manage the on-going tussle between the customers and DRM vendors. The current technological setting in the DRM industry has failed to address these problems resulting in large number of failures for DRM vendors. We also discussed how changing requirements in services and rapidly changing content rendering platforms are making it difficult for DRM vendors to implement stable solutions. The separation of DRM services from the rights enforcement technologies greatly facilitates the development of stable solutions. Finally, we considered how a layered DRM framework can have a major influence on DRM vendor economics. Such a framework provides a space for competition among existing vendors as well as a space for potential entrants into the DRM industry. A layered DRM framework can thus facilitate the transition of vendors from the second phase of the DRM market to the third phase.

(Pramod A Jamkhedkar is from Department of Computer Science, University of New Mexico, Albuquerque, NM.

Gregory L Heileman is from Department of Electrical & Computer Engineering, University of New Mexico, Albuquerque, NM.)

References

1. Harald Alverstrand. "The role of the standards process in shaping the internet". *Proceeding of the IEEE*, 92(9):1371-1374, 2004.
2. D D Clark, J Wroclawski, K R Sollins, and R Braden. "Tussle in cyberspace: Defining tomorrow's Internet". *In SIGCOMM*, pages 347-356, Pittsburg, Pennsylvania, USA, Aug. 2002.
3. "The DRM vendor graveyard", *http://www.info-mech.com/drm_vendor_graveyard.html.*
4. P A Jamkhedkar and G L Heileman. "DRM as a layered system". In *Proceedings of the Fourth ACM Workshop on Digital Rights Management*, pages 11-21, Washington, DC, Oct. 2004.
5. Marc A. Kaplan. "IBM cryptolopes, superdistribution and digital rights management", 1996. *http://researchweb.watson.ibm.com/people/k/kaplan/cryptolope-docs/crypap.html.*
6. Geoffery A Moore. *Crossing the Chasm: Marketing and Selling High-Tech Products to Mainstream Customers.* Harperbusiness, 1999.
7. Bill Rosenblatt, Bill Trippe, and Stephen Mooney. *Digital Rights Mangement: Business and Technology.* M&T Books, New York, NY, 2002.
8. SealedMedia. Core Technology, Jun. 2004.

9

DRM, Trusted Computing and Operating System Architecture*

Jason F Reid and William J Caelli

Robust technological enforcement of DRM licenses assumes the prevention of direct access to the raw bit representation of decrypted digital content and the license enforcement mechanisms itself is possible. This is difficult to achieve on an open computing platform such as a PC. Recent trusted computing initiatives namely, the Trusted Computing Group (TCG) specification, and Microsoft's Next Generation Secure Computing Base (NGSCB) aim in part to address this problem. The protection architecture and access control model of mainstream operating systems makes them inappropriate as a platform for a DRM content rendering client because decrypted content cannot be protected against a privileged process. If a DRM client is to be deployed on an open computing platform, the operating system should implement the reference monitor concept, which underpins the mandatory access control model. The TCG model of trusted computing has important limitations when combined with an operating system enforcing discretionary access control. We argue that

* This paper appeared at the Australasian Information Security Workshop 2005 (AISW2005), Newcastle, Australia.

the TCG services of sealed storage and remote attestation which are important in DRM applications, cannot operate in a secure and efficient manner on such an operating system.

1. Introduction

Advances in digital compression technology coupled with the reduced cost and increased capacity of storage media and network bandwidth have combined to make the distribution of digital content over the Internet a practical reality. The owners of copyrighted works, particularly in the entertainment area, have become increasingly anxious to ensure that evolving digital technology does not limit or reduce their capacity to enforce their copyrights for financial reward. This concern has motivated a steadily growing interest in the field of Digital Rights Management (DRM).

DRM has been defined as "the management of rights to digital goods and content, including its confinement to authorized use and users and the management of any consequences of that use throughout the entire life cycle of the content" (CEN/ISSS, 2003).

This definition encompasses two distinct aspects of DRM that are independently recognised as being worthy of protection in the World Intellectual Property Organisation's copyright treaty (WIPO, 1996): firstly, rights management information, which includes "information which identifies the work, the author of the work, the owner of any right in the work, or information about the terms and conditions of use of the work", and secondly, technological enforcement, which encompasses effective technological mechanisms used to enforce the terms and conditions of use for a work.

Although these two aspects of DRM cannot be cleanly separated, it is the second aspect that is the principle focus of this paper. In particular, we consider the difficult challenge of technological enforcement on open computing platforms such as a general purpose personal computer (PC).

The essential premise of DRM is that a rights' owner wishes to license digital content (which is represented as binary digits or bits) to a licensee or customer who agrees to be bound by the terms of the license. Note that the customer is not buying the bits themselves. Rather, they are buying the right to use the bits in a defined and restricted manner, as authorised in the terms of the license. Hence, the license defines a type of usage policy. A hypothetical license might authorise a single playing of the content on a nominated platform. Copying, multiple 'plays', redistribution and modification may be prohibited. Technological enforcement is necessary because the rights' owner does not necessarily trust the customer, yet they would like to have a reasonable level of assurance that the license terms will be complied with even though the content is stored and used on devices that they do not own or control. Digital information can be protected from unauthorised access in transit and storage by well-understood cryptographic techniques. As Schneck (1999) argues, the more complicated challenge presented by DRM flows from the observation that the content bits must be in the clear (i.e., not protected by encryption) on the client platform in order to be rendered in a manner perceptible to a user. If the decrypted content bits can be accessed, (for example by using a kernel debugger or modified device driver), the technological enforcement of the license conditions can be circumvented. Once dissociated from its protection, the content can be freely copied, played, modified and redistributed, albeit in violation of the license terms.

Consequently, to reliably enforce typical DRM policies, it must not be possible for the platform user to access the plaintext bits that represent the content, despite the practical reality that the platform is under the user's direct control[1]. This is an access control problem that cannot be solved purely by cryptography. On open computing platforms that can run arbitrary software, it is a difficult problem to which there is currently no practical, deployed solution, particularly in terms of 'software-only' techniques. Recent trusted computing initiatives, namely Microsoft's Next Generation Secure Computing Base (NGSCB) (Microsoft, 2004) and the Trusted Computing Group (TCG) specification, (Trusted Computing Group, 2003) formerly known as TCPA aim in part, to address this issue through both hardware and software based methods (Anderson, 2003).

The goal of trusted computing is to deliver systems that are highly resistant to subversion by malicious adversaries, allowing them to operate reliably and predictably in almost any circumstance. Trusted computing is an important ingredient in DRM because it provides a sound basis for license enforcement. Given the way the NGSCB and TCG initiatives have been promoted, one could be forgiven for thinking that trusted computing is an entirely new concept. As we discuss in Section 3.1, trusted computing actually has a long history but the lessons this history can teach have been largely ignored over the last 20 years, particularly in the design of mainstream PC operating systems[2]. As a consequence, such systems are fundamentally ill-equipped to provide the level of protection that a robust DRM system demands.

1.1 Contribution

In this paper, we explain in detail why mainstream, commercial grade operating systems are an inappropriate platform on which to base a DRM client. We clarify why DRM platforms require an operating system that can enforce mandatory access control. We aim to address common misunderstandings as to the extent to which the TCG specification implements DRM. A key conclusion of our analysis is that the addition of TCG components to a discretionary access control enforcing operating system does not result in a 'trusted system' that can reliably enforce DRM licenses. We identify problems with DRM related applications of the TCG sealed storage feature that flow from the non-deterministic order of execution of a multi-tasking operating system. We highlight issues that undermine the effectiveness of the TCG remote attestation feature when it is deployed on mainstream operating systems.

1.2 Overview

The remainder of this paper is organised as follows. Section 2 provides background on the relevance of trusted systems to DRM. Section 3 examines operating system properties that are necessary to support secure DRM client applications, highlighting the deficiency of mainstream operating systems in relation to these requirements. Section 4 presents an analysis of the TCG specification and the degree to which it can improve the trustworthiness of mainstream operating systems. Section 5 examines Microsoft's NGSCB initiative and Section 6 provides conclusions to this analysis.

2. DRM Client Security and Trusted Systems

Stefik (1997) argues that trusted systems are a basic requirement for robust DRM. Stefik defines a trusted system as one "that can be relied on to follow certain rules. In the context of digital works, a trusted system follows rules governing the terms, conditions and fees for using digital works." The rules or license terms are expressed in a computer-interpretable format, (known as a rights expression language) and the content rendering client ensures that the content is protected and manipulated in a manner consistent with the rules. Stefik does not describe the properties a trusted system should have to reliably enforce the rules. However it is implicit from the functional description that the trusted system must protect the underlying bit representation of the content from direct access by a user. If this were not the case, bypassing rule enforcement would be trivial.

According to Lacy *et al.* (1997), the license interpretation and enforcement components of the client's content rendering platform, (which we will refer to as the DRM client) must be implemented within the boundaries of a Trusted Computing Base (TCB). Lacy does not consider the complications that are introduced if the DRM client is an open computing device capable of running arbitrary software.

Biddle *et al.* (2003) identify the following necessary enforcement properties for a DRM client:

1. The client cannot remove the encryption from the file and send it to a peer.
2. The client cannot 'clone' its DRM system to make it run on another host.
3. The client obeys the rules set out in the DRM license.
4. The client cannot separate the rules from the payload.

When the DRM client is implemented in application software on a mainstream operating system, Hauser and Wenz (2003) contend that policy enforcement can be bypassed with relative ease. They document a number of successful attacks on deployed schemes. Properties 1, 3 and 4 are particularly difficult to implement in application level clients that run on mainstream operating systems. In the next section, we discuss reasons for the inadequacy of application level policy enforcement, in the absence of certain operating system features.

3. DRM, Trusted Systems and Mandatory Access Control

This section examines the relationship between operating system architecture and the effectiveness of DRM license enforcement.

According to Loscocco *et al.*, (1998) "current security efforts suffer from the flawed assumption that adequate security can be provided in applications with the existing security mechanisms of mainstream operating systems." They identify two important operating system mechanisms that are necessary for effective application-level security policy enforcement: firstly, the ability to enforce a mandatory security policy; and secondly, a trusted path for user input and output. Since neither property is implemented in current mainstream operating systems, they argue that the security of applications based thereon can be nothing more than "a fortress built on sand". This contention is certainly consistent with the results reported by Hauser and Wenz (2003).

The terms mandatory security policy and Mandatory Access Control (MAC) are used in a broader sense than their more common association with Multi-Level Security (MLS) systems that are based on the work of Bell and La Padula (1973). As Loscocco *et al.* (1998) describes, a system must be capable of enforcing a defined security policy in a mandatory fashion. This means that policy enforcement must be assured. To achieve mandatory security, security policy must be established, configured and maintained by an authorised security policy administrator (as opposed to Discretionary Access Control (DAC) systems, which allow ordinary users to configure access policy). The policy may be expressed in MLS terms or it may be role based[3] or it may be based on Domain and Type enforcement (DTE)[4]. The key requirement is that the operating system and underlying hardware are designed so that it is not possible for software or users to reconfigure or subvert the enforcement of the policy. Loscocco *et al.*, argues that carefully controlled memory segregation is critically important in achieving this requirement. When it is attained, mutually distrustful applications are able to execute on the same platform without being able to access each other's resources (if the policy does not allow it). This is a crucial requirement for DRM clients if Biddle's enforcement properties, as described in Section 2, are to be met.

3.1 Architecture Flaws in Mainstream OSs

A key limitation of mainstream operating systems that renders them inappropriate as platforms for a DRM client is their enforcement of an identity based discretionary security policy rather than a mandatory security policy. The DAC model is incompatible with the trust relationship that exists between a content provider and a content consumer, who is not assumed to be trustworthy. Since content is locally rendered, the content provider is forced to rely on the customer's DRM client to enforce their license terms but the environment that this client operates in is under the customer's control. In a DAC system, control of the execution environment gives the customer the ability to subvert the policy enforcement mechanisms of their DRM client[5]. The system owner can run privileged software such as a modified device driver that is able to access the memory space of the DRM client[6]. In a MAC system based for example, on DTE, it is possible to configure the MAC policy so that the DRM client's memory space cannot be accessed, even by other parts of the operating system. If the content provider can evaluate the MAC policy configuration to confirm that it enforces DRM client isolation, they can establish a degree of trust in the DRM client's ability to enforce the license terms – on the grounds that the application's technological enforcement measures cannot be tampered with or bypassed and its address space cannot be snooped by other privileged processes to copy decrypted content bits.

A MAC capability provides a sound basis for policy enforcement through rigorous control over information flows between subjects and objects (see Badger *et al.,* 1995). MAC systems rely on the concept of a reference monitor, (Anderson, 1972) which is responsible for enforcing the policy. The reference monitor mediates every access to system resources and data, (collectively known as objects) deciding whether the requested access is consistent with the policy. To ensure that every access is mediated, it must not be possible to bypass the reference monitor. The reference monitor mechanism also needs to be protected against tampering to ensure that an attacker cannot subvert or influence its access decisions. Finally, the reference monitor needs to be small enough to allow it to be validated via analysis and testing. These properties can be achieved by software in concert with hardware protection mechanisms (Schell *et al.,* 1985). The totality of software and hardware that is responsible for enforcing the security policy is known as the Trusted Computing Base (TCB).

A further critical weakness in mainstream operating systems is their inability to implement the security principle of least privilege, described for example, by Saltzer and Schroeder (1975). As the name suggests, least privilege requires a program or user to be given only the minimum set of access rights necessary to complete a task. To achieve this, a system needs to be able to express and enforce fine-grained access rights. In today's mainstream operating systems, privileges are bound to the so-called user 'IDs' so that access decisions are based on user identity. As a consequence, all of a user's privileges are granted to each program running on behalf of that user.

There is no efficient mechanism to reduce the set of available privileges to those that are actually needed.

To make matters worse mainstream operating systems have only two major categories of users: the root or super-user, and normal users. As the name 'super-user' implies, processes with super-user privilege cannot be constrained by access controls as there is no reference monitor. This operating system architecture creates a serious problem for DRM applications, because the platform owner typically has access to the super-user account. Without access controls, a DRM license cannot be enforced against the super-user and plain text content bits cannot be reliably protected. Observance of the principle of least privilege and enforcement of MAC underpin effective domain confinement through reliable control over information flows within the operating system (Saltzer and Schroeder, 1975). A DRM client based on an open computing platform cannot successfully maintain Biddle's minimum enforcement properties, (listed in Section 2) without the confinement and information flow control that a reference monitor enables.

Device drivers in mainstream operating systems present a particular problem because they must be totally trusted but they are not necessarily trustworthy. Drivers are tailored to a specific piece of hardware (e.g., a particular sound or graphics card) so they are normally provided by the hardware vendor. This creates a problem of trust. Solomon and Russinovich (2000) note: "device driver code has complete access to system memory space and can bypass Windows 2000 security to access objects." Thus, device driver code is like application code in that it is supplied by a range of sources. But it is effectively operating system code since it has unrestricted access to system resources. To further complicate matters, device drivers can be dynamically loaded at runtime. Thus, a malicious or buggy driver can be used for example, to compromise cryptographic keys and the plaintext of protected content. A digitally signed driver provided by a trusted vendor is a common approach to combat this problem. Unfortunately, this offers only a partial solution because drivers are typically too large and complex to evaluate to attain a reasonable degree of assurance that they do not contain exploitable bugs or unexpected behaviours. A signature does not guarantee correct operation. It is also difficult to ensure that the integrity of the signature verification mechanism and signer's public key are protected.

Early trusted systems such as Multics, (Corbato *et al.* 1972) addressed the device driver trust issue via a hierarchy of hardware enforced execution domains known as rings. Building on the Multics approach, Intel x86 processors have supported a ring based protection architecture (Figure 1) since the 286 chip. This four level design, with ring 0 being the most privileged and ring 3 the least, is intended to allow the operating system kernel, (which implements the reference monitor) to operate at a higher level of hardware enforced privilege than device drivers, other operating system components and code libraries which, in turn, can have higher privilege than users and application processes. The higher level of privilege ensures that the reference monitor mechanism is more resistant to bypass or tampering by other less trusted processes running in rings of lesser privilege. The quantity and complexity of code that must be trusted to enforce the mandatory security policy is thereby substantially reduced. This makes it easier to establish confidence in its correctness. The x86 hardware architecture is capable of supporting highly secure and trustworthy operation. When correctly utilised, its ring-based architecture combined with its fine-grained memory segmentation allow it to enforce effective domain separation and confinement at the hardware level. Unfortunately, with rare exceptions, (e.g. the GEMSOS OS described in Schell *et al.* (1985)) the protection rings and memory segmentation/capability features of the Intel x86 have not been used by mainstream, general purpose operating system designers as they were intended. Mainstream operating systems use only the most and least privileged rings for system and user space respectively, emulating two state machines. While PC operating systems may not have been designed with security as a high priority, the same cannot be said of the processor on which they are based.

Figure 1: The Intel x86 Ring Architecture

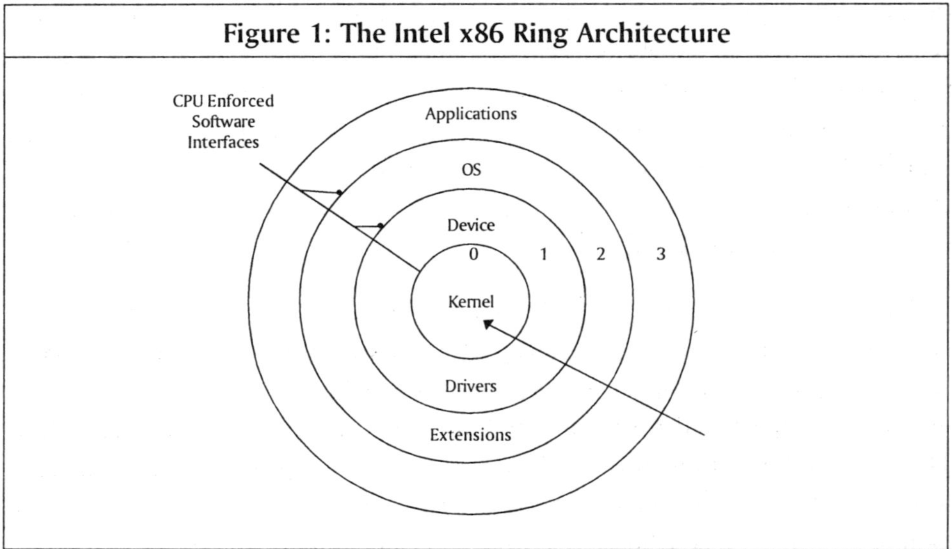

The failure of mainstream operating systems to correctly utilise the ring structure of the x86 processor explains Intel's announced intention to release a new chip with what is effectively a 'ring –1'. According to Peinado, *et al.,* (2004) the reason for this is that Microsoft's new NGSCB trusted computing architecture requires a higher level of privilege to enable effective domain separation within ring 0 which, for reasons of backward compatibility must continue to host device drivers of questionable provenance and other potentially insecure operating system components. This is discussed in more detail in Section 5.

In summary, mainstream operating systems lack the essential features that are required to protect decrypted content and thereby support the enforcement of DRM licenses. They do not enforce a mandatory access policy, and they fail to observe the principle of least privilege, which greatly magnifies the threat presented by software bugs and privileged but malicious code. In addition, the sheer volume and complexity of privileged code, (including device drivers) means that there is no possibility of gaining any reasonable level of assurance that a platform will obey DRM license terms. Trust mechanisms based on signed code and drivers do not alter this situation since the problem flows from the access control model and operating system architecture.

4. Trusted Computing Group – Formerly TCPA

In response to myriad problems created by the insecurity of open computing platforms, the Trusted Computing Group (TCG) has proposed a trusted computing platform specification (Trusted Computing Group 2003). In this section, we briefly describe key aspects of the specification. In the context of a DRM client application, we analyse the operating system features that are necessary to make meaningful use of TCG services, particularly remote attestation and sealed storage.

The Trusted Computing Group (TCG), successor to the Trusted Computing Platform Alliance (TCPA), is an initiative led by AMD, Hewlett-Packard, IBM, Intel, Microsoft, Sony, and Sun Microsystems. The TCG aims to "develop and promote open, vendor-neutral, industry standard specifications for trusted computing building blocks and software interfaces across multiple platforms" [7].

The novelty of the TCG architecture lies in the range of entities that are able to use TCG features as a basis for trust. These include not only the platform user and owner but also, remote entities wishing to interact with the platform. The mechanism of remote attestation allows remote third parties to challenge a platform to report details of its current software state. On the basis of the attestation, third parties can decide whether they consider the platform's configuration to be trustworthy. If correctly implemented, remote attestation promises to be an important feature for DRM clients on open platforms since it may assist a content provider in deciding whether the client is currently configured to enforce the license terms reliably before the content is actually provided.

A closely related TCG objective is to provide reliable, hardware-based protection for secrets such as cryptographic keys. Since open computing platforms can run arbitrary software, this objective aims to ensure that protected secrets will not be revealed unless the platform's software state meets clearly defined and accurately measurable criteria. TCG's sealed storage feature can be used to bind a protected secret such as a content decryption key to a particular software configuration. If the configuration is not as specified, the sealed key will not be released.

4.1 TCG Architectural Modifications

The architectural modifications required by the TCG specification include the addition of a cryptographic processor called a Trusted Platform Module (TPM). The TPM must be a fixed part of the computing device that cannot (easily) be transferred to another platform. The TPM provides a range of cryptographic primitives including random number generation, SHA-1 hashing, asymmetric encryption and decryption, signing and verification using 2048 bit RSA, and asymmetric key pair generation[8]. There is also a small amount of protected key storage. Currently available TPMs are based on smart card processors.

4.2 Integrity Measurement and Reporting

The TCG security services of remote attestation and sealed storage build on an integrity protected boot technique that was introduced by Arbaugh *et al.* (1997). Integrity protected booting is fundamental to the design of the TCG architecture. Figure 2 illustrates the process with numbers in parentheses denoting the sequence of events.

The boot process starts in a defined state with execution of the BIOS 'boot block' code. The BIOS boot block is called the Core Root of Trust for Measurement (CRTM). Since it initiates the booting and measurement process, it is implicitly trusted. The core idea behind integrity protected booting is that a precise hash-

Figure 2: TCG Integrity Protected Boot Sequence

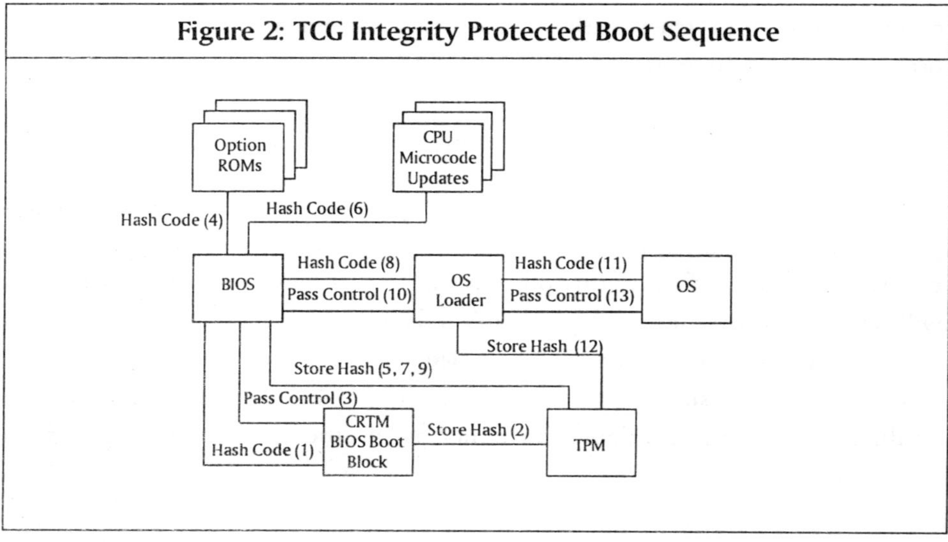

based measurement or fingerprint of all executable code in the boot chain should be taken and securely stored immediately before that code is given control of the processor. Accordingly, the CRTM takes a hash of the BIOS code (1) and stores the value in a protected hardware register in the TPM (2), called a Platform Configuration Register (PCR). PCRs cannot be deleted or arbitrarily overwritten within a boot cycle. They are 'update only' using a simple chained hash technique, based on the SHA-1 secure hash algorithm that works as follows (where || denotes concatenation):

Updated PCR Value = Hash(Previous PCR Value || Current Measurement To Store).

This operation is known as extending a PCR. It allows a practically unlimited number of measurements to be stored or committed in a fixed size register.

The CRTM then passes control to the BIOS code (3) which stores measurements of option ROM, CPU microcode updates and the OS loader before passing control to the latter. The boot process continues following the same pattern until the kernel is loaded. If any executable stage in this chain has been modified, the change will be reflected in the hash value. Since the PCRs can only be extended, not overwritten, the modified code cannot hide itself when it is given control of the CPU.

Remote attestation allows a TCG enabled platform to assert the state of its current software environment to a third party. The TPM uses a certified key pair that identifies the platform as a genuine TCG platform, to sign the current PCR values. Figure 3 illustrates the attestation procedure in a DRM setting. Before delivering protected content, a content provider can challenge a requesting TCG platform to attest on its current configuration. The platform sends the signed PCRs together with a log containing each of the individual measurements that have been extended into the PCR hash chains. The provider reviews each individual measurement to ensure that it corresponds to a component that it considers 'trusted'. If satisfied with the platform's state, the content can be delivered.

4.3 Operating System Support for TCG Trusted Computing

In this section we examine the types of operating system support that are necessary to meaningfully make use of remote attestation and sealed storage features.

Figure 3: TCG Remote Attestation Protocol

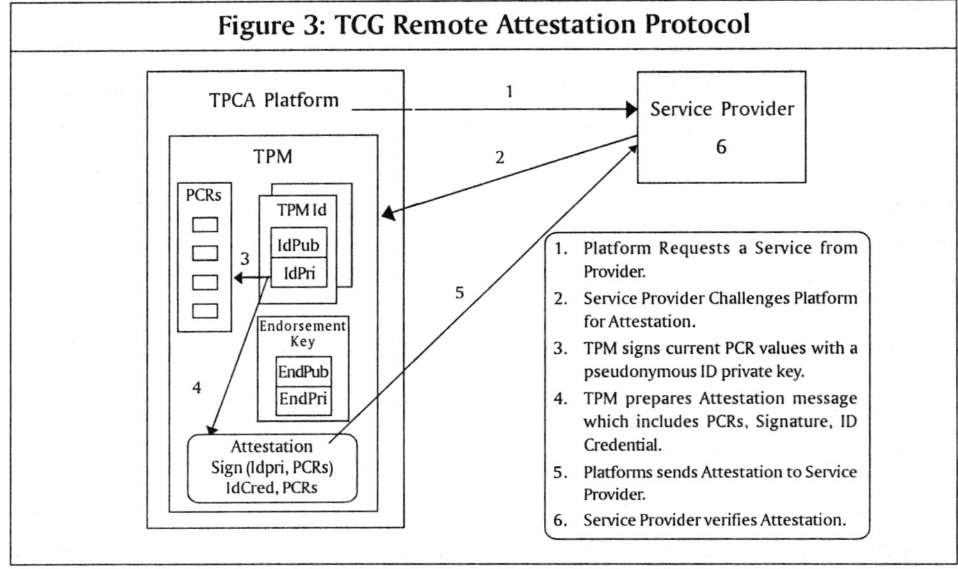

We highlight a number of serious challenges in applying TCG concepts of trusted computing to mainstream operating systems.

The TCG specification is claimed to be operating system neutral. It defines lowest common denominator functionality for a range of platform types including PDAs, mobile phones and PCs. Consequently, it does not deal with operating system architecture issues and it does not mandate or suggest operating system security features necessary for TCG services to work reliably. The specification defines requirements as far as the operating system (or bootstrap) loader. Despite the TCG specification's understandable silence in this regard, we contend that a multi-tasking operating system cannot meaningfully implement TCG functions, particularly remote attestation and sealed storage unless it has the 'classical' trusted computing features that were described in Section 3. The TCG's integrity verification approach is not a substitute for sound operating system architecture.

To understand why this is so, consider a typical DRM content delivery scenario wherein a TCG enabled DRM client platform wishes to connect to a content provider to download and subsequently view a movie. In exchange for payment, the provider will transfer an encrypted copy of the movie and a license for a single viewing. The license prohibits copying, modification and transfer to other platforms. Note that these license terms implicate all of Biddle's enforcement properties (listed in Section 2). Building on TCG features, the content provider takes a number of steps to ensure the integrity of the policy enforcement mechanisms on the client's platform. We use the term integrity to refer to the ongoing ability of the platform to reliably enforce the license terms. There are three main types of verification requirement to determine and preserve integrity:

1. The content provider requires client platforms to establish via remote attestation that they have booted according to TCG principles. The content provider assesses the booted software environment against a list of 'trusted' components to ensure that the client booted into a trusted state.
2. The content provider must ensure that the client has not executed untrusted software after the boot process completed but before the remote attestation was initiated.
3. The content provider must ensure that a trusted version of the DRM client is executing at the time of the remote attestation, and that client cannot execute untrusted software while the protected content is being accessed or viewed.

We will now analyse the practical implications of addressing these requirements in the context of a mainstream operating system.

The motivation for the first requirement is self-evident. However, it is worth emphasizing that the TCG design is based on the premise that a system can be trusted if the PCR registers match values expected by a relying party. The expected values must be those of a known secure configuration. This assumes that a secure and trusted configuration actually exists and that the configuration is trusted because it is trustworthy. As we argued in Section 3.1, this assumption is not well founded in the case of mainstream operating systems because complexity and architecture defeat assurance of integrity. TCG does not solve code quality or operating system architecture problems. This is a critical and often overlooked limitation of the TCG model of trusted computing.

The second and third requirements reflect the fact that the integrity of a platform (running a mainstream operating system) is dependent on its runtime behaviour. A theoretically trustworthy state immediately post-boot provides no guarantee that integrity will be maintained, since software executing post-boot can affect the integrity of the platform. For example, a dynamically loaded kernel module, device driver or privileged application can potentially execute at any time and violate protection requirements. As we noted in Section 3.1, this is possible because there is no mandatory control over information flow among and within processes running at the highest level of privilege.

To support requirements two and three, the operating system itself needs to be modified to include a measuring function that fingerprints the executable code and configuration data of any system or user level process before it is launched. Sailer *et al.,* (2004) propose a 'TCG based integrity measurement architecture' based on Linux in which they describe a number of operating system modifications to this end. They describe the instrumentation of functions that initiate the loading of code and data that may impact platform integrity. In a DAC-based operating system not enforcing the principle of least privilege, there are many such places where the measuring function must be called. Relatively simple candidates include functions that load kernel modules, dynamically loadable libraries, and user-level executables. Other more problematic candidates include script interpreters, virtual machines, (e.g., the java class loader) privileged applications and network services. The instrumentation itself is relatively simple. It requires a call to a 'hash and store' function immediately prior to code execution. The problem lies in the practical difficulty of ensuring that all code is instrumented – particularly privileged application code. The source code of legacy and proprietary applications is not always available and software vendors may not be motivated or able to issue instrumented versions of all software that is still in use. Arguably, the impracticality of instrumenting all script interpreters, virtual machines, just in time compilers, and privileged applications calls into question the viability of the whole approach. The failure to instrument results in potential avenues for integrity violation.

The third requirement is the most challenging since it requires that the PCR values always reflect the current configuration. Therefore, to be able to verify the integrity of any one process all other processes must be measured on an ongoing basis (Sailer *et al.,* 2004). Since the integrity of a process may be violated at any moment, an attestation is only meaningful at the instant of the last measurement.

By the time a challenger has evaluated an attestation response, the integrity status may have changed in a material way. The challenger has no way to know if this has happened except to continually rechallenge the platform, a highly inefficient and unsatisfactory option that in any case can only provide retrospective assurance.

This problem also impacts sealed storage. A platform may have been in the configuration mandated in a sealed storage policy (as reflected in the required PCR values) at the time a protected cryptographic key was released to the operating system but this configuration can subsequently change (i.e., within the same boot cycle) putting the key and decrypted cipher text at risk of compromise.

In the absence of MAC based domain confinement, what is needed is a reliable way for the platform to revoke its trusted status and immediately purge any protected content or keys from memory if an integrity-relevant change occurs. The insurmountable difficulty lies in distinguishing a change that should result in trusted status revocation from an integrity preserving one. The reason we consider the problem to be insurmountable relates to how unrecognised fingerprints that have been extended into PCRs should be handled. This is discussed in the next section.

4.4 Maintaining Integrity Assurance

In the TCG remote attestation protocol, the challenged platform sends the current PCR values together with a log of the individual fingerprints that have been chained together to produce these values. The challenger can use the log to determine whether it trusts the components that are identified by each individual measurement that makes up a hash chain. To identify any tampering with the log, it can recalculate the chain to ensure it produces the reported PCR value. From a challenger's perspective, the presence of any unrecognised fingerprint in the log should result in the platform being considered untrustworthy – the unknown fingerprint could be that of a malicious component such as a modified device driver or a program that provides the same functionality as an instrumented program but without the instrumentation, e.g., a kernel module loader that can violate the integrity of the platform by loading malicious code that will not be reflected in the current PCR values.

This will only present a problem if unrecognised fingerprints can be legitimately expected from an otherwise 'trustworthy' platform. Unfortunately they are highly likely because loosely structured data, (including scripting files, configuration files etc.) must be fingerprinted. This is necessary because the runtime behaviour of a program is commonly determined by the configuration files it parses at start up, and also, the data consumed as inputs once running. Therefore, to assess the integrity impact of executable code, its inputs must be measured. The measurement of semi-structured and unstructured input data and configuration files is particularly problematic in the context of the TCG architecture since they are not as amenable to integrity verification via fingerprinting, as is static code. Non-executable files of this type can tolerate subtle differences such as extra white space characters, comments or the same elements in a different order, with no impact on integrity. Nonetheless, any such difference will produce a completely different fingerprint. Differences of this type can be reasonably expected in the real world as users tailor the system behaviour to meet their individual needs via configuration files. Without access to the measured file itself, the challenger will be unable to determine whether an unrecognised fingerprint results from an irrelevant formatting difference in a semi-structured file as opposed to a malicious component or an un-instrumented component loader. Hash-based integrity measurement may be practical for executable code but it is very unforgiving when applied to semi-structured data – arguably so unforgiving as to call the whole approach into question.

This line of reasoning applies equally to TCG's sealed storage feature. We noted that sealed storage allows the release of a protected key to be conditional on the current status of PCR registers matching some predefined and trusted values. The presence of an unknown measurement in the PCR hash chains will render a sealed object inaccessible. New measurements can be introduced by changes in the software or hardware configuration (e.g., an upgrade of a video card).

We believe the use of sealed storage for DRM content protection in mainstream operating systems is impractical for two reasons. The first relates to the order PCRs are extended in. With hash chains, the order of element chaining determines the resulting output value. Therefore, to access a sealed object, all the fingerprints that have been extended into a PCR must be trusted and they must be chained together in precisely the same order that produced the reference PCR values to which the object is sealed. In mainstream operating systems, the order of PCR extension is deterministic up to the operating system loader. After this point, order depends on individual runtime behaviour as the operating system kernel proceeds to launch multiple concurrent processes which themselves may be multithreaded. In such a multitasking environment, execution order is not deterministic.

The second reason why sealed storage is impractical flows from the observation in Section 4.3 that to maintain integrity, all executable code needs to be measured before it is loaded. This means that PCRs continue to be extended as new applications are run. Therefore, in typical usage they do not stabilise to a predetermined value[9]. This problem could be ameliorated by sealing an object to a subset of PCR values that only reflects the early stages of the boot process, perhaps up to the loading of the operating system kernel. This would be more likely to produce the deterministic result that sealed storage requires. It will not, however, capture post boot platform configuration changes such as the loading of kernel modules that can materially impact integrity.

The impracticality of remote attestation and sealed storage on mainstream operating systems is a serious drawback. It underlines the fact that the TCG building blocks cannot remedy problems that flow from operating system architectural deficiencies. Secure DRM clients cannot be deployed on multi-tasking operating systems that are unable to provide isolation and confinement of mutually distrustful and potentially hostile processes. The application of TCG components does not change this fact. Sailer *et al.,* (2004) assert that "many of the Microsoft NGSCB guarantees can be obtained on today's hardware and today's software and that these guarantees do not require a new CPU mode or operating system but merely depend on the availability of an independent trusted entity, a TPM for example." We contend that while a number of guarantees may be possible, the important ones, (not necessarily delivered by NCSGB either) cannot be achieved, since critical elements of a trusted system must be enforced by a combination of the operating system mapped to CPU hardware-based protection structures. They cannot be provided by add-on hardware.

The addition of TCG components to mainstream operating systems does not result in a 'trusted system' in the traditional sense of the term. It does not introduce trusted paths, or a reference monitor, and it does not alter the problems created by the failure to observe the principle of least privilege. The TPM allows integrity measurements to be stored in a trusted fashion but it does not provide any mechanism to prevent integrity violations. It does allow known versions of compromised software to be identified by their fingerprints and this is definitely useful. It also provides a more secure environment for the storage of cryptographic keys, particularly asymmetric signing keys. However, effective domain confinement and mandatory access control are fundamental requirements for trusted computing and reliable license enforcement in DRM clients. For these reasons we believe that the security benefits gained by applying TCG components to mainstream operating systems that enforce purely discretionary access control are worthwhile but modest.

TCG components combined with MAC-based operating systems such as SELinux (Loscocco, 2001) have significant advantages over their DAC based counterparts – advantages that may make sealed storage and remote attestation considerably more practical. In a MAC based system, a challenger needs to verify the integrity of the security policy interpretation and enforcement mechanism, the policy configuration itself and the DRM client application. If these components are trusted to enforce isolation of the DRM client, no further measurements are required to establish the ongoing integrity of the DRM client. Thus, the impractical requirement for ongoing measurement in DAC architectures is avoided. Since integrity assurance is based on isolation, detailed measurements of other loaded executables and configuration data is not required.

4.5 Privacy Impacts

Remote attestation reveals particularly fine-grained details of a platform's configuration that are likely to be sufficient to distinguish different platforms from each other and to recognise the same platform across different sessions. In DAC enforcing architectures in particular, the privacy protection mechanisms detailed in the TCG specification, including the zero-knowledge authentication protocols introduced in version 1.2 are at great risk of being rendered ineffective.

5. Next Generation Secure Computing Base (NGSCB), formerly Palladium

'Next Generation Secure Computing Base' (NGSCB) is the name for Microsoft Inc.'s trusted computing program, formerly known as Palladium. According to the designers of the system Peinado *et al.,* (2004) NGSCB is a "high assurance runtime environment for trustworthy applications on a regular personal computer". NGSCB builds on the TCG specification and a number of significant planned modifications to the CPU and chipset that have been announced by Intel Inc. under their 'LaGrande' program. The chipset modifications are apparently designed to introduce a trusted path for keyboard, mouse and other input, and secure display output. The CPU modifications introduce a new mode akin to a 'ring-1' and a number of new instructions to support it. The new mode is required for reasons of backward compatibility with existing Microsoft 'Windows' operating systems.

Backward compatibility was stated as a key requirement for NGSCB. As we noted in Section 3.1, the Windows kernel, device drivers and operating system operate at the highest level of hardware privilege, in ring-0. Due to the untrustworthy bug-prone nature of some operating system components and drivers running in this ring, there is no way to introduce a "high assurance runtime environment" because there is no tamper resistant space in which to implement a domain separation mechanism. Virtual Machine Monitors (VMM), a well understood approach to isolating mutually distrusting systems on the same CPU are not an option in this case because, according to Robin and Irvine, (Robin and Irvine, 2000) the Intel x86 cannot be securely virtualised. In the simplest version of the VMM approach, multiple operating systems can be simultaneously hosted in ring-1 by a VMM that runs in ring 0. The VMM presents the same interface to the hosted operating systems as the native hardware and provides domain isolation between them.

Full virtualisation of the x86 chip may not be possible but, nonetheless, the type of isolation that NGSCB demands requires something roughly equivalent to a VMM and a VMM requires a higher level of privilege than the hosted operating systems in order to work. This is the reason behind the new mode, 'ring -1' that Intel announced for their 'LaGrande' project.

Peinado *et al.*, (Peinado *et al.* 2004) describe the NGSCB equivalent of a VMM as an isolation kernel. The isolation kernel protects the memory and device resources of a domain from access by other domains. The isolation kernel is not itself a fully featured operating system, it merely manages the coexistence of multiple operating systems on the same machine. Again, for reasons of backward compatibility, the isolation kernel does not boot before the standard Windows operating system and it does not run beneath it. This somewhat unconventional approach is a key difference to the TCG style of trusted computing, which bases its assurance on an assessment of the integrity of the entire boot chain. NGSCB also takes a different tack in not assuming that the BIOS is trustworthy. In a sense, the NGSCB approach has abandoned any premise of making the traditional Windows operating system 'trusted' and opted instead to construct a secure environment that can run along side it – "a tight sanctuary on an otherwise bug-prone system" in the words of Peinado *et al.*, (2004). This tight sanctuary can be launched and terminated multiple times in the same boot cycle and multiple sanctuaries can simultaneously coexist.

Like TCG, the NGSCB design supports remote attestation, and sealed storage. Unlike the basic version of TCG described in the previous section, it supports hardware enforced domain isolation and trusted paths. As between domains, this is a form of MAC since, once activated, neither users nor administrators can turn the hardware protection off. Microsoft has asserted that the code for the isolation kernel will be sufficiently small and simple to provide assurance of its correctness through independent evaluation. Thus NGSCB's 'sanctuary' appears to embody the important features that are required of a trustworthy computing platform. However, Microsoft has not described in any detail the trusted operating system that the isolation kernel actually launches – the trusted sanctuary itself. This sanctuary is intended to support multiple applications or 'applets' which do not necessarily trust each other. Thus, an operating system capable of the functions described in Section 3 will also be required.

According to Rooney (Rooney, 2004) the future of NGSCB is far from certain. Application developers have expressed reluctance to rewrite code to take advantage of NGSCB features and Microsoft is reportedly reviewing the design to make the task of application integration more streamlined. The impact that this will have on the trustworthiness of NGSCB is unclear. As at the time of writing, the Microsoft NGSCB web page states, "Microsoft is currently evolving the NGSCB architecture to expand the benefits to customers in terms of applicability and flexibility". (See: Microsoft, 2004). Experience has shown that flexibility tends to undermine security, but certainly, no conclusions can be drawn until the revised design is clarified. Rooney notes that Microsoft is shifting emphasis to support No Execute (NX) technology that has been implemented by Intel in its recent processors. NX allows memory pages to be marked as non-executable to limit common attacks that exploit buffer overflow. We note that a strategy based purely on NX falls well short of the requirements for trusted computing. It is also worth noting that if the Intel segmentation/capability architecture were correctly utilised, NX would be unnecessary as a no-execute control bit is already available at the segment level.

6. Conclusion

We began by emphasizing the importance of trusted computing for robust DRM license enforcement. The license validation, interpretation and enforcement functions of a DRM client need to be implemented within the bounds of a trusted computing base. With reference to the early trusted computing literature, we reviewed the critical features that define a trusted computing platform. Enforcement of a mandatory access control policy, observance of the principle of least privilege and provision of trusted paths were identified as key requirements. These are absent in mainstream operating systems. For this reason, we argued that such operating systems are inappropriate to host DRM client applications. We then analysed the degree to which the TCG model of trusted computing can be applied to mainstream operating systems to improve their trustworthiness. We concluded that the addition of TCG components to such systems does not result in a trusted system. The TCG specification cannot substitute for the absence of MAC and the associated domain confinement it supports. We identified specific problems that make the TCG features of sealed storage and remote attestation impractical when they are used in conjunction with a DAC enforcing operating system. We concluded that the TCG specification in conjunction with a MAC enforcing operating system may offer a considerably more robust platform on which to deploy a DRM client.

(Jason F Reid and William J Caelli are with Information Security Research Centre, Queensland University of Technology, Australia. They can be reached at if.reidaqut.edu.av and w.caelli@qat.edu.av respectively.)

Endnotes

1 An alternative policy enforcement strategy relies on the detection of policy descriptive watermarks embedded in content. To be effective, all content rendering devices must detect these watermarks and process the content accordingly. Biddle *et al.* (2003) argue that the requirement for all computing devices to implement and enforce such protections is impractical.

2 We adopt the term mainstream operating system to refer to popular commercial operating systems such as Windows 95, NT, 2000 and XP from Microsoft Inc. (USA), Linux from various distributions of this open source system and various versions of Unix that implement a discretionary access control policy.

3 See: Ferraiolo, *et al.* (1995)

4 See: Badger *et al.* (1995)

5 A DAC architecture cannot reliably enforce a mandatory security policy (Harrison *et al.*, 1976).

6 TCG integrity measurement capabilities do not effectively address this problem. See Section 4.3

7 See: *https://www.trustedcomputinggroup.org/home*

8 See: Menezes *et al.*, (1996) for a description of these terms.

9 Version 1.2 of the TCG Specification introduced PCRs that can be reset within a boot cycle.

References

Anderson, J P (1972). "Computer Security Technology Planning Study". ESD-TR-73-51, Air Force Electronic Systems Division, Hanscom AFB, Bedford, MA.

Anderson, R J (2003). "Cryptography and competition policy: issues with 'trusted computing'". In *Proceedings of the Twenty-Second ACM Symposium on Principles of Distributed Computing* (PODC 2003), July 13-16, Boston, Massachusetts, pp 3-10.

Arbaugh, W A, Farber, D J *et al.* (1997). "A secure and reliable boot strap architecture". In *Proceedings of 1997 IEEE Symposium on Security and Privacy*, pp 65-71, May 1997.

Badger, L Sterne, DF *et al.* (1995). "Practical domain and type enforcement for Unix". In *Proceedings of the 1995 IEEE Symposium on Security and Privacy*, page 66, IEEE Computer Society.

Bell, D E and LaPadula, L J (1973). "Secure computer systems: Mathematical foundations and model". Technical Report M74 244, The MITRE Corp., Bedford MA.

Biddle, P, England, P, Peinado, M and Willman, B (2003). "The Darknet and the future of content protection". In *Digital Rights Management- Technological, Economic, Legal and Political Aspects. LNCS* 2770, Springer, pp 344-365.

Corbato, F J, Saltzer, J H and Clingen CT (1972). "Multics - the first seven years". In *Proceedings of the Spring Joint Computer Conference*, pages 571-583, AFIPS Press.

CEN/ISSS, (2003). Digital Rights Management Report *http://europa.eu.int/comm/enterprise/ict/policy/doc/drm .pdf.* Accessed 18 August 2004.

Ferraiolo, D Cugini, J and Kuhn, R (1995). "Role Based Access Control (RBAC): Features and motivations". In *Proceedings of the Annual Computer Security Applications Conference*, New Orleans, Louisianna, December 11-15, IEEE Computer Society Press.

Harrison, M, Ruzzo, W and Ullman, J (1976). "Protection in Operating Systems". *Communications of the ACM*, 19(8) pp. 461-471.

Hauser, T and Wenz, C (2003): "DRM Under Attack: Weaknesses in Existing Systems". In *Digital Rights Management – Technological, Economic, Legal and Political Aspects. LNCS 2770*, Springer, pp 206-223.

Lacy, J, Snyder, J H and Maher, DP (1997). "Music on the Internet and the intellectual property protection problem". In *Proceedings of the IEEE International Symposium on Industrial Electronics (ISIE 97)*, Vol 1, pp 77-83.

Loscocco, P A Smalley, S D *et al.* (1998). "The inevitability of failure: The flawed assumption of security in modern computing environments". In *21st National Information Systems Security Conference*, Arlington, VA., August.

Loscocco, P A Smalley, S D (2001). "Meeting critical security objectives with Security-Enhanced Linux". In *Proceedings of the 2001 Ottawa Linux Symposium.*

Menezes, A J Van Oorschot, P C and Vanstone, S A (1996). *Handbook of Applied Cryptography,* CRC Press, ISBN 0849385237.

Microsoft, (2004), Next Generation Secure Computing Base – Product Information, available at: *http://www.microsoft.com/resources/ngscb/productinfo.mspx*, accessed 20 July 2004.

Peinado, M Chen, Y *et al.* (2004), NGSCB: A Trusted Open System. In Proceedings of 9th Australasian Conference on Information Security and Privacy ACISP, Sydney, Australia, July 13-15.

Robin, J and Irvine, C (2000). Analysis of the Intel Pentium' s ability to support a secure virtual machine monitor. In Proceedings of the 9th USENIX Security Symposium, Denver, Colorado, USA, August 14-17.

Rooney, P (2004). Microsoft Shelves NGSCB Project as NX Moves to Centre Stage. 5 May 2004, *http://www.crn.com/sections/BreakingNews/dailyarchives.as p?ArticleID=49936* accessed 7 May 2004.

Sailer, R Zhang, X. *et al.* (2004). "Design and implementation of a TCG-based integrity measurement architecture". In *Proceedings of the 13th Usenix Security Symposium*, San Diego, August 9–13.

Saltzer, J H and Schroeder, M.D. (1975). "The protection of information in computer systems". *Proceedings of the IEEE*, 63(9):1278-1308, Sept.

Schell, R, Tao, T and Heckman M (1985). "Designing the GEMSOS security kernel for security and performance". In *Proceedings of National Computer Security Conference*, Gaithersburg.

Schneck, P (1999). "Access Control to Prevent Piracy of Digital Information". *Proceedings of the IEEE*, 87(7):1239-1250.

Solomon, D A, and Russinovich, M (2000). *Inside Microsoft Windows 2000.* Microsoft Press, 2000. ISBN 0735610215.

Stefik, M (1997). "Shifting the Possible: How Trusted Systems and Digital Property Rights Challenge Us to Rethink Digital Publishing". *Berkeley Technology Law Journal* Vol. 12. No.1. pp 137-159.

Trusted Computing Group, (2003), Trusted Platform Module Main Specification, Part 1: Design Principles, Part 2: TPM Structures, Part 3: Commands, October 2003, Version 1.2, Revision 62, available at *http://www.trustedcomputinggroup.org*, accessed 26 May 2004.

WIPO, (1996). World Intellectual Property Organization. Wipo copyright treaty. *http://www.wipo.org/eng/diplconf/distrib/treaty01.htm* Accessed 15 April 2004.

10

A Trusted Key Management Scheme for Digital Rights Management

Yeonjeong Jeong, Kisong Yoon and Jaecheol Ryou

In this paper, we propose a key management scheme which can provide delivery of the key used to encrypt a digital content from the package server to digital rights management (DRM) clients in a secure manner. The proposed scheme can protect digital content from attacks since an encrypted digital content is sent by a package server and only DRM clients can decrypt the encrypted digital content. It protects the key not only from purchasers but also among the other principals who manage the distribution and license servers.

I. Introduction

Current digital rights management (DRM) provides content protection from purchasers and key management transparently to users. It adopts a license-based mechanism which separates the keys from encrypted contents. The encrypted content is delivered to a player from a distribution server while the license including the keys is transported to the DRM client from a license server. Although the contents are downloaded, users cannot use the contents if they do not have a

Source: www.etrij.etri.re.kr ETRI Journal Volume 27, Number 1, February 2005.

license [1]-[3]. In Microsoft's DRM, a package server and a license server share a secret seed and can generate their key by using that secret [4]. In a DRM developed by InterTrust, at each moment a package server encrypts a digital content, the package server transmits his encryption key to a license server [5], [6]. Because the license servers of Microsoft's DRM and InterTrust's DRM have or can generate the key used in encryption, it may be possible to extract a raw digital content by using the key.

The current DRM systems have focused on content protection from the purchaser. However, they do not provide a way to protect a digital content from the license server. If the owners of the package server and the license server are not the same, the principal of the package server cannot choose but trust the principal of the license server.

Therefore, we need to provide a way to protect digital content among the other principals who manage the distribution servers and license servers. To protect digital content from attacks, we can use encryption technology. After content is encrypted, only DRM clients can decrypt the content while other clients cannot. This indicates how a content encryption key is protected from its generation to consumption. The key management of a DRM system deals with content encryption, distribution of the content encryption key, delivery of the content encryption key, and authentication among DRM components. In this paper, we propose a key management scheme which can provide secure delivery of the key used to encrypt a digital content from the package server to DRM clients.

II. DRM System

The typical and basic components of a DRM system are a package server, distribution server, license server, and DRM client [1], [2]. The package server encrypts content and generates encryption information such as the seeds of the encryption keys and the encryption length. It provides encrypted content to the distribution server and encryption information to the license server. The distribution server sets up a web site for content and provides encrypted content to the purchaser. The license server issues a license to the DRM client. The DRM client analyzes the license and decrypts the content. Figure 1 shows the components of a DRM system and the flow of DRM service among them.

The proposed key management scheme will deal with key management among the four components of a DRM system.

Figure 1: Service Flow in a DRM System

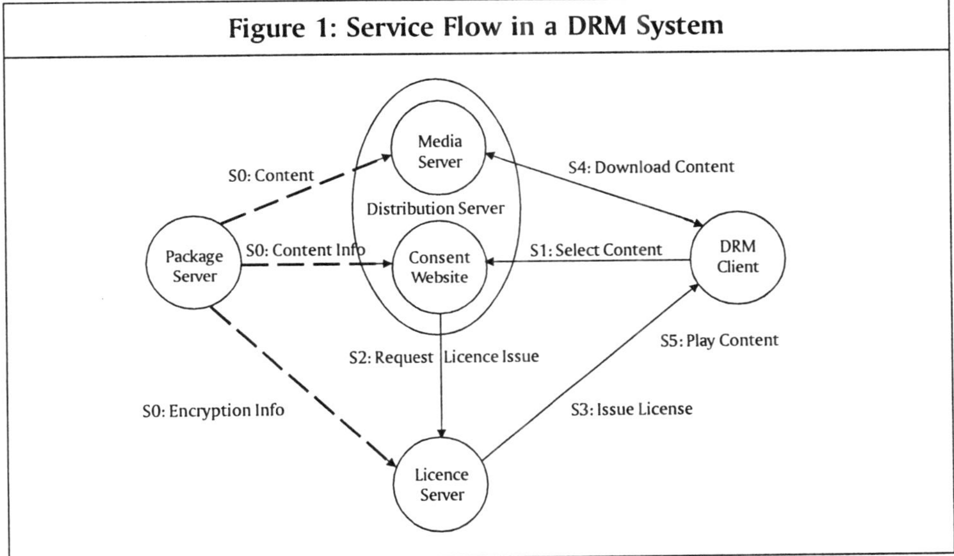

III. Trusted Key Management Scheme

Based on the results of previous studies [1]-[3], [7]-[11] on a content distribution model and DRM system, we propose a key management scheme in which only package servers and DRM clients can decrypt a digital content while, one that authenticates DRM clients cannot. Further, we provide a security analysis of the key management in which one can assume certain actions by an adversary. The proposed key management scheme will deal with key management among the four components of a DRM system.

1. Encryption Key

Encryption technology is used to protect data from a user who does not have the rights to use them. A symmetric key is usually used to encrypt content because it has a large data volume and needs high performance for encryption. The digital content is encrypted with a symmetric key. For each digital content, a different symmetric key is used to minimize the risk of a key leak. To protect against the illegal use of symmetric keys, the seeds of symmetric keys are encrypted with a public key and delivered to a principal who owns a secret key. Therefore, the principal who owns a secret key and the seeds encrypted with a public key can generate a symmetric key and decrypt the encrypted digital content.

- A symmetric key is used to encrypt digital content and has seed 1 and seed 2 to generate it.
- An asymmetric key is used to encrypt the seeds of symmetric keys.

2. Key Distribution Scheme

The principals of the package server, distribution server, and license server generate their own secret/public keys and send the public key to the certificate authority (CA) to get a certificate, which is a usual process in a public key infrastructure environment. The components of a DRM system can use the public key, secret key, and public key certificate of the principals. Figure 2 shows the key distribution of asymmetric keys which are used to encrypt the seeds of symmetric keys and mutually used to authenticate the components of a DRM system. To have a certificate issued, the principals of the package server, distribution server, and license server must apply for a certificate at a registration authority (RA) and receive a "reference number" and "authentication code" after the RA verifies the identity of the principals. Then, the principals generate their own secret key and

Figure 2: Asymmetric Key Distribution

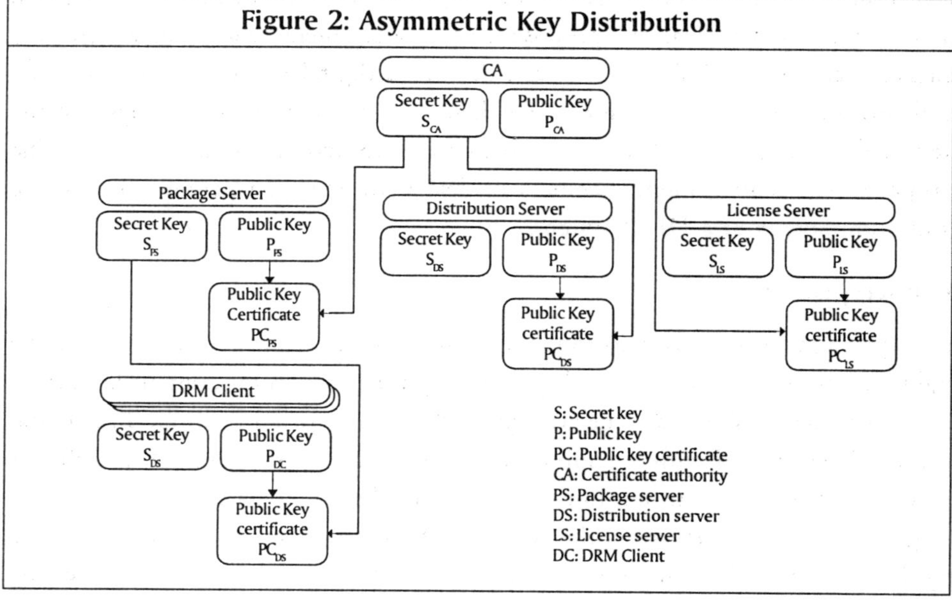

public key and request the certificate of the public key from the CA with the reference number and authentication code sent by the RA. The CA issues the certificate by signing the public key of the principals with the CA's secret key.

The package server issues the certificate of a DRM client to authorize the DRM client but not the purchaser, who is the principal of the IMPRIMATUR business model [7]. There are two reasons why a package server does this. First, the owner of the package server has raw content and wants to protect it. None of the principals except him should know how to decrypt the content. The components of a DRM system which have a content decryption key are the package server and DRM client. Thus, the owner of the package server needs to authorize the DRM client. Second, it is difficult to authenticate the purchaser and request a public key certificate of the CA from him. He is a customer who simply needs to pay a fee to watch a movie but is not a service provider [12].

3. Key Delivery Scheme

The delivery of key seeds from the package server to the distribution server and license server is described in the following steps. It occurs when the package server packages content. Figure 3 shows the flow of the steps. Because the two key seeds are separated and stored at different servers, neither the distribution server nor the license server can generate a decryption key.

Figure 3: Key Delivery When Packaging

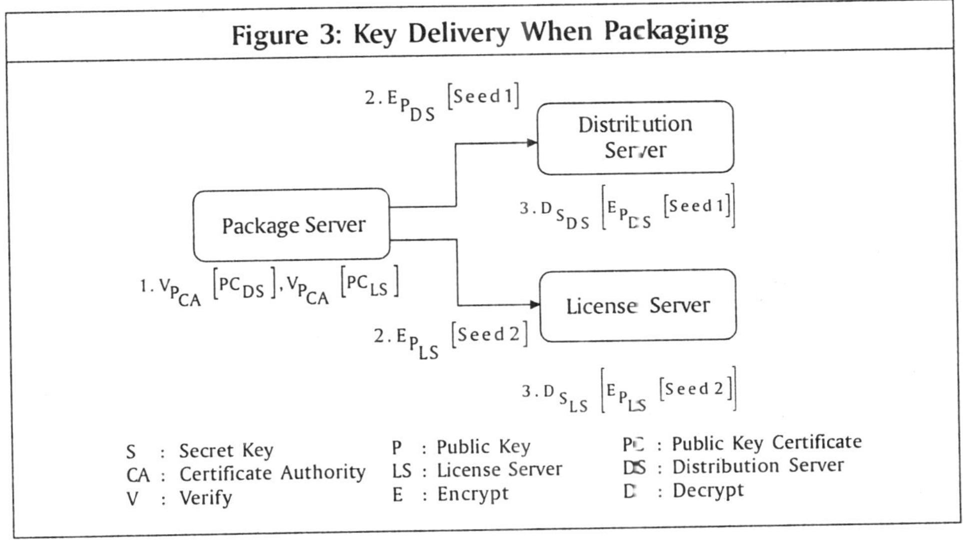

Step 1. The package server verifies the public key certificates of the distribution server and license server.

Step 2. The package server sends a message which contains an encrypted seed to the distribution server and license server after it encrypts one (seed 1) of the seeds with the distribution server's public key and the other (seed 2) with the license server's public key.

Step 3. The distribution server and license server verify the public key certificate of the package server with the public key of the CA. The distribution server and license server verify the message which includes an encrypted seed. Then, each server can decrypt the encrypted seed with its own secret key and store the decrypted seed to its secure database.

The delivery of key seeds to the DRM client is described in the following steps. It occurs to provide a content service to a purchaser when he requests the content service from a distribution server. Figure 4 shows the flow of the steps.

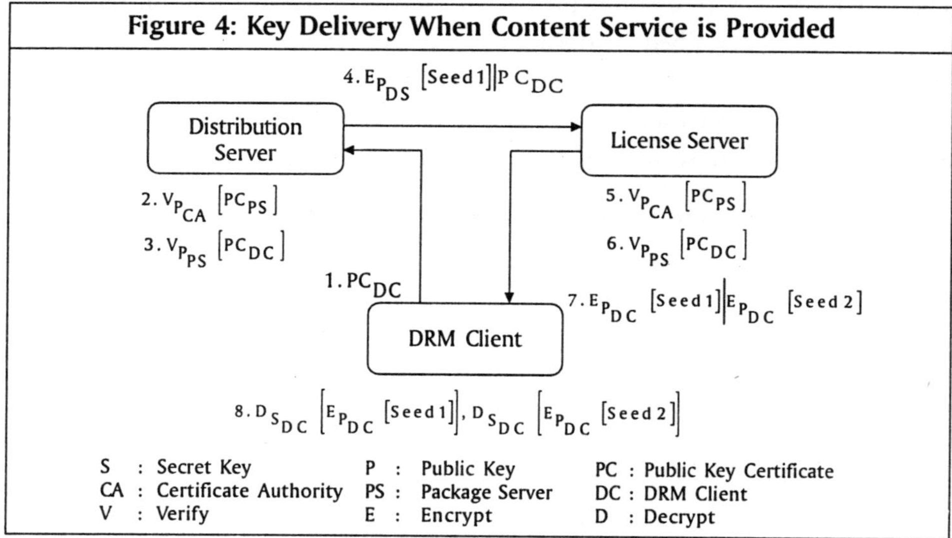

Figure 4: Key Delivery When Content Service is Provided

The distribution server and license server can verify whether the DRM client is a legal component to which a seed can be given. The DRM client does not have its public key certificate from the CA. However, the distribution server and license server can verify it with the package server's public key according to steps

2, 3, 5, and 6. Because the distribution server encrypts seed 1 with the public key of the DRM client and sends it to the license server, the license server cannot generate a decryption key. The license server also encrypts seed 2 with the DRM client's public key and builds a license which has encrypted seed 1 and seed 2. Thus, the decryption key seeds are decrypted by only one DRM client who has a secret key and not the others.

Step 1. The DRM client sends his public key certificate to the distribution server.

Step 2. The distribution server verifies the public key certificate of the package server with the CA's public key.

Step 3. The distribution server verifies the public key certificate of the DRM client with the package server's public key.

Step 4. The distribution server sends a message which contains encrypted seed1 to the license server after it encrypts seed1 with the DRM client's public key.

Step 5. The license server verifies the public key certificate of the package server with the CA's public key.

Step 6. The license server verifies the public key certificate of the DRM client with the package server's public key.

Step 7. The license server issues a license to the DRM client after encrypting seed 2 with the public key of the DRM client. The license contains both encrypted seed 1 and seed 2.

Step 8. The DRM client verifies the public key certificate of the license server with the CA's public key. Then, it parses and analyzes the license which contains two encrypted seeds, rights, content URL, and so forth, and decrypts both encrypted seeds with its secret key. Finally, it obtains a symmetric key which will be used to decrypt the content.

4. Analysis

The forgery of a component of a DRM system can be detected by its certificate. One component of a DRM system can authenticate another component by its certificate to determine whether it is a legal component to which a seed can be given. An attack on the two key seeds during delivery from the packager server to the distribution server and the license server is prevented because a seed is encrypted with a public key and delivered to a server who owns a secret key. The two key seeds are separated and stored at different servers; neither the distribution server nor the license server can generate a decryption key by itself. And a decryption key can be protected from an attack on the distribution server or the license server since the two key seeds are separately stored at different servers. Because the distribution server encrypts seed 1 with the DRM client's public key and sends it to the license server, the license server cannot generate a decryption key. It also encrypts seed 2 with the DRM client's public key. Thus, the decryption key seeds are decrypted by only one DRM client who has a secret key and not the others.

IV. Conclusion

Current DRM has focused on content protection from the purchaser. While the key used in encryption is delivered to DRM clients from a package server, it is not protected from the principals who manage the distribution server and license server. We propose a key management scheme which can provide delivery of the key used to encrypt a digital content from the package server to DRM clients in a secure manner. The key is protected from its generation to consumption. The proposed scheme protects the key from not only the purchaser but also other principals. It can protect the digital content from attacks during the content distribution since the encrypted digital content is sent by the package server and only the DRM client can decrypt the digital content.

(Yeonjeong Jeong and Kisong Yoon are with Digital Content Research Division, ETRI, Daejeon, Korea.

Jaecheol Ryou is with the Department of Computer Science, Chungnam National University, Daejeon, Korea.)

References

1. G Hanaoka, K Ogawa, I Murota, G Ohtake, K Majima, S Gohshi, K Oyamada, S Namba, and H Imai, "Managing Encryption and Key Publication Independently in Digital Rights Management Systems," *IEICE Trans. on Fundamentals of Electronics, Communications, and Computer Sciences*, vol.E87-A, no.1, Jan. 2004.

2. Q Liu, R Safavi-Naini, and N P Sheppard, "Digital Rights Management for Content Distribution," *Proc. Australasian Information Security Workshop Conference on ACSW Frontiers 2003*, vol. 21, Jan. 2003.

3. J Lee, S Hwang, S Jeong, K Yoon, C Park, and J Ryou, "A DRM Framework for Distribution Digital Contents through the Internet," *ETRI* J., vol. 25, Dec. 2003, pp.423-436.

4. Microsoft, *http://www.microsoft.com/wondows/windowsmedia/drm/default.aspx.*

5. O Sibert, "DigiBox: A Self-Protecting Container for Information Commerce," *1st USENIX Workshop on Electronic Commerce,* 1995.

6. InterTrust, *http://www.intertrust.com/main/research/index.html.*

7. ISO/IEC, JTC 1/SC 29/WG 11, Information Technology – Multimedia Framework (MPEG-21) - Part 1: Vision, Technologies, and Strategy, N3939, Jan. 2001.

8. L J Camp, "First Principles of Copyright for DRM Design," *IEEE Internet Computing*, vol.7, May-June 2003, pp. 59-65.

9. D K Mulligan, J Han, and A J Burstein, "How DRM-Based Content Delivery Systems Disrupt Expectations of Personal Use," *Proc. 2003 ACM Works. Digital Rights Management*, Oct. 2003, pp.77-88.

10. M Valimaki and O Pitkanen, "Digital Rights Management on Open and Semi-Open Networks," *Proc, WIAPP 2001.* July 2001, pp.154-155.

11. F Hartung and F Ramme, "Digital Rights Management and Watermarking of Multimedia Content for M-Commerce Applications," *IEEE Comm.*, vol. 38, Nov. 2000, pp.78-84.

12 J E Cohen, "DRM and Privacy," *Communications of the ACM*, vol. 46, issue 4, Apr. 2003.

11

Controlled Sharing of Personal Content Using Digital Rights Management

Claudine Conrado, Milan Petkovic, Michiel van der Veen and Wytse van der Velde

This paper describes a system which allows controlled distribution of personal digital content by users. The system extends an existing Digital Rights Management system for the protection of commercial copyrighted content by essentially allowing users to become content providers. This fact, however, makes the system vulnerable to illegal content distribution, i.e., distribution by users who do not own the content. To solve this problem, a solution is proposed which involves the compulsory registration with a trusted authority of a user's personal content. During registration, the association between user identity and content is securely recorded by the authority, but users have the possibility to remain anonymous towards any other party. Moreover, in case the initial content identification fails and content is illegally registered, the authority can ensure user accountability.

Source: Journal of Research and Practice in Information Technology Vol.38, No.1, February 2006.

1. Introduction

Recent developments in digital technologies, along with increasingly interconnected high-speed networks and the decrease in prices for high-performance digital devices, have established digital content distribution as one of the fastest emerging activities nowadays. This trend of digital content distribution gives great opportunities for commercial content providers but also poses threats as digital content can be illegally copied and distributed very easily. Therefore, commercial content providers need technologies, accompanied by legislation, that can protect digital content from illegal use. Digital Rights Management (DRM) is a collection of technologies that provides content protection by enforcing the use of digital content according to granted rights. It enables content owners and content providers to protect their copyrights and maintain control over distribution of and access to content.

In parallel to the introduction of multimedia download services, there is also a clear increase in production of personal digital information by consumers including digital photos, home-video, text, etc. This is inspired by the ever decreasing prices of digital cameras, camcorders, mobile phones, storage devices, as well as cheaper high-speed Internet. As a consequence, consumers have to deal with an ever growing amount of personal digital data, alongside the downloaded commercial content. Some of this personal content might be highly confidential and in need of protection; therefore, users may want to share it in a controlled way. This means that the content owner should be able to control the use of his content by other users with whom he shares it. For instance, the owner could specify rights such as play, play once and copy, which are enforced when those users access the content. More importantly, the owner could control further distribution of his content by preventing the users with whom he shares the content from spreading it further. However, in contrast to a lot of effort which has been put into the protection of copyrighted commercial content in a number of different DRM systems currently available, controlled sharing of personal content is often ignored.

In this paper, an approach to controlled sharing of personal content is described which reuses the concepts defined in DRM systems used by the commercial content owners. However, when personal content and commercial content are managed together in one system, the clear line between producers and consumers of content (or content providers and users) fades. Every user of the system is a potential content provider and is able to create and introduce new content into the system. As a consequence, numerous new issues arise such as the requirement that the security of the system should remain the same as before the introduction of personal content. This means that the system should prevent illegal distribution of commercial content as well as personal content. Further requirements are that content owners should be able to protect their privacy and the security of their content, even when jointly owning content. Therefore, while extending the DRM system to support controlled sharing of personal content, focus is put on preserving the system's security.

The remainder of the paper is organized as follows. In Section 2, the related work is reviewed. Section 3 discusses a solution that extends an existing DRM system for commercial content to support controlled sharing of personal content. In Section 4, a description of a method that prevents illegal sharing of commercial content and its security's aspects is given. Section 5 describes an extension of the system that enhances user privacy and allows private multiple ownership of the content. Finally, Section 6 draws conclusions.

2. Related Work

Sharing of digital personal content, especially over the Internet, is nowadays widespread. For instance, P2P distribution networks have become one of the most used technologies for sharing content between people, which is attested by the popularity of applications such as KaZaa. However, these applications do not provide any control over the distribution of content and therefore, allow illegal distribution of commercial content, in particular copyrighted music and movies.

From the commercial content industry's content is one of the major downsides of the P2P technology. However, P2P networks do have the potential to provide an industry-compliant distribution model. The success of Apple's iTunes (iTunes, 2005) provides some evidence that there are possibilities of using copyright-compliant systems profitably, provided that the incentives for using such a system are high enough. In the case of iTunes, these incentives are quality, availability and price of music.

Other proposals for providing such incentives have been presented, e.g., the Music2Share system (Kalker, Epema, Hartel, Lagendijk and van Steen, 2004). It uses quality control of music and combines this with relatively free usage conditions and an easy payment structure to make it interesting for users.

Another proposal by Grimm and Nützel (2002) combines the idea of DRM and P2P file sharing with the idea that a user who has paid for content can redistribute this content against payment. Users that do not pay are unable to redistribute content, thus providing an incentive for payment.

In this paper, a different way to create an incentive is proposed: users of a commercial content protection system can utilize the same protection mechanisms which are used for commercial content also for their own personal content. In this way, the DRM system, instead of only restricting users, also helps those users by protecting their personal content. This presumably gives a much more positive image to DRM as a technology which can support and be in fact beneficial to users. Moreover, it gives an incentive to users to support the system and prevent that its security be compromised in any way.

3. A DRM System for Personal and Commercial Content

In this section, a DRM system for controlled distribution and usage of commercial as well as personal content is presented. The basics of the system, its components and settings are described in the next section, while Section 3.2 explains how the system is used for content protection and sharing.

3.1. System Components and Authorization Hierarchy

The system is an extension of the DRM framework for protection of commercial content introduced by van den Heuvel, Jonker, Kamperman and Lenoir (2002). In the extended DRM system, users are able to protect and controllably share their personal content. This effectively means that the user who is the owner of the content takes over a role of content and license provider and therefore, becomes involved in the content and license creation as well as content protection tasks. Considering personal content, owners will most likely be sharing content with other users, so the person-based DRM model (Conrado, Kamperman, Schrijen and Jonker, 2003), in which rights to access content are granted to persons rather than devices, is used as a basis for the presently described DRM system.

While describing the system, components and properties are highlighted which are relevant for the protection and sharing of personal content. Most of these system components are also part of the original DRM system for protection of commercial content and are described below:

i) *Personalized Smartcard*: A device used for user identification. The smartcard contains a private key which corresponds to the public key of the user. The public key is certified by some Trusted Third Party (TTP). Therefore, the TTP knows the link between the user's identity and his public key.

ii) *Compliant Device*: A device that behaves according to the DRM rules. It can identify a user by means of a personalized smartcard. The compliant devices provide a secure and robust computing platform for the DRM operations and offer a secure storage for keys and state information used in the system.

iii) *Content Container*: Personal digital content is stored in encrypted form together with a unique content identifier (the "content container" abstraction) and can be retrieved from anywhere in the network.

iv) *Content Right:* A certificate issued by the content provider containing the content identifier, a content encryption key (CEK), the User Right Authority's public key and the content provider's signature. The Content Right is securely stored in the compliant device or securely obtained from a content provider.

v) *User Right*: A certificate issued by the User Right Authority authorizing a person to use content according to granted rights. It consists of content identifier, user identifier, rights expression and the User Right Authority's signature, User Rights may reside anywhere in the system and normally not stored in a secure way. Moreover, Content Right and User Right may be merged in one license (OMA-DRM, 2004).

vi) *Content ID Certificate:* A certificate that creates a secure link between content, its identifier and the content owner, who becomes also content

Figure 1: Certificate Authorization Hierarchy

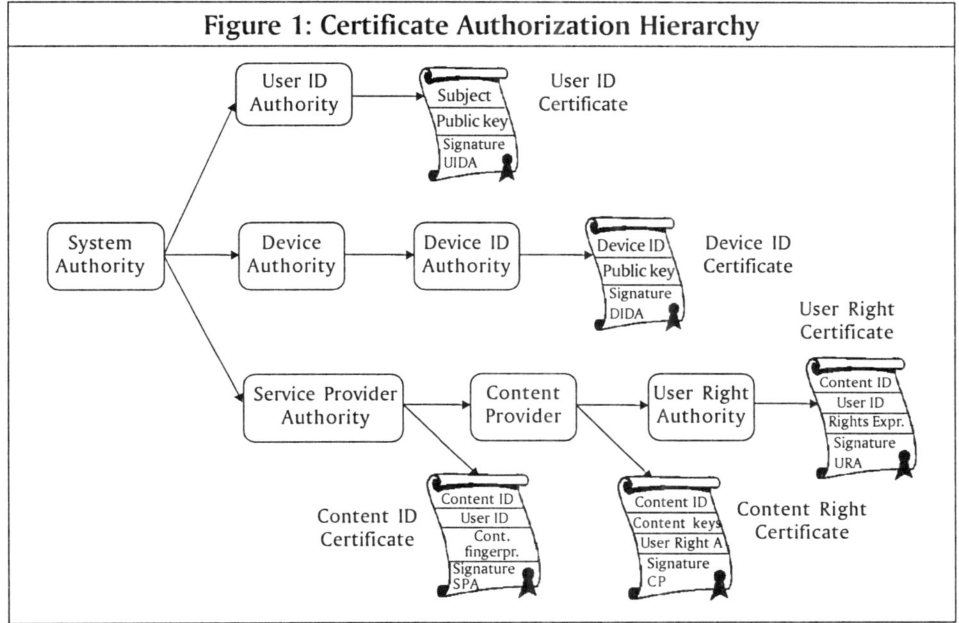

provider. This certificate is needed for personal content, since the content provider may be any user in the system and needs, thus, to be explicitly linked to the content.

The certificates used in the system are issued by different authorities, which organize an authorization hierarchy depicted in Figure 1. The System Authority is the root of the hierarchy. Each compliant device has a built-in key of this authority. The Service Provider Authority (SPA) authorizes different content providers (users) by certifying their public keys and linking them with content items by means of the Content ID Certificate. Content providers are allowed to issue Content Rights. A Content Right contains in turn the public key of the User Right Authority. This construction allows content providers to delegate the issuing of User Rights. The User Right Authority issues User Rights for a certain piece of content. The Device Authority authorizes Device ID Authorities, e.g. device manufactures, to issue Device ID Certificates that give a unique identity to a device. The User ID Authority issues User ID Certificates. This certificate typically contains user identity information and a public key that identifies a user within the system.

3.2. Content Protection and Sharing

During the content protection and sharing procedures, a number of different transactions, schematically depicted in Figure 2, are performed within the system. The described transactions for content protection refer specifically to personal content: a user can act as a content provider, therefore, this must be certified by means of the Content ID Certificate. The described transactions for content sharing, on the other hand, are essentially the same for both, personal and commercial content, except that in the latter, a (recognized) commercial content provider takes the role of the user. These transactions are described below, where references to the numbered links in Figure 2 are made at the appropriate points.

Figure 2: Representation of the Various Interactions in the DRM System

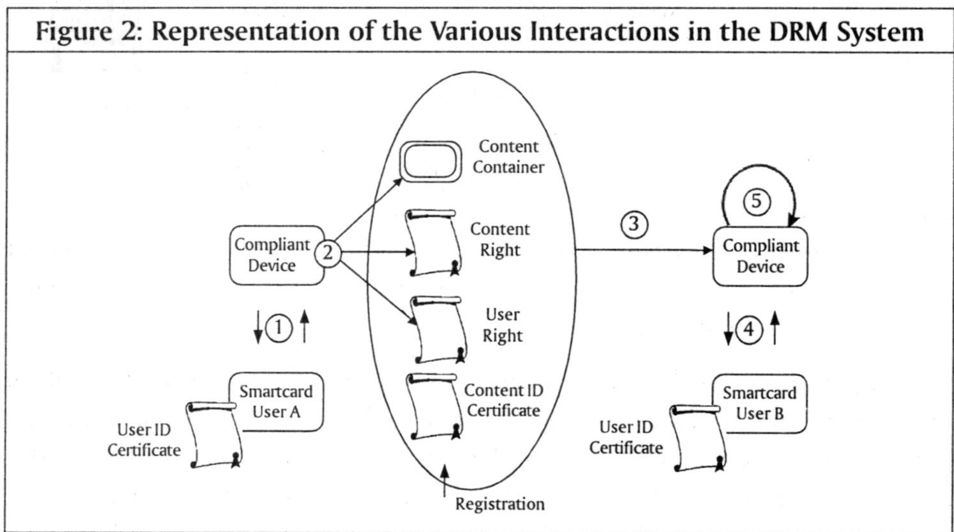

When a user Alice wants to protect a personal content item, in order to be later on able to share it in a controlled way, she registers the content with the SPA (content registration is discussed in the next section) and obtains a Content ID Certificate. The certificate consists of the fields Content ID, User ID, Content Fingerprint and Signature SPA. The Content ID field refers to the content itself. The User ID field contains the public key of Alice, who is then considered the owner of the content (as well as content provider). The Content Fingerprint is a short "summary" of the multimedia content which can uniquely identify that content. It usually consists of robust features extracted from the content (see van der Veen, Lemma and Kalker, 2004). Finally, the Signature SPA is the digital signature of the SPA on the certificate. The next step in the content protection process is creation of the Content Right together with encryption of the content. Before allowing Alice to create a Content Right, a compliant device authenticates her (step 1 in Figure 2) and checks whether she is authorized to do so by inspecting the Content ID Certificate, which must contain Alice's ID (her public key). If so, the compliant device proceeds with the creation of the Content Right certificate (step 2 in Figure 2) by randomly choosing a symmetric key (CEK), which is used to encrypt the content, and placing the key in the certificate. Additional information in the Content Right certificate includes the Content ID and the public key of the User Right Authority. Typically, this authority will be the content owner Alice, but she may also create a Content Right for other users allowing them to sign User Rights (i.e., to share the content). Finally, Alice signs the Content Right.

If Alice wants to share such protected content item with another user Bob, she creates a User Right certificate that includes the public key of Bob and sends the secure content container together with the necessary certificates (User Right and Content ID Certificate) to Bob (step 3 in Figure 2). The Content Right certificate is also needed but it should be securely sent directly to the compliant device that will be handling the content access action with Bob, since that certificate has the CEK, which can be used to decrypt the content. When Bob wants to access the content, he must have a valid User ID Certificate. He authenticates to a compliant device using his smartcard (step 4 Figure 2) and presents the obtained certificates from Alice together with the secure content container. The compliant device must check the validity of the certificates before allowing access to the content (step 5 Figure 2). Moreover, the device will compare the User ID from the User Right with the User ID in the User ID Certificate. It also has to verify that all certificates are used for the content whose identifier is in the Content ID Certificate. To do so, the compliant device obtains the CEK from the Content Right certificate, decrypts the content, calculates the fingerprint of that content and finally matches the fingerprint of the content with the fingerprint in the Content ID Certificate. If the fingerprints do not match, the device will detect a content substitution attack, which means that the original encrypted content in the content container has been replaced with a different content, but assigned the same identifier. The device in this case will not allow Bob to access the content.

4. Registration of Personal Content

Any content which is to be protected under a DRM system must be recognizable within that system. In the case of commercial content, typically each content item is assigned a unique content identifier within that specific DRM system. This assignment can be thought of as the registration of the content item in the DRM system.

The DRM system described in the previous section is used to protect both commercial and personal content. The assignment of a unique content identifier to every piece of content that enters the system is still necessary. However, as of now every user can become a content provider and sign certificates in such a system, there is a danger regarding illegal distribution of commercial content. The problem exists because there are no explicit measures to prevent commercial content from being distributed as personal content by users of the DRM system. Without preventive measures, a malicious user who has obtained an illegal copy of commercial content is able to distribute that content within the DRM system as his own personal content.

A solution to the problem above is to introduce a secure registration procedure that not only assigns a unique identifier to content, but also verifies the identity of content by using fingerprint technology (van der Veen *et al*, 2004). The registration procedure as well as its security aspects are discussed below.

4.1. The Registration Steps

To introduce a new content item into the system, the user Alice has to follow a number of steps which are described below and shown in Figure 3.

Step 1: Alice imports to her compliant device a content item that she wants to introduce. The device calculates the fingerprint of the content item.

Step 2: The device provides the SPA with the fingerprint of the content item and the public key of Alice.

Step 3: The SPA matches the fingerprint of Alice's known commercial content and already registered personal content.

Step 4: If there is a match the SPA refuses to register the content item. Otherwise, the SPA proceeds by generating a Content ID Certificate and a database entry, with a time stamp on it, linking Alice's ID to the content (i.e., to its fingerprint). This allows SPA to prevent other users from trying to later on register Alice's as their own. Optionally a watermark identifier and a watermarking key (van der Veen *et al*, 2004) are also generated by the SPA to allow the possibility of "forensic tracking" outside the DRM system, as discussed below.

Step 5: The SPA sends the Content ID Certificate (and the watermark identifier and watermarking key in case watermarks are used) to the compliant device.

Step 6: Finally, all the necessary certificates are created so as to make the content suitable for distribution using the DRM system. When watermarks are

Figure 3: The Registration Phase

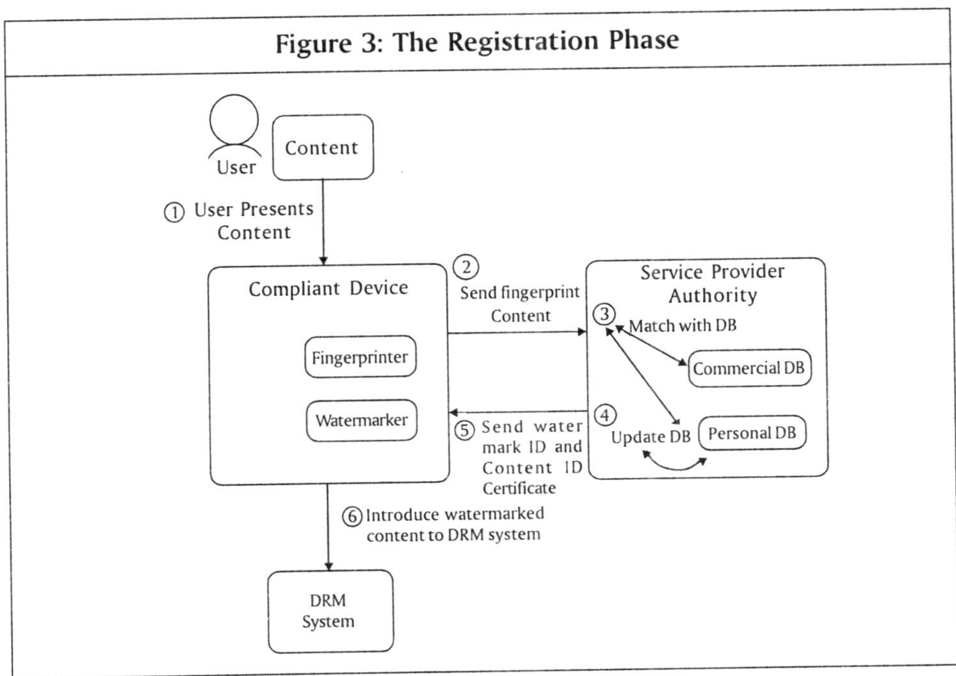

used, the compliant device also watermarks the content with the watermark ID using the watermarking key.

4.2. Security Analysis

The threat model used for the present security analysis is as follows. A casual-copying model is assumed as described by Felten (2003). This means that the security of the system is not concerned with widespread copying and distribution by organized groups of criminals, but with small-scale and disorganized copying amongst small groups of ordinary users. The security of the system tries to frustrate and create barriers for would-be infringers. In the threat model, it is assumed that if the barriers for illegal distribution are high enough and there is an incentive for users to behave in accordance with the system, then most of the users will behave in such a way. Therefore, if only a few users manage to distribute illegal content within the system, the system itself does not fail regarding the threat model. With such a threat model in mind, specific system security aspects are discussed below.

Fingerprint Check and DRM Infrastructure. The goal of fingerprint identification at the beginning of the registration procedure is to prevent malicious users from registering commercial and pre-registered personal content as their personal content. It is assumed that the SPA has a database with the fingerprints of all existing commercial content as well as pre-registered personal content. In a more realistic setting, the SPA may use a distributed system in which the query to match a given fingerprint is forwarded to other parties with their databases. The management of such databases is, however, outside the scope of this paper.

After the fingerprint check has been performed, content is rejected in case a match is found, otherwise it is accepted for registration in the system. However, the fingerprint identification may fail, for instance, if the checked fingerprint databases are incomplete and therefore, unable to recognize all registered content, or if the malicious user manages to tamper with the content and changes its fingerprint so that it cannot be recognized. In the latter case, however, the robustness of the fingerprint should be sufficient to substantially degrade the quality of the changed content. In any of these cases, the consequence of fingerprint identification failure is that content is successfully and illegally registered and can be distributed within the DRM system as belonging to the malicious user.

The very infrastructure of the DRM system, however, can be used as a mechanism against illegal registration of content. This infrastructure is based on digital certificates issued by competent authorities, as depicted in Figure 1. In order for a registered content item to be distributed within the DRM system, certificates must be issued and presented to compliant devices for verification. In particular, a Content ID Certificate is issued by the SPA which contains the User ID (public key) of the content introducer. Moreover, this public key can also be used to check signatures on Content Rights and possibly User Rights. Therefore, if illegal content is detected within the DRM system, the original content introducer can be found via his public key and the corresponding User ID Certificate.

Watermark Extraction – A further measure which can be used to increase the system's security is the use of watermarks. During the registration phase, the content may be optionally watermarked by the compliant device with a watermark ID which is created and sent to the device by the SPA. This acts as a pointer to a user's ID to serve as a "stamp" of ownership which the content item carries wherever it goes. Therefore, in case of a dispute, for instance, over content ownership, it can always be determined by means of the watermark.

The watermark also allows the possibility of the so-called "forensic tracking" outside the DRM system. This covers the situation in which illegal content has been introduced into the DRM system by a malicious user and has been, later on, brought outside the DRM system. In this case, the infrastructure of the DRM system can no longer be used to identify the malicious user. Moreover, tampering with the content may lead to changes in its fingerprint in a way that it can no longer be recognized. By means of the watermark ID, however, the malicious user's identity can be recovered from the SPA's database.

Illegal content in this context may be (i) commercial content, which typically is not originally watermarked but has its ownership certified by other means, and (ii) other user's registered personal content, which will in this case include an additional watermark ID pointing to the original owner's ID and therefore with an earlier time stamp on it. In either of these cases, ownership had been established prior to the registration performed by the malicious user, so malicious behaviour, i.e., the illegal registration of content, can be proved.

Forensic tracking outside the DRM system is performed with participation of the SPA (for the watermark extraction and database check) as well as participation of the User ID Authority (which knows the real identity of the user whose public key is in the SAP's database).

5. Private and Controlled Ownership Sharing

In order to register a content item, the user has to authenticate with the SPA, so he is not (and should not be) anonymous towards the SPA. However, he does not need to identify himself to any other party in the system. In particular, a user may require that he cannot be linked to a given content (anonymous publishing) nor linked to other users for whom he creates User Rights. Moreover, a user may require that all his content items cannot be linked to one another and to his identity. These are user privacy requirements which can be fulfilled by means of content registration with user pseudonyms. Additionally, if a different pseudonym is used for each different piece of registered content, unlinkability of content items can also be achieved.

A further requirement is that shared ownership of personal content amongst multiple users be possible. For instance, a family vacation movie in principle belongs to the group of family members. In this case, the whole group participates in the registration of the content and therefore acquires all rights implied by content ownership. It is important to notice that ownership sharing, which is established at the registration phase and addressed in this section, is distinct from the sharing of the content itself, which is performed via the DRM system as described in Section 3.2. The rights implied by content ownership include, e.g., access to the decrypted content as well as the power to determine who can distribute the content as User Right Authority. But as personal content is likely to contain private information about its owners, an additional privacy requirement is that further sharing of ownership with outsiders (who would then acquire owners' rights) be jointly decided by all owners. This requirement aims to limit the dissemination of personal content in a large and uncontrollable scale since, via a content ownership sharing chain, the content may get out of the control of the DRM system.

5.1. Registering Content with Controlled Anonymity

Pseudonyms generated from a user's public key can be easily obtained from the SPA in the following way. Assuming that the public/private key pair is built according to the Diffie-Hellman key agreement, let x be the user's private key and $h=g^x$ be the corresponding public key, where g is a group generator (for further details see Menezes, van Oorschot and Vanstone, 1997). To generate a pseudonym h', the SPA generates a random value a and computes the new public key $h'=h^a$ whose corresponding private key is $x'=xa$. The value a is then securely sent to the user, so that he is able to calculate his new key pair (x', h'), with no other party learning his pseudonym.

Content can now be registered under the user's pseudonym h', which no party (except the SPA) can link to the original public key h. For any new piece of content, a new pseudonym can be generated in the same way and used for registration. When ownership of a given content is shared between N owners, the procedure above is repeated for all owners. Upon registration, all owners i (where $i \in \{1, 2, ..., N\}$) obtain from the SPA distinct pseudonyms which are unlinkable to one another, to the owners' real identities and to further pseudonyms the owners may get. The registration procedure proceeds as described in the previous section with a few modifications. After content fingerprint checking, the SPA generates random values a_i and computes the pseudonyms $hi'=hi^{ai}$. Each value a_i is sent to (and only to) owner i. The Content ID Certificate now comprises a unique content identifier, the content fingerprint and the new pseudonyms h_i' of each registered owner. This certificate serves also to ensure that all the pseudonyms h_i' are constructed in the correct way. Moreover, information stored in the SPA's database now must include the original identifiers h_i as well as the generated random values a_i for each of the owners.

Because the SPA stores the values h_i and a_i for all owners of a given content, any pseudonym and/or any content can be traced back to any of the owners' real identities. This provides revocable anonymity which is important to provide accountability in the system. For instance, illegal import of content into the DRM system can be traced back to the culprits, even if they are normally anonymous in the system.

5.2. Controlled Ownership Sharing

A further privacy issue is how to control the further sharing of ownership. This sharing should be allowed only if jointly decided by all owners (in which case the registration process is carried out again with an extra owner added to the data). Sharing, however, may happen without the approval of all owners. This can happen via the disclosure by one of the owners, say i (the "leaker"), to an outsider of the pseudonymous private key x_i'. With this key, the outsider has all rights of the leaker in the DRM system. And since the outsider does not learn anything about the leaker's original private key x_i (given that x_i' is randomly related to x_i), a deterrent mechanism is needed to stop such potential leakers. Such a mechanism is described below.

The SPA is set up such that it will reveal the value a_i (of any of the owners i) to any party who comes to it and proves knowledge of the private key x_i' corresponding to the pseudonym h_i'. The party may do so completely anonymously. The idea behind this is that only one of the two, the owner i himself or an outsider who received the private key x_i' from owner i, is able to authenticate with pseudonym h_i'. In the first case, there are no consequences since owner i should in fact know a_i. He may need to ask this value in case, e.g., he loses it. In this case, he must authenticate with his original public key h_i, in order to prove that the request is legitimate. The second case, however, has major implications since the outsider is able to learn the leaker's original private key by calculating $x_i = x_i'/a_i$. Given that the outsider may considerably profit from the knowledge of *xi*, with no liabilities on his part, he is likely to do so. A further implication of the outsider's action is the fact that the SPA is immediately notified that owner i has leaked his private key to an outsider. The SPA can then warn the other owners about the fact and, furthermore, can tell them who the leaker was.

6. Conclusion

This paper presents and discusses a system for the protection of users' privacy when sharing personal digital content with other users. The system allows the controlled sharing of personal content, which is achieved by means of an extension of a DRM system originally devised to protect commercial content. The idea behind extending an existing DRM system to protect both types of content is twofold. First, the whole infrastructure (e.g., compliant devices and certificate authorities) of the existing system, which is already in place, can be re-used for personal content. Second, the use of a DRM system for protecting personal content is thought to create for users a more positive view of DRM in general, and this can contribute to the acceptance by users of controlled distribution of commercial content.

The original DRM system involves an authorization hierarchy implemented by means of competent authorities that create and sign digital certificates. This authorization hierarchy is modified in the extended DRM system to accommodate the fact that consumers can now be content providers as well. For this reason, a new digital certificate (i.e., a "certificate of ownership") is introduced which establishes a secure link between a user and his personal content.

The fact that consumers become content providers has security implications as well. Consumers are now able to control the usage of their personal content in the system, but this also opens the door for potential misuse of commercial content (e.g., its illegal introduction in the system as personal content). To prevent such a threat, the extended DRM system requires that users register their content with a competent authority, at which point they obtain the certificate of ownership and may have their content marked with their identity, but only after the identity of the content itself has been checked and the content certified as new.

The extended DRM system can provide further user privacy by providing users with the possibility of private ownership of content with private and controlled multiple ownership. This means that users are able to register their personal content under pseudonyms, with unlinkability of pseudonyms also supported (i.e., a unique pseudonym per content item). Moreover, multiple users may own a content item, with their privacy protected in two ways: (i) pseudonyms, a different one for each user, can be used for content registration, and (ii) transfer of ownership of their content must be decided jointly by all owners.

Privacy of content ownership can be achieved as described above, except towards the registration authority which always keeps a record of the original user identifier and all the content registered under the corresponding pseudonyms. This is done in order to enforce accountability in the system but may be seen as a downside of the system. This lack of privacy can be alleviated by means of a mechanism of distribution of trust. In this case, the original user identifier can be replaced by temporary identifiers which are then used by the registration authority. The temporary identifiers are, in their turn, generated by another trusted third party which must then (to enforce accountability) keep a record of the user's real identity. As long as the authority do not collude, the association between users and their personal content is not known by any of the parties in the system. Of course, trust can be further distributed to diminish the possibility of collusions between authorities.

While the mechanism described above would increase user's privacy, it would also make the technological solution more complex, certainly from the architectural point of view. This trade-off between system's privacy provision systems with the strong requirement that security levels be preserved after addition of privacy enhancements. This is certainly the case for the original system considered, i.e., a DRM system for the protection of commercial content. Its extension to protect personal content, as well as further extensions to provide user's privacy, must include mechanisms to ensure user accountability, otherwise commercial content providers will certainly object to such extensions. Therefore, privacy protection has limitations in such systems. This means that it is unrealistic for any user, specially the user who values the freedom of anonymous publishing above the right to claim content ownership, to expect completely anonymity in the system.

References

Conrado, C., Kamperman, F., Schrijen, G.J. and Jonker, W. (2003): "Privacy In An Identity-based DRM System". *Proceedings of the 14th International Workshop on Databases and Expert Systems Applications*, Prague, Czech Republic.

Felten, E.W. (2003): "DRM", and the first rule of security analysis. *Freedom to Tinker*. http:// *www.freedom-to-tinker.com/archives/000317.html.* Accessed 12 May 2005.

Grimm, R. and Nutzel, J. (2002): "A friendly peer-to-peer file sharing system with profit but without copy protection". In *Innovative Internet Computing Systems* 2346:133-142, Lecture Notes in Computer Science, Springer-Verlag. ITUNES (2005): iPod+iTunes for Mac and Windows. *http://www.apple.com/itunes.* Accessed 12-May-2005.

Kalkert, T., Epema, D.H.J., Hartel, P.H., Lagendijk, R.L. and Van Steen, M. (2004): Music2Share - Copyright – Compliant Music Sharing in P2P Systems. *Proceedings of the IEEE* 92(6).

Menezes, A.J., Van Oorschot, P.C. and Vanstone, S.A. (1997): *Handbook of Applied Cryptography.* CRC Press. OMA-DRM (2004): Specifications: DRM Specification V2.0. Open Mobile Alliance. *http://www.openmobilealliance. org/release_program/drm_archive.html.* Accessed 12 May 2005.

Van Den Heuvel, S.A.F.A., Jonker, W., Kamperman, F.L.A.J. and Lenoir, P.J. (2002): "Secure content management in authorised domains". IBC 2002.

Van Der Veen, M., Lemma, A. and Kalker, T. (2004): "Watermarking and fingerprinting for electronic music delivery system". *SPIE 2004*, San Jose, USA.

(Claudine Conrado obtained her PhD degree in 1993 in theoretical non-linear physics from the Niels Bohr Institute in Copenhagen Denmark. Currently she is working at the Information and System Security Department of Philips Research on Privacy Enhancing Technologies. Her areas of interest include privacy and security in electronic interactions and ubiquitous systems, in particular in digital content distribution systems and healthcare applications.

Milan Petkovic is a senior scientist in the Information and System Security department at the Philips Research in the Netherlands. Dr. Petkovic received his Dipl-Ing. and MSc degrees in Computer Science from University of Niš, and his PhD degree in Computer Science from University of Twente. Among his research interests are information security, secure content management, privacy protection, multimedia information retrieval, and database systems. His publication records include a book on Content-Based Video Retrieval, as well as a number of book chapters and research articles.

Michiel van der Veen received his MSc in physics (with honours) from Utrecht University in 1996. He obtained his PhD degree from the ETH-Swiss Federal Institute of Technology. In January 2000, he joined Philips Research Eindhoven and since then worked on projects related to Information Security, Privacy, Digital Watermarking and Biometrics. In these fields, he published over 30 scientific papers and filed more than 20 patent applications.

Wytse H van der Velde has been a student at the University of Twente, Enschede, the Netherlands since 1998 and is close to receiving his MS degree in Computer Science. From 2004 to 2005 he was a member of the Information and System Security research group at Philips Research in Eindhoven and has done research for his thesis in the fields of privacy in ambient intelligence and content sharing in DRM systems. His other research interests include distributed systems and computer architectures.)

12

A Novel Watermarking Algorithm for Resistant Geometric Attacks Using Feature Points Matching

Jin Cong

A digital watermarking is an imperceptible signal embedded directly into the media content, and it can be detected from the host media for some applications. The insertion and detection of digital watermarking can help to identify the source or ownership of the media, the legitimacy of its usage, and the type of the content or other accessory information in various applications. The paper aims to report a novel method of estimating the geometric manipulation to which present day data hiding is subjected. It finds that the purposed scheme does not require the original image because reference point information on the original image has been contained in the secret key.

1. Introduction

There has been a lot of interest in the digital watermarking research over the last few years, mostly due to the fact that the digital watermarking might be used as a tool to protect the copyright of multimedia data. A digital watermarking is an

Source: www.emeraldinsight.com. Information Management and Computer Society, Vol. 14, No.1 2006.

imperceptible signal embedded directly into the media content, and it can be detected from the host media for some applications. The insertion and detection of digital watermarking can help to identify the source or ownership of the media, the legitimacy of its usage, and the type of the content or other accessory information in various applications. Specific operations related to the status of the watermarking can then be applied to cope with different situations.

As a copyright protection tool, the digital watermarking has several requirements. First of all, the watermarking must be robust against watermarking attacks. Watermarking attacks are referred to those procedures applied to the media content for the purposes of editing, storage or even circumventing watermarking detection. The watermarking must survive all possible attacks that degrade the data to the extent that the commercial value of the media is still maintained. These attacks include but are not limited to compression, noise-adding, geometrical modification, and even anti-watermarking software. Second, the watermarking must be embedded in a sophisticated way to avoid degrading the perceptual quality of the host media. Users should not sense the existence of the watermarking by viewing or listening to the watermarked media. Besides, watermarking detection should be done without the original data as a reference. Detection algorithms that require the original data restrict the applicability of digital watermarking since it is impractical to search the original data file in a huge database, whenever we would like to detect the watermarking from a suspected media. Watermarking detection without the original media is called "blind" watermarking detection.

Recently, quite a few schemes (Barni *et al.,* 2003; Shih and Wu, 2003; Furon and Duhamel, 2003) have been proposed for digital image watermarking. However, in watermarking applications; the robustness of the watermarking to geometric manipulations is a critical issue. This is due to the fact that changing the image size or its orientation, even by slight amount, could reduce the receiver ability to correctly detect the watermarking. This can be compared to losing synchronization in a communication system. Correction of geometric transformations has not been studied extensively in the past.

By geometrical modifications, we refer to all image manipulations that change the image spatially. In this research, we consider geometrical modifications that most image users can apply easily while the value of the image is still preserved. In particular, we focus on the affine transform, which can be defined by a 2 × 2 affine matrix plus translation. Given the input position (x, y), the new position (x', y') can be determined by using six parameters in the following model:

$$\begin{pmatrix} x' \\ y' \end{pmatrix} = \begin{pmatrix} a_{00} & a_{01} \\ a_{10} & a_{11} \end{pmatrix} \begin{pmatrix} x \\ y \end{pmatrix} \begin{pmatrix} t_1 \\ t_2 \end{pmatrix} + A. \begin{pmatrix} x \\ y \end{pmatrix} + t = \{A, t\}$$

In Mitiche and Aggarwal (1983), shape-specific points (SSPs) are computed in spatial or image domain for the purpose of contour registration. This technique is translation, rotation, and scale change independent. In this research, we present a new watermarking algorithm, in which SSP is used for resisting geometry attack.

We first introduce the following notation. Integer $I(i,j)$ and $I'(i,j)$ indicate (grayscale or) luminance of the original image I and the watermarked image I' with coordinates (i, j), $(1 \leq i \leq N_1,\ 1 \leq j \leq N_2)$, respectively.

In this research, according to the approaches proposed by Cox *et al.*, watermarking embedding is achieved by modifying a set of full-frame DCT coefficients of the image. The amount of modification each coefficient undergoes is proportional to the magnitude of the coefficients itself as expressed by the following rule

$$I'(i, j) = I(i, j) + \omega \cdot W(i, j). \tag{1}$$

Where, ω indicates a parameter controlling the watermarking strength, and $W(i, j)$ is watermarking data.

2. Definition and Properties of SSP

We introduce the definition of SSPs (Mitiche and Aggarwal, 1983) at first.

In the following discussion, Γ is a discrete set of points $\{(x_i, y_i), i = 1, \ldots, n\}$ in a planar. If σ is a transformation on Γ, then σ induces a transformation on the individual points of Γ. For convenience, in this paper, we will designate this transformation and the corresponding induced point transformation by the same name.

Definition: Given a point set Γ in a plane Θ and a set Σ of transformations in Θ, let $\rho = f(\Gamma)$ be a point in Θ computed from Γ according to procedure *f*. Also, let $\Gamma' = \sigma(\Gamma)$ where $\sigma \varepsilon \Sigma$ and let $\rho' = f(\Gamma')$. Then ρ is a SSP of Γ with respect to Σ if and only if $\rho' = \sigma(\rho)$ (Mitiche and Aggarwal, 1983).

The above definition simply says that if transformation σ takes Γ onto Γ′, then it takes ρ onto ρ'. By Mitiche and Aggarwal (1983), we know that SSP is invariant with respect to translations, rotations, and scale changes. We are interested in just these transformations.

To points set Γ, there are two kinds of most frequently used calculation SSP methods (Mitiche and Aggarwal, 1983). The calculation methods are as follows:

1. Given points set Γ described by the discrete set of points $\{(x_i, y_i), i = 1, \ldots, n\}$, considering the unweighted mean point (centroid) *G*, the coordinates of which are given by

$$x_G = \frac{1}{n}\sum x_i, \qquad y_G = \frac{1}{n}\sum y_i \tag{2}$$

   It is very easy to know that (x_G, y_G) is a SSP of Γ with respect to Σ.

2. Another example of a SSP is the radius weighted mean point *H*, the coordinates of which are

$$x_H = \frac{1}{R}\sum r_i x_i, \qquad y_H = \frac{1}{R}\sum r_i y_i \tag{3}$$

   where r_i is the distance from the centroid *G*, as defined in the previous example, to the point (x_i, y_i) on the Γ and $R = \sum r_i$. It is very easy to know that (x_H, y_H) is a SSP of Γ with respect to Σ, too.

Note that using any SSP and radii from it to the points on the Γ, one can obtain a new SSP.

In this paper, we adopt block-based methodologies, i.e., the image is divided into blocks for extracting the feature points of image. With divided blocks and their local SSP, we can estimate the parameter of geometry transformation undergone by watermarked image. Once detected, these transformations are inverted and then synchronization can be realized. The goal of resisting geometry attack can be achieved.

3. Feature Points Extraction and Matching

3.1 Feature Points Extraction

It is well known that feature point detectors find salient points in natural images. These points are often located near corners and edges of the image. Feature points detectors were first developed for computer vision and reconstruction (Boufama *et al.*, 1998; Faugeras *et al.*, 1998), but they are also employed in database retrieval as a descriptor of the image (Loupias *et al.*, 2000; Dufournaud *et al.*, 2000).

To design a feature points-based method, we first have to select an appropriate tool to extract an image feature point descriptor. In this research, this representation has to be robust to geometric transformations. We orient our choice towards tools commonly used in pattern recognition: feature points detectors.

We focus our study on Canny edge detector (Bas *et al.*, 2000) that are commonly used in pattern recognition and vision systems. The Canny operator was designed to be an optimal edge detector (according to particular criteria, there are other detectors around that also claim to be optimal with respect to slightly different criteria). It takes as input a gray scale image, and produces as output an image showing the positions of tracked intensity discontinuities.

The Canny operator works in a multi-stage process. First of all the image is smoothed by Gaussian convolution. Then a simple 2D first derivative operator (somewhat like the Roberts Cross) is applied to the smoothed image to highlight regions of the image with high first spatial derivatives. Edges give rise to ridges in the gradient magnitude image. The algorithm then tracks along the top of these ridges and sets to zero all pixels that are not actually on the ridge top so as to give a thin line in the output, a process known as non-maximal suppression. The tracking process exhibits hysteresis controlled by two thresholds: T_1 and T_2, with $T_1 > T_2$. Tracking can only begin at a point on a ridge higher than T_1. Tracking then continues in both directions out from that point until the height of the ridge falls below T_2. This hysteresis helps to ensure that noisy edges are not broken up into multiple edge fragments.

In the application of image watermarking, the ideal feature points should be invariant to geometrical transformation. That is, once an image undergone geometric transformation, we expect the feature points can still indicate the same local features. Moreover, when only partial information of an image is available, using feature points is advantages over other features (such as edges or regions) to capture local information. For example, if image I_A is a portion of the image I_B, the interest points of I_B will also include that of I_A.

Therefore, in our research, it is divided into $n \times n$ blocks after getting the Canny edge image. We calculate SSPs of every block, and the feature point set of the image may be obtained. The feature point set of the original image is called reference point set, denoted by $P = \{P_j = (p_{j1}\ p_{j2})^T | j = 1, 2, \ldots, m\}$.

3.2 Feature Points Matching

For tested image generated by geometric manipulating watermarked image, we obtain its feature point set, denoted by $Q = \{ q_j = (q_{j1}\ q_{j2})^T | j = 1, 2, \ldots, m\}$, using the same method with original image. In other words, sets of points P and Q related by an affine transformation $\{A, t\}$.

In this research, we define a set of correspondence variables $\{m_{jk}\}$ – match matrix M – such that:

$$m_{jk} = \begin{cases} 1 & \text{if point } P_j \text{ correspondes to point } q_k \\ 0 & \text{otherwise;} \end{cases}$$

Now our problem may be defined as: given two such sets of points P and Q, find the affine transformation $\{A, t\}$ – and the match matrix M – that best relates them. Often a point matching algorithm will attempt to find either the $\{A, t\}$ or the correspondence M, since knowledge of one relatively easily determines the other; i.e., given the $\{A, t\}$ one can determine the correspondence or given the correspondence one can determine the $\{A, t\}$.

Therefore, given two sets of points *P* and *Q*, according to the approaches proposed by Canny (1986), we formulate the following objective to find the affine transformation $\{A, t\}$, which best maps some points of *P* onto some points of *Q*.

$$E(M, t, A) = \sum_{j=1}^{m}\sum_{k=1}^{m} m_{jk} \| p_j - t - Aq_k \|^2 + g(A) - \alpha \sum_{j=1}^{m}\sum_{k=1}^{m} m_{jk} \tag{4}$$

subject to

$$\forall j,\ \sum_{j=1}^{m} m_{jk} \leq 1,\quad \forall k,\ \sum_{k=1}^{m} m_{jk} \leq 1,\ \forall jk$$

$$m_{jk} \in \{0, 1\} \text{ and } g(A) = \gamma(a^2 + b^2 + c^2)$$

Where t is translation variable, and A (composed of four separate parameters $\{a, \theta, b, c\}$) is decomposed into scale, rotation, and two components of shear as follows:

$$A = s(a)R(\theta)Sh_1(b)Sh_2(c)$$

where,

$$s(a) = \begin{pmatrix} e^a & 0 \\ 0 & e^a \end{pmatrix},\ Sh_1(b) = \begin{pmatrix} e^b & 0 \\ 0 & e^{-b} \end{pmatrix}\ Sh_2(c) = \begin{pmatrix} \cosh(c) & \sinh(c) \\ \sinh(c) & \cosh(c) \end{pmatrix}$$

$R(\theta)$ is the standard 2 × 2 rotation matrix. $g(A)$ serves to regularize, by Gold *et al.*, (1998), the affine transformation by penalizing large values of the scale and shear components. Three separate regularization parameters, γ, κ, and λ can also be used for this purpose. If different bounds are desired for the different components of A, we could set $g(A) = \gamma a^2 + \kappa b^2 + \lambda c^2$. However, in all the experiments in this paper, only one parameter γ was used to set the bound on the scale and shear components. α is the threshold value of matching error, and it can be determined according to different matching require.

In above way, the feature point matching is turned into an optimizing problem of solving match matrix and transformation parameter jointly. We notice that, when objective function (4) is solved, it is very easy to get trapped in local minima of objective function (4) since match matrix is binary. So we relax all elements of match matrix M from binary turning into continuous real number (i.e., $m_{jk} \in \{0, 1\} \rightarrow m_{jk} \in [0, 1]$). It shows that match partly is permitted. Such match matrix is called the fuzzy match matrix.

We notice that the constraint conditions of rows and columns are inequalities. Through introducing a relaxation variable, inequality constraint may be turned into equality constraint, i.e.,

$$\forall j, \sum_{j=1}^{m} m_{jk} \leq 1 \rightarrow \sum_{j=1}^{m+1} m_{jk} = 1 \ \forall k, \sum_{k=1}^{m} m_{jk} \leq 1 \rightarrow \sum_{k=1}^{m+1} m_{jk} = 1 \qquad (5)$$

3.3 Matching Algorithm by Simulated Annealing Algorithm

In this research, simulated annealing (SA) algorithm will be used for solving objective function (4). SA has been used by a number of researchers for matching and model fitting (Girosi *et al.*, 1995; Blais and Levine, 1995). SA is a Monte Carlo approach for minimizing such multivariate functions. The term SA derives from the roughly analogous physical process of heating and then slowly cooling a substance to obtain a strong crystalline structure.

In simulation, a minimum of the objective function corresponds to this ground state of the substance. The SA process lowers the temperature by slow stages until the system "freezes" and no further changes occur. At each temperature, the simulation must proceed long enough for the system to reach steady state or thermal equilibrium.

In deterministic SA technique, it was required that the global minimum of objective function (4) can be solved very easily when temperature is high enough. According to the optimality theory, objective function (4) should be convex. Therefore, we introduce a damping factor in objective function (4), i.e.,

$$T \sum_{j=1}^{m+1} \sum_{k=1}^{m+1} m_{jk} \log m_{jk},$$

where T is control anneal temperature. The functions of this kind of damping factor are:

- Under high anneal temperature, objective function (4) should be convex, and convex degree can be controlled by anneal temperature T.
- It may be guaranteed that all elements of match matrix are un-negative.

The equality constraint equation (5) and damping factor are added to objective function (4), objective function of the feature point matching problem can obtained as follows

$$E(M,t,A)=\sum_{j=1}^{m}\sum_{k=1}^{m} m_{jk}\,\| p_j - t - Aq_k \|^2 + g(A) - \alpha\sum_{j=1}^{m}\sum_{k=1}^{m} m_{jk} \tag{6}$$
$$+\sum_{j=1}^{m}\mu_j\left(\sum_{k=1}^{m+1} m_{jk}-1\right)+\sum_{k=1}^{m}v_k\left(\sum_{j=1}^{m+1} m_{jk}-1\right)+\mathrm{T}\sum_{j=1}^{m+1}\sum_{k=1}^{m+1} m_{jk}\log m_{jk},$$

where μ_j and ν_k are Lagrange factor.

Through minimize objective function (6), we can obtain match matrix and the transformation parameter between sets of points P and Q. At first, suppose transformation parameter be known already, by $(\partial E/\partial m_{jk})' = 0$, and minimizing match matrix M of objective function (6) is:

$$m_{jk}=\exp\left\{-\frac{1}{\mathrm{T}}\left(\| p_j - t - Aq_k \|^2 - \alpha + \mu_j + v_k\right)\right\} \tag{7}$$

By the equation (7), we know that Lagrange factor μ_j and ν_k mast is determined at first for solving M under certain annealing temperature. If solving μ_j and ν_k by gradient method directly, the solution speed is very slow and the efficiency is very low. Therefore, in this research, deterministic SA algorithm (Hoff *et al.*, 1997) will be used for solving objective function (6). A kind of fast and high-efficient algorithm that was proposed by the literary (Hoff *et al.*, 1997) is used to replace the complicated solving process of M. By Peterson and Soderberg (1989), we know that the process of solving μ_j and the rows normalizing process of M is uniform, and the process of solving ν_k and the columns normalizing process of M is uniform, too. So, the complicated solving process of M is turned into the rows and columns normalizing process of match matrix M. It may improve the matching speed greatly.

The structure of the fixed point solution allows a Lagrange factor updating scheme where all the μ_j are updated, followed by the ν_k. Let the $(n + 1)$th update of the Lagrange parameter μ_j be associated with the $(2n + 1)$th update of M and nth update of the Lagrange parameter ν_k be associated with the $2n$th update of M.

Now

$$m_{jk}^{(2n+1)} = \exp\left(-\frac{1}{T}\left(\| p_j - t - Aq_k \|^2 - \alpha + \mu_j^{(n+1)} + \nu_k^{(n)}\right)\right), \text{ and}$$

$$m_{jk}^{(2n)} = \exp\left(-\frac{1}{T}\left(\| p_j - t - Aq_k \|^2 - \alpha + \mu_j^{(n)} + \nu_k^{(n)}\right)\right). \tag{8}$$

Taking ratios, we get

$$\frac{m_{jk}^{(2n)}}{m_{jk}^{(2n+1)}} = \exp\left(-\frac{1}{T}\left(\mu_j^{(n)} - \mu_j^{(n+1)}\right)\right). \tag{9}$$

Setting the derivative of the energy function in equation (6) with respect to μ to zero, we solve for the row constraint

$$\sum_k m_{jk}^{(2n+1)} = 1 \Rightarrow \exp\left(\frac{1}{T}\mu_j^{(n+1)}\right)$$

$$= \sum_k \exp\left(-\frac{1}{T}\left(\| p_j - t - Aq_k \|^2 - \alpha + \nu_k^{(n)}\right)\right) \tag{10}$$

From equations (8)-(10), we get

$$m_{jk}^{(2n+1)} = \frac{m_{jk}^{(2n)}}{\sum_k m_{jk}^{(2n)}}$$

A similar relationship is obtained between the ν_k, update and column normalization. Therefore, the pseudocode for the feature point set matching algorithm using SA is as following:

Initialize: $t = [0\ 0]^T$, $\theta = 0$, $T = T_0$, $m_{jk} = 1 + \varepsilon$, $\gamma = \gamma_0$, $a = 0$, $b = 0$, $c = 0$, where ε is a small positive random variable.

Begin A: Do A until ($T \leq T_{final}$)

Begin B: Do B until iterations steps > I_0

Begin C:

$$P_{jk} \leftarrow -\left(\| p_j - \mathrm{t} - Aq_k \|^2 - \alpha\right), \quad m_{jk} \leftarrow \exp\left(\frac{P_{jk}}{T}\right)$$

Begin D: Do D until iterations steps > I_1

Update M by normalizing across all rows:

$$m_{jk} \leftarrow \frac{m_{jk}}{\sum_{k=1}^{m+1} m_{jk}};$$

Update M by normalizing across all columns:

$$m_{jk} \leftarrow \frac{m_{jk}}{\sum_{j=1}^{m+1} m_{jk}};$$

End D

End C

Begin E: Calculate transformation parameters between the feature point sets

Update θ using analytical solution

Update t using analytical solution

Update a using Newton's method

Update b using Newton's method

Update c using Newton's method

End E

End B

$T \leftarrow Tr$, $\gamma \leftarrow \gamma\, r$, where r is anneal rate at which the control temperature T is descended

End A

In the following, we let $\Psi \underset{def}{=} s(a)Sh_1(b)Sh_2(c)$ using equation (4). Then update equations for θ and t in step E of the algorithm are

$$\theta = \tan^{-1} \frac{\sum_{jk} m_{jk}\left(\left(p_{j2}-t_2\right)\Psi_{k1}-\left(p_{j1}-t_1\right)\Psi_{k2}\right)}{\sum_{jk} m_{jk}\left(\left(p_{j1}-t_1\right)\Psi_{k1}-\left(p_{j2}-t_2\right)\Psi_{k2}\right)}$$

$$t_1 = \frac{\sum_{jk} m_{jk}(p_{j1}-[\mathrm{AQ}]_{k1})}{\sum_{jk} m_{jk}} \quad \text{and} \quad t_2 = \frac{\sum_{jk} m_{jk}(p_{j2}-[\mathrm{AQ}]_{k2})}{\sum_{jk} m_{jk}}$$

To update a, b and c in step E, the first and second partial derivatives of equation (4) are calculated with respect to a, b and c and these first and second partial derivatives are then used in Newton's method to calculate the fixed points.

4. Design of Watermarking

In our research, watermarking is generated by secret key. After referenced point set P obtained, the secret key may be generated. Given m feature points of P in the original image, i.e., (p_{11}, p_{12}), (p_{21}, p_{22}),. . ., (p_{m1}, p_{m2}), Table I shows the detailed construction of a secret key. Here, each p_{j1} or p_{j2} is represented by a binary code denoted by $c = \{c_i | c_i \in \{0, 1\}\}$; $i = 1; 2; \ldots ; L\}$, where L is the length of the binary sequence of each p_{j1} or p_{j2}. Usually we use $c' = \{c' | c' = 1 - 2c_i$, $i = 1, 2, \ldots, L\}$. So c' is a binary polar sequence of { -1, 1}.

Where $p^{(1)}$, $p^{(2)}$, . . . , and $p^{(m)}$ are 2D pseudo-random binary sequence of {-1, 1} with zero mean, generated using the key as the seed. So the whole secret key is 2D binary sequence of {–1, 1} too. This binary sequence of {–1, 1} is denoted B. The length of B is defined Ξ, where

$$\Xi = \text{Length } p^{(1)} + \text{Length } p^{(2)} + \cdots + \text{Length } p^{(m)} + 2mL = N_1 \times N_2.$$

Table 1: Construction of the Secret Key

... ... p_{11} p_{12} ... ... p_{21} p_{22} ... ... p_{m1} p_{m2}
$p^{(1)}$ |← $p^{(2)}$ →| ... $p^{(m)}$ |← →| |← →|

In other words, Ξ equals the size of the original image. Suppose d is a secret message hidden in an original image, where $d = \{d_i | d_i \in \{0, 1\}\}$, $i = 1, 2, \ldots, V\}$. We let still $d' = \{d'_i \,|\, d'_i = 1 - 2d_i$, $i = 1, 2, \ldots, V\}$. So d' is a binary polar sequence of $\{-1, 1\}$ too. There are V binary sequences of $\{-1, 1\}$ the same as size of B using different key as the seed, respectively. The watermarking will be W (i, j) = B · $d' = \sum_{k=1}^{V} B_{i,j}(k) d'_k$.

The watermarking can be embedded into an original image additively by equation (1). A simple detection can be performed using correlation detector. The correlation is calculated as

$$C_l = \sum_{i,j} B_{i,j}(l) I'(i,j) = \sum_{i,j} B_{i,j}(l) I(i,j) + \omega \sum_{i,j} B_{i,j}(l) \sum_{k=1}^{V} B_{i,j}(k) d'_k$$

$$= \omega \sum_{k=1}^{V} \sum_{i,j} B_{i,j}(l) B_{i,j}(k) d'_k = \omega \sum_{i,j} | B_{i,j}(k) |^2 d'_l,$$

where $l = 1, 2, \ldots, V$. In the above deduction, because $B_{i,j}(l)$ is a zero mean pseudo-random binary sequence of $\{-1, 1\}$, and it is independent with $I(i, j)$, term $\sum_{i,j} B_{i,j}(l) . I(i,j)$ is supposedly close to zero. Other terms are all zeros when $k \neq l$, because pseudo-random patterns $B_{i,j}(l)$ are uncorrelated with each other. So secret message can be decoded by $d'_l \approx (C_l)$.

5. Experiment Results

In these experiments, we will investigate the blind decode problem of the secret message. Let us consider 256 × 256 grayscale images. Let Figure 1 be an original image, and Figure 2 a secret message. Figure 3 is the watermarked image after embedding the secret message into Figure 1 according to equation (1), when $\omega = 0.03$ (Figures 4-19).

Figure 1: Original Image

Figure 2: Secret Message

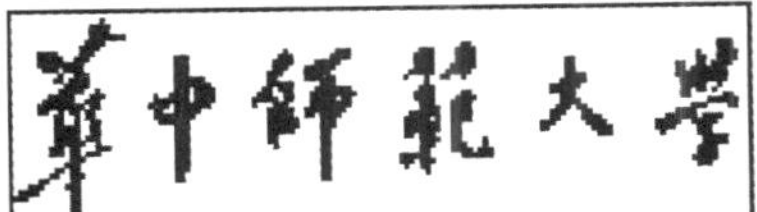

Figure 3: Watermarked Image, when w = 0.03

Figure 4: The Canny Edge of Figure 1

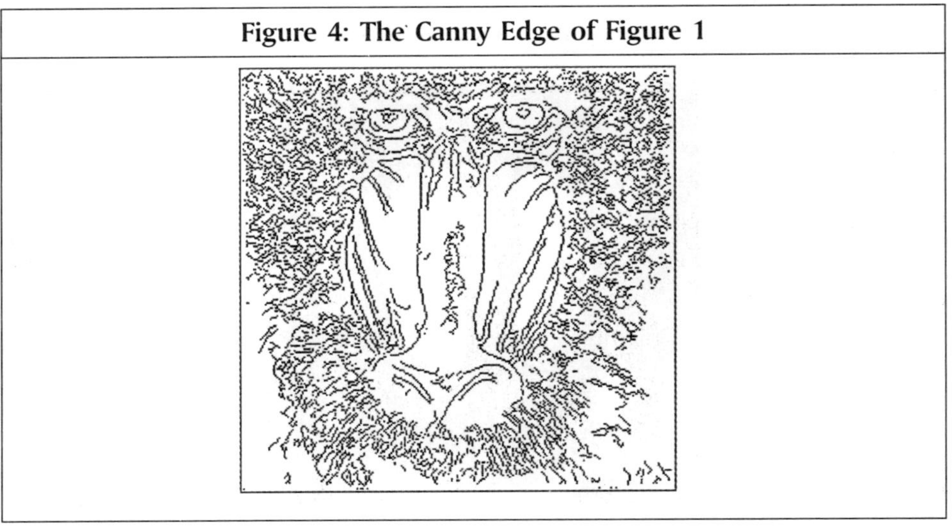

Figure 5: Referenced Points set of Figure 4

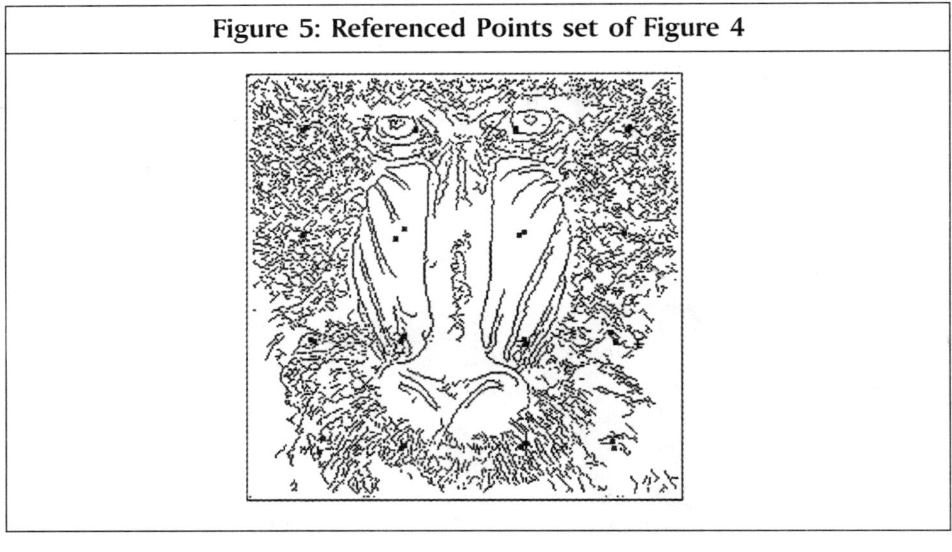

Figure 6: This is a Tested Image by Scaling Figure 3 According to 85 percent

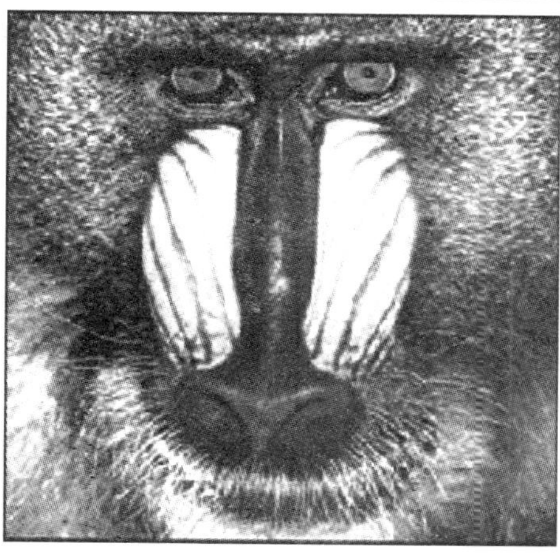

Figure 7: Feature Points Set of Figure 6

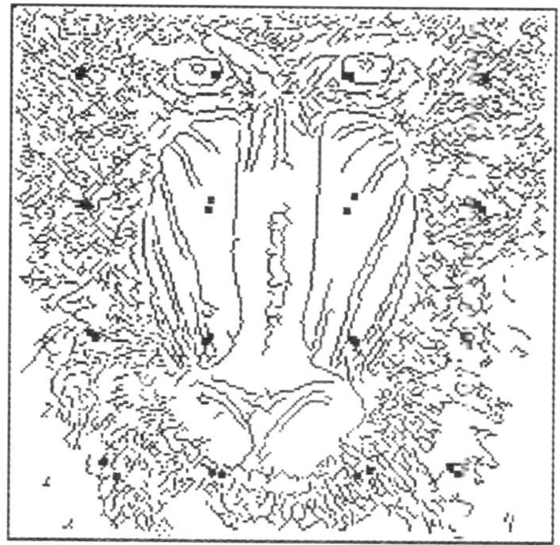

Figure 8: This is a Test Image by Rotating Figure 3 According to 4^0

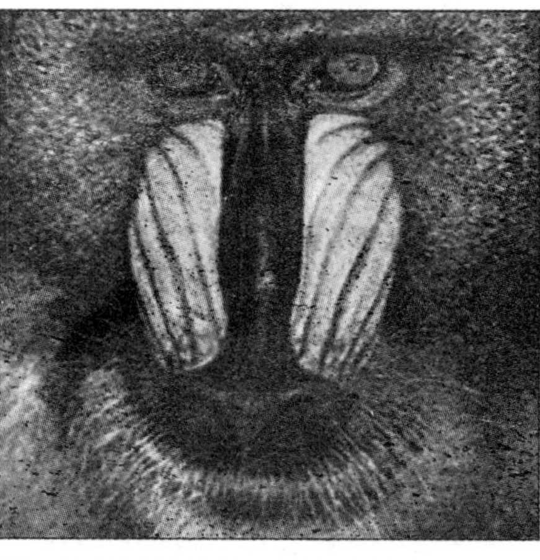

Figure 9: The Canny Edge of Figure 8

Figure 10: Feature Points Set of Figure 8

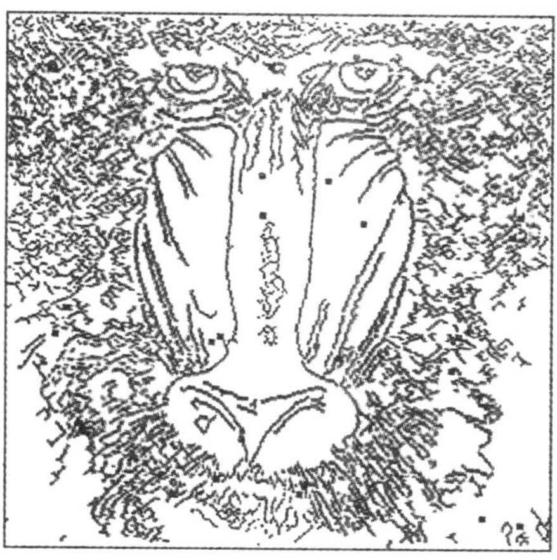

Figure 11: This is a Watermarked Image Attacked by Zero-mean Gaussian Noise with Variance 0.01

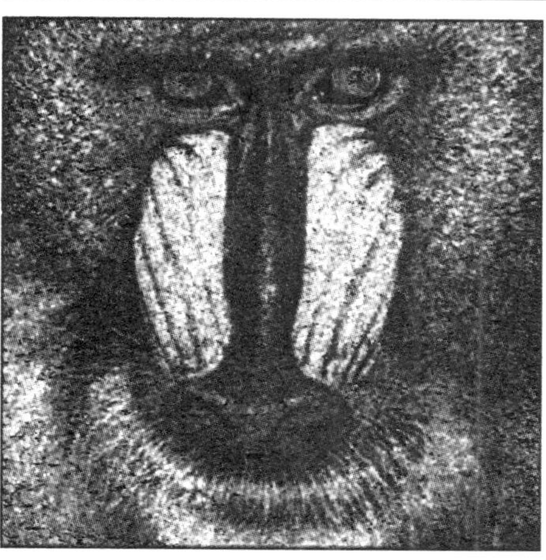

Figure 12: The Canny Edge of Figure 11

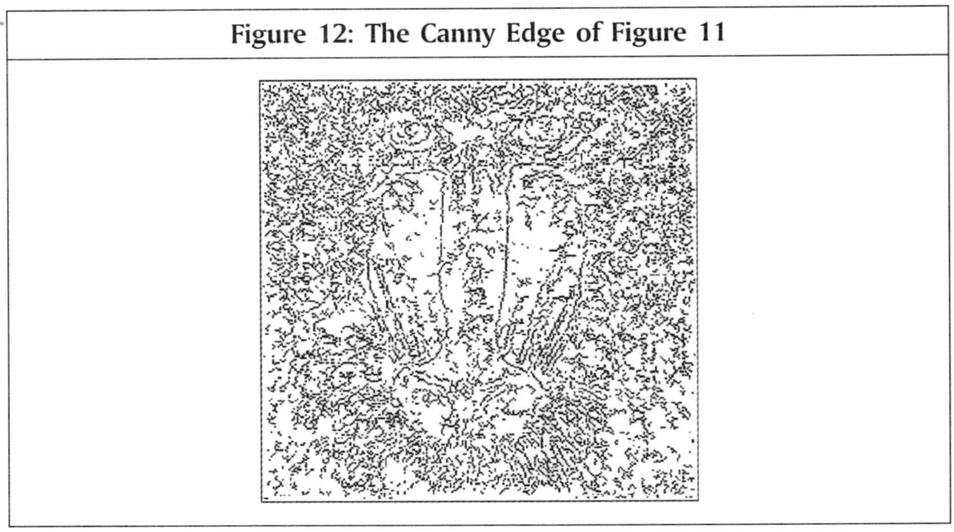

Figure 13: Feature Points Set of Figure 12

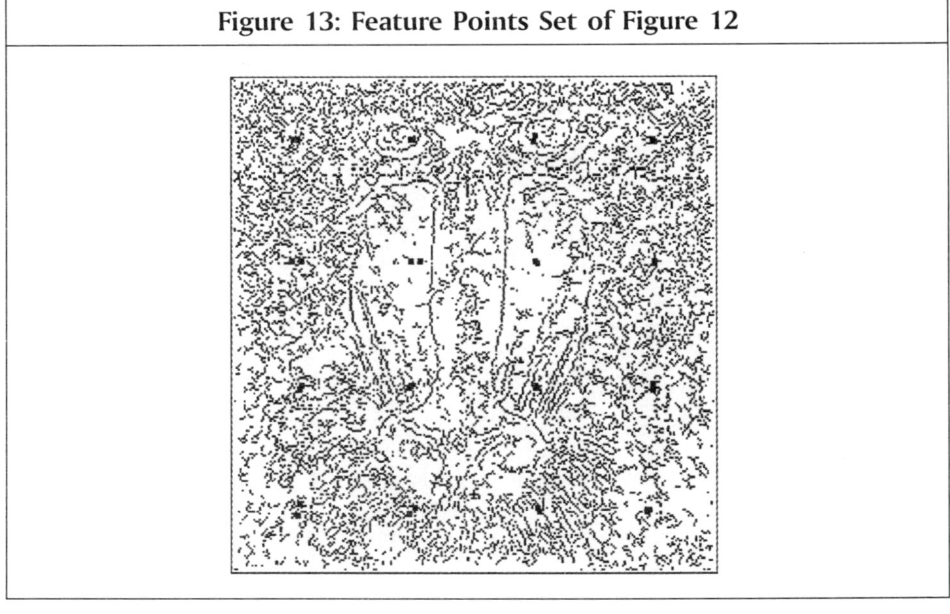

Figure 14: This is a Watermarked Image Compressed According to JPEG Quality 65

Figure 15: The Canny Edge of Figure 14

Figure 16: Feature Points Set of Figure 14

Figure 17: This is a Tested Image by Cropping Figure 3

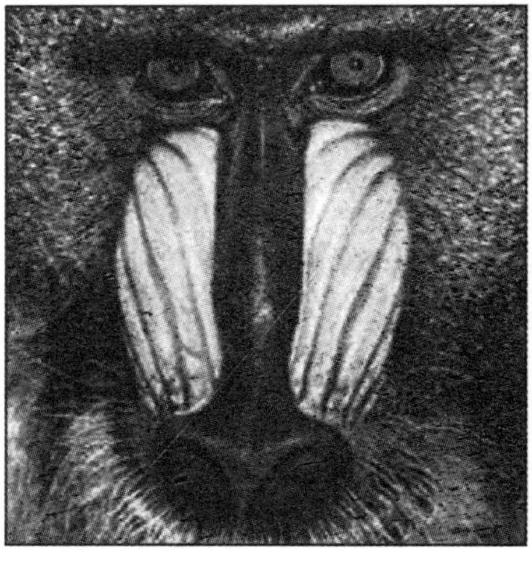

Figure 18: The Canny Edge of Figure 17

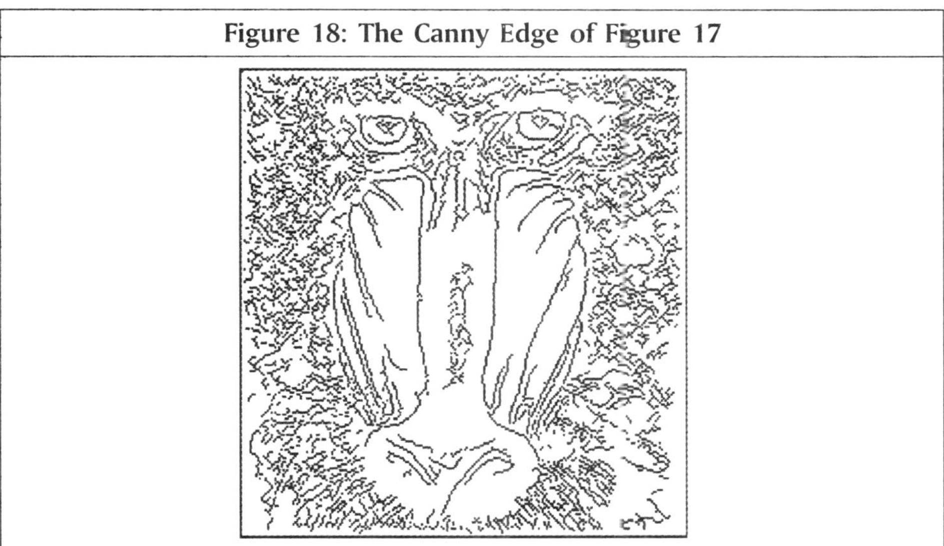

Figure 19: Feature Points Set of Figure 17

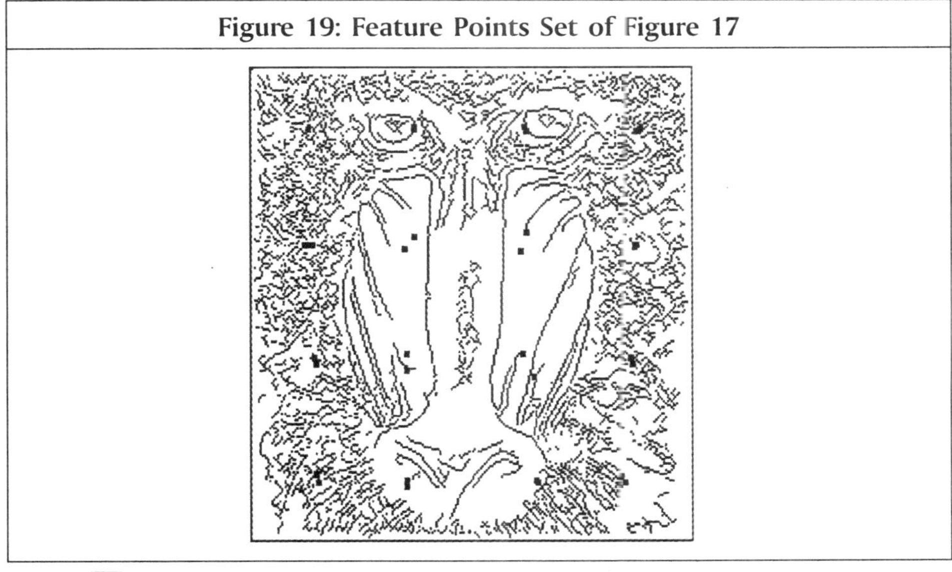

In the experiments, the parameters of our algorithm are set as, original image divided into 64 $\times$ 64 blocks. We calculate SSPs of every block. Table II shows the coordinates of these points. The length of binary code for each coordinate is 9. For the experiments, the following values for the constants were used: T_0 = 0.4, T_{final} = 0.0009, r = 1.065, γ_0 = 0.4, α = 0.03, I_0 = 8, I_1 = 40.

In the experiments, because the size of secret message is $41 \times 141 = 5{,}781$, we produce 5,781 *B* random matrices, and all its elements are binary random variables of $\{-1, 1\}$ with zero mean. The size of B equals the size of the original image. According to the design method of watermarking, after some elements of *B* are replaced by referenced point set *P*, we received new *B* matrix.

After running our algorithm, to Tables II-VII, respectively, the decoded secret messages are Figures 20-24, respectively.

Here, similarity between secret message and decoded secret message is simply expressed in terms of the fraction $y = X/N$, where *N* is the total number of secret message points in both figures and *X* is the count of points from either secret message that have at least one point from the other secret message in their 3×3 neighborhood. Refer to Table VIII.

Table II: Referenced Point Coordinates of Figure 5

	Pj_1	Pj_2
1	34	33
2	32	35
3	33	100
4	34	100
5	35	159
6	33	159
7	34	225
8	33	226
9	96	34
10	97	33
11	93	93
12	99	88
13	95	164
14	97	161
15	96	223
16	96	223
17	160	38

Contd...

Contd...

18	161	40
19	161	91
20	158	93
21	163	165
22	160	164
23	156	215
24	162	216
25	220	45
26	228	43
27	224	93
28	226	91
29	223	165
30	225	162
31	222	216
32	226	217

Besides above experiments, we let other five images be original images selected from USC-SIPI Image Database (1977) (Figure 25) for testing the new watermarking algorithm. The experiment results show that this watermarking algorithm is a good method for resisting various attacks.

6. Conclusion

In this paper, a blind image watermarking algorithm is designed using feature points matching. Key of this algorithm is that referenced points information of the original image is contained in secret key. By utilizing referenced points information, we can realize the blind secret message decoding. Through experiment, we know that the blind secret message decoder has the good robustness to scaling, rotation, Gaussian noise, JPEG compression, and cropping attacks, and it has very high similarity between the decoded secret message and the original secret message. It points out a new way for designing the better blind secret message decoder.

Table III: Feature Point Coordinates of Figure 7

	qj_1	qj_2
1	29	27
2	27	28
3	28	81
4	28	82
5	28	135
6	28	133
7	28	189
8	29	189
9	81	29
10	82	31
11	79	80
12	83	79
13	77	137
14	83	134
15	80	186
16	82	188
17	133	32
18	135	34
19	136	78
20	134	80
21	136	138
22	135	137
23	133	181
24	137	183
25	185	38
26	191	43
27	189	81
28	190	85
29	190	139
30	188	144
31	186	176
32	189	179

Table IV: Feature Point Coordinates of Figure 10

	qj_1	qj_2
1	44	24
2	45	26
3	49	125
4	35	127
5	49	153
6	27	166
7	36	241
8	33	242
9	107	32
10	99	32
11	88	127
12	107	129
13	88	158
14	107	176
15	108	246
16	98	249
17	159	41
18	172	37
19	167	114
20	160	110
21	168	159
22	173	170
23	158	225
24	175	223
25	215	52
26	218	54
27	236	118
28	245	96
29	240	157
30	236	159
31	247	261
32	245	243

Table V: Feature Point Coordinates of Figure 13		
	qj_1	qj_2
1	33	33
2	33	35
3	33	96
4	33	95
5	31	161
6	34	160
7	34	224
8	33	223
9	96	32
10	96	37
11	96	100
12	96	95
13	97	162
14	96	161
15	96	224
16	97	224
17	162	36
18	160	37
19	161	94
20	160	95
21	161	162
22	160	161
23	159	223
24	162	223
25	221	36
26	227	35
27	223	97
28	226	94
29	223	162
30	225	163
31	224	221
32	225	220

Table VI: Feature Point Coordinates of Figure 16

	qj_1	qj_2
1	34	33
2	33	33
3	32	95
4	34	94
5	34	162
6	33	162
7	34	223
8	33	225
9	96	33
10	97	36
11	95	93
12	98	93
13	92	171
14	101	160
15	95	223
16	96	225
17	160	39
18	159	42
19	162	91
20	160	91
21	162	164
22	160	165
23	157	217
24	161	219
25	220	45
26	227	47
27	223	95
28	225	91
29	225	165
30	224	172
31	222	216
32	226	220

Table VII: Feature Point Coordinates of Figure 19

	qj_1	qj_2
1	30	30
2	30	30
3	29	85
4	30	85
5	31	143
6	29	142
7	31	200
8	30	202
9	86	29
10	86	32
11	82	85
12	88	80
13	80	143
14	89	140
15	87	199
16	86	200
17	141	33
18	144	34
19	147	81
20	139	81
21	150	147
22	139	141
23	141	197
24	144	198
25	197	34
26	201	35
27	203	81
28	200	81
29	201	149
30	200	148
31	198	192
32	201	194

Figure 20: Decoded the Secret Message from Figure 6

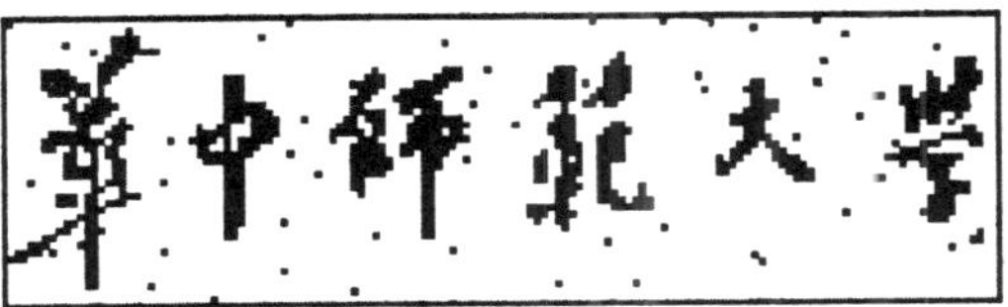

Figure 21: Decoded the Secret Message from Figure 8

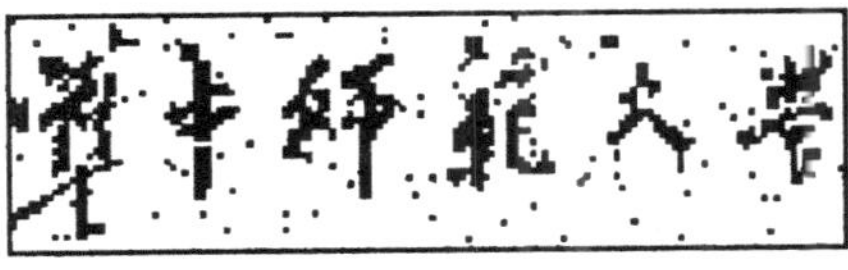

Figure 22: Decoded the Secret Message from Figure 13

Figure 23: Decoded the Secret Message from Figure 16

Figure 24: Decoded the Secret Message from Figure 19

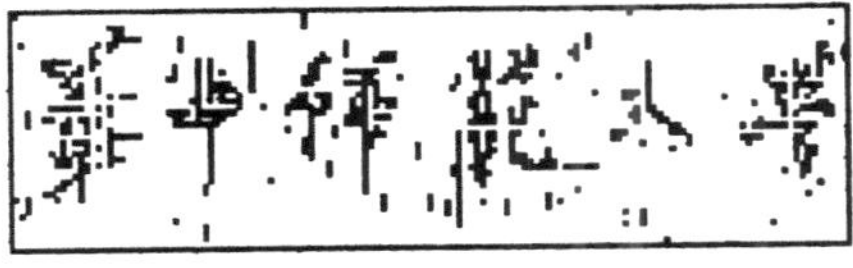

Table VIII: Similarity Measure for Figures 20-24

Experiment	Similarity
Figures 2 and 20	0.9310
Figures 2 and 21	0.7928
Figures 2 and 22	0.9277
Figures 2 and 23	0.9485
Figures 2 and 24	0.7610

Figure 25: Original Images

(Jin Cong is from Department of Computer Science, Central China Normal University, Wuhan, People's Republic of China).

References

Barni, M, Bartolini, F and Furon, T (2003), "A general framework for robust watermarking security", *Signal Processing*, Vol. 83, pp. 2069-84.

Bas, P, Chassery, J-M and Macq, B (2000), "Robust watermarking based on the warping of pre-defined triangular patterns", *Proceedings of SPIE*, pp. 99-109.

Blais, G and Levine, D (1995), "Registering multi-view range data to create 3D computer objects", *IEEE Transactions on PAMI*, Vol. 17 No. 8, pp. 820-4.

Boufama, B, Mohr, R and Morin, L (1998), "Using geometric properties for automatic object positioning", *Image and Vision Computing*, Vol. 16 No. 1, pp. 27-33.

Canny, J (1986), "A computational approach to edge detection", *IEEE Transactions on Pattern Analysis and Machine Intelligence*, Vol. 8 No. 6, pp. 679-98.

Dufournaud, Y, Schmid, C and Horaud, R (2000), "Matching image with different resolutions", *Computer Vision and Pattern Recognition*, Vol. 1, pp. 612-8.

Faugeras, O, Quan, L and Sturm, P (1998), "Self-calibration of a 1D projective camera and its application to the self-calibration of a 2D projective camera", *Proceedings of the 5th European Conference on Computer Vision, Freiburg, Germany*, June, pp. 36-52.

Furon, T and Duhamel, P (2003), "An asymmetric watermarking method", *IEEE Trans. Signal Processing*, Vol. 51 No. 4, pp. 981-95.

Girosi, F, Jones, F and Poggio, T (1995), "Regularization theory and neural network architectures", *Neural Computation*, Vol. 7, pp. 219-69.

Gold, S, Rangarajan, A and Lu, C P (1998), "New algorithms for 2D and 3D point matching: Pose estimation and correspondence", *Pattern Recognition*, Vol. 31 No. 8, pp. 1019-31.

Hoff, W A , Hood, F W and King, H (1997), "An interactive system for creating object models from range data based on simulated annealing", *Proceedings of International Conference on Robotics and Automations, IEEE, Albuquerque, NM, April 21-27*, pp. 2559-64.

Loupias, E., Sebe, N, Bres, S and Jolion, J M (2000), "Wavelet-based salient points for image retrieval", *Proceedings of ICIP*, September.

Mitiche, A and Aggarwal, J K (1983), "Contour registration by shape-specific points for shape matching", *Computer Vision, Graphics, and Image Processing*, Vol. 22, pp. 396-408.

Peterson, C and Soderberg, B (1989), "A new method for mapping optimization problems onto neural networks", Intl. *Journal of Neural Systems*, Vol. 1 No. 1, pp. 3-22.

Shih, F Y and Wu, Y T (2003), "Combinational image watermarking in the spatial and frequency domains", *Pattern Recognition*, Vol. 36, pp. 969-75.

USC-SIPI Image Database (1977), available at: *http://sipi.usc.edu/services/database/Database.html*

Further Reading

Sinkhorn, R (1964), "A relationship between arbitrary positive matrices and doubly stochastic matrices", *Ann. Math. Statist., Vol.* 35, pp. 876-9.

13

Hash-based Counter Scheme for Digital Rights Management

Mikko Löytynoja and Tapio Seppänen

This paper describes a counter scheme that uses hash functions to count how many times the user is allowed to play protected content in a DRM-enabled player. The proposed basic scheme can be used in scenarios where the user cannot be assumed to have online connection. We discuss the weaknesses of the proposed scheme and present alternatives to the basic scheme, which increases the security of the counter.

1. Introduction

Content such as music and video is increasingly in digital form. This increases the risk of illegal copying, as it is very easy to make perfect copies from digital content, whereas when copying analog content, the quality of each generation is worse than the previous one. Digital rights management (DRM) tries to find a solution to this problem inside a triangle set by technology, economics and law.

DRM is not just copy protection of content; it enables new business possibilities as the users can be granted many kinds of usage rights to content, e.g. limited number of usages, limited period of usage, and different cost for

Source: www.mediateam.oulu.fi. Proceedings 2005 IEEE International Conference on Multimedia and Expo, Amsterdam, The Netherlands.

viewing and printing. These rights can be used to create flexible billing schemes, e.g. user pays certain amount if he/she prints document less than 10 times, but after that the price of printing is cheaper. Limiting period of usage enable network based video rental business, where user is allowed to play movie for one day. These rights are usually defined using rights expression languages (REL), such as ODRL [1], XrML [2] and MPEG-21 REL [3].

The biggest vulnerability of any DRM system is that any software-based system, if not running on tamper-proof hardware, can be modified and thus the protection mechanism can be circumvented. Encryption protects from these kinds of attacks to a certain level and watermarking can be used to protect the content after decryption. But if the attacker has the key available, e.g. by purchasing one license to the content, he/she can then freely distribute the content to other users using cracked players. Frequent updating and patching the security holes in players can be used as countermeasures against these attacks. A trusted computing platform could be used to prevent users from modifying the player; the trusted platform module can calculate hash of the player software and verify that it has not been tampered. It still remains to be seen when and what kind of trusted computing platforms will emerge. [4] Additionally, it is always possible to record the content in analog form while it is presented to the user. The only way to protect against this DA/AD attack is to insert something to the content itself such as watermark.

The rights expression languages define what the user can do with the content and under what conditions, but they do not define how these rights are enforced. One of these conditions that are presented in RELs and in DRM solutions from e.g. Microsoft, RealNetworks, Adobe, is a limited number of usages. Since the most present or upcoming DRM products have the feature to restrict number of times content can be consumed, it is very important to create secure way to count the usages. In the XrML specification examples, the condition of a limited number of usages is implemented with a reference to some external service and the ODRL does not specify how the limit is implemented in practice either. The implementation of this condition is much more complex than what it first seems. In a scenario, in which the user is online during the content consumption, a specific server can be used to count the remaining usages. But this is not a feasible solution in a scenario where the user cannot be assumed to be online all the time, e.g. mobile use or with a dial-up connection to the network.

In DRM systems, the user's terminal must be considered as hostile, since the user benefits, if he/she can break the protection and e.g. get unlimited playback of the content. How to count the remaining usages on a user's terminal, if the user is able to access and modify all the data stored on that terminal? Encryption is not a feasible solution, because the keys must be stored on that same device, hence they are available to the user. There are ways to obfuscate encryption keys into application, so that it is very hard to retrieve them as shown in [5][6][7]. It is still possible to attack against the obfuscation [8] and the computational complexity increases when using obfuscation [7], which might restrict its usage in mobile devices.

In this paper, we propose a hash-based counter scheme that can be used to count the number of remaining usages. The basic counter scheme that is presented in Section 2 can be used in an offline scenario. In Section 3, we discuss the vulnerabilities in the proposed scheme and present improvement to basic scheme when using NTFS file system. Section 4 presents some experimental results of the implementation in mobile phone. Section 5 concludes the discussion.

2. Basic Counter Scheme

The license for content can limit the number of times that the user is allowed to consume the content. Our proposed basic hash-based counter scheme can be used to count the number of usages left in a scenario, in which we assume that the user does not necessarily have an online connection and that the licenses which describe what the user can do with the content are protected by digital signatures and the signatures can be verified with public-key certificates. We also assume that the player software is trusted, i.e., it is not hacked and it will adhere to the license terms.

In our current implementation of the DRM system, we use XML-based licenses. The test system is presented in more detail in Section 3. The proposed scheme is based on a scheme originally developed as micropayment mechanism proposed simultaneously by [9][10][11]. These micropayment schemes enabled the user to have a number of tokens that could be used to pay very small amounts.

The scheme uses hash function, which takes variable length input and turns it to fixed length output. The hash function is a one-way function, i.e., it is very hard to guess its input if only the output is given. Examples of cryptographically strong hash functions are MD5 [12] or SHA-1 [13]. When the license is first created, a random string t0 is generated. The hash function *h* is the applied *n* times recursively

$$t_{i+1} = h(t_i)$$

for $i = 0, 1, \ldots, n-1$, where n is the number of times that the user is allowed to consume the content. The license is divided into two parts, one of which is digitally signed by the DRM license server and the other one is not. The t_0 and n are stored in the unsigned part of the license and the t_n and n are stored in the signed part of the license. When the user consumes the content, the player applies the hash function to t_0 and replaces the value stored in the unsigned part of the license with t_1 and updates the counter value in unsigned part to $n-i$ etc. The remaining amount of usages left in the license can be validated by hashing the value in the unsigned part $n-i$ times and checking that the output equals t_n.

Figure 1: XML License Showing Counter.

```
<License>
<Signature>loDet09DTwestFS</Signature>
<SignedPart>
        <Count count="5">2Q9ksZ4jd8</Count>
        ...
        </SignedPart>
<UnsignedPart>
        <Counter count="3">uCkZm6vuk=</Counter>
</UnsignedPart>
</License>
```

Figure 1 shows an example of the XML license file used to mark the number of usages in our test system. The Signature element contains signature information about the SignedPart of the license. The value of Count element is the t_n and it also has an attribute, which defines what the value of n is. The value of n is needed to check that the count attribute, which is $n-i$, in Counter element is not greater than initial number of usages. This ensures that the user cannot modify the t_i in unsigned part and calculate how many times the hash function needs to be performed to get t_n and so increase the value of counter.

The difference of the proposed scheme compared to the original micropayment schemes is that counting is reversed in the DRM counter scheme. In the micropayment scheme, the client sends the last hash value to the vendor, signed by a trusted third party. After that the client sends the previous hash values to the vendor when he/she wants to pay something, as shown below.

$t_n, t_{n-1}, t_{n-2}, \ldots$

The DRM counter functions by calculating the next hash value and replacing the previous one with the new one. Since the previous counter values must be permanently erased, the DRM counter is more vulnerable against attacks.

3. Improving the Basic Counter Scheme

The proposed scheme needs quite strict restrictions in order for it to be secure. The biggest weakness of the scheme is that previous counter values must be erased to prevent the user from resetting the counter to an earlier value. The proposed scheme prevents the user from increasing the number of usages left in the license. In a case where the counter is simply a value stored in the license, a malicious user could freely change the value to whatever he/she wishes. In our scheme, the user would need to find the value that produces the hash functions output in order to increase the counter, which is very hard if the hash function used is cryptographically strong. Although the basic scheme is not very secure, it is more secure than storing the counter value in plaintext, since the value cannot be increased. Additionally, the scheme is not computationally heavy, since the calculation of remaining usages requires only a few hash operations. In the following, we present what restrictions the scheme sets to the scenario, in order to prevent the user from attacking the counter.

3.1. Replay Attack

The basic counter scheme prevents the user from increasing the counter value, but the user is still able to keep the counter from decreasing. The basic scheme assumes that the user is offline and hence the counter must reside on the user's terminal. The easiest way to attack the proposed counter scheme is by a method that we call replay attack.

Since the user is usually able to access the data stored on the terminal, he/she can make a backup copy of the licenses. After the backup, the user plays the content normally and the DRM counter decreases the remaining usages normally. When the license has run out of usages, the user restores the license from the backup. This undoes all the changes that the DRM enabled player has made to the licenses and the license can be used again to play the content. In other words, the counter never decreases.

The replay attack can be used in all scenarios where the counter must reside on the user's terminal and it is impossible to protect against it, if the user has write access to all the data stored in the terminal. One solution to this attack is to store the counter in the server, but this would prevent offline use of protected content. Trusted computing platform could also be used to check that the user has not modified the license files or to provide storage space where only the player software is able to store data. [14] The latter solution requires that the hardware and the operating system support this kind of features.

3.2. NTFS File Last Access Attribute

When using NTFS file system, each file has three date attributes; creation, modification and last access. [15] The last access date is changed each time the file is moved, copied, backed up or modified etc. This fragile nature of the attribute could be used to make replay attack more difficult. The player software stores, in addition to counter data, the date and time when the counter was last decreased. This same date and time are stored in file's last access date attribute. Next time the user tries to play protected content, the player checks that the two dates match, if they differ the license has been tampered.

This method can naturally be attacked. Easiest way is to use file management application that enables to change the last access date of the file. If the date stored inside the license is obfuscated, the user cannot simply check what is the correct date and set it as the last access date attribute. So the user must first get the utility software and he/she must also store the current date of each license file before playing them. This at least makes the replay attack more tedious.

The drawback of this method is that the last access attribute could be changed by some application even if the user has not been tampering the license, so the user should not even read the contents of the license files. This same kind of approach could be used with file systems if there is date attribute that is changed each time the file is copied. Preferably that date attribute would not change if the file is read, as sometime is the case with NTFS's last access date.

4. Experimental Results

We have implemented the proposed scheme in our DRM architecture.[16] The computational cost of the hash function is very low even with a player running in mobile phone. We implemented the basic counter scheme to a player running in Nokia 660, which was released Q4 2003. On average, with the hash functions implemented with Java 2 ME in Nokia 6600, it is possible to process 200 kb of data with MD5 and 100 kb with SHA-1 using block sizes from 8 bytes to 8192 bytes. So, calculating the counter value takes less than millisecond.

Unfortunately, the implementations of the secure counters in current DRM products are not publicly available information, which makes it hard to compare their implementations to ours.

5. Conclusions

Without a secure platform, a perfect copy control may be impossible. Our pragmatic goal is, therefore, to create technology that complicates content copying in varying degrees. In this paper, we presented a counter scheme, which uses a hash function to prevent the user from increasing the number of remaining usages. The scheme is feasible in a scenario, where users cannot be assumed to have an online network connection, but it is wished that content consumption be limited to a certain number of usages.

In this offline case, the counter data must be stored on user's terminal, which must be considered as hostile environment. The proposed scheme enables counting usages and prevent user from increasing the counter value. The drawback of the scheme is that counting the usages on the user's terminal is open to replay attacks, if the user is able to access all the data on the terminal. This can be countered with limiting the user's access to license files with the help of the operating system and secure hardware. Moving the counter to a server, limits the use scenario to online use, which is not feasible in many cases. We also presented a method that utilizes NTFS's last access date attributes. Because the attribute is changed each time the file is copied, it can be used to make replay attack harder.

Acknowledgments

The financial support from the National Technology Agency of Finland (Tekes), Graduate School in Electronics, Telecommunications and Automation (GETA), and the Stardust project consortium is gratefully acknowledged.

(Mikko Löytynoja and Tapio Seppänen are from MediaTeam Oulu, Department of Electrical and Information Engineering, University of Oulu, Finland. They can be reached at mikkolöytynoja@oulu.fi and tapioseppänen@oulu.fi respectively).

References

1. The Open Digital Rights Language, *http://www.odrl.net/*
2. The eXtensible Rights Markup Language, *http://www.xrml.org/*
3. DeMartini T, Wang X & Wragg B (ed.) MPEG-21 Rights Expression Language. MPEG-21 Working Documents Parts 5 & 6, March 2003.
4. Becker E, Buhse W, Günnewig D & Rump N "Trusted Platforms, DRM and Beyond". In *Digital Rights Management: Technological, Economic, Legal and Political Aspects.* Springer LNCS, v. 2770, pp. 178-205.
5. Chow S, Eisen P, Johnson H & van Oorschot P C, "White-Box Cryptography and an AES Implementation", In *Proceedings of the Ninth Workshop on Selected Areas in Cryptography*, Springer-Verlag, 2003, pp. 250-270.
6. Chow S, Eisen P, Johnson H & van Oorschot P C, "A White-Box DES Implementation for DRM Applications", In *Proceedings of 2nd work ACM Workshop on Digital Rights Managements* (DRM 2002), Springer-Verlag, 2003 November 18, pp. 1-15.
7. Link H E & Neumann W D, "Clarifying Obfuscation: Improving the Security of White-Box Encoding". In *Cryptology ePrint* Archive, Report 2004/025. *http://eprint.iacr.org/2004/025.pdf*

8. Jacob M, Boneh D & Felten E, "Attacking an Obfuscated Cipher by Injecting Faults", In *Proceedings of 2nd work ACM Workshop on Digital Rights Management* (DRM 2002), Springer-Verlag, 2003 November, pp. 16-31.

9. Anderson R J, Manifavas C & Sutherland C "NetCard – A Practical Electronic Cash Scheme". In *Security Protocols* (1996), Springer LNCS, v. 1189, pp. 49-57.

10. Pedersen T P "Electronic Payments of Small Amounts". In *Security Protocols* (1996), Springer LNCS, v. 1189, pp. 59-68.

11. Rivest R L & Shamir A "PayWord and MicroMint: Two Simple Micropayment Schemes". In *Security Protocols* (1996), Springer LNCS, v. 1189, pp. 69-87.

12. Rivest R L "The MD5 message-digest algorithm". Internet Request for Comment (RFC 1321), April 1992.

13. National Institute of Standards and Technology (NIST) "Secure Hash Standard". In *FIPS* Publication 180, May 11 1993.

14. Cram E "Next-Generation Secure Computing Base: Development Considerations for Nexus Computing Agents" Microsoft, October 2003.

15. Microsoft, "File Times", Platform SDK: Windows System Information, MSDN Library, *http://msdn.microsoft.com/library/default.asp?url=/library/en-us/sysinfo/base/file_times.asp*

16. Löytynoja M, Seppänen T & Cvejic N "Experimental DRM architecture using watermarking and PKI". In proceedings of 1st *International Mobile IPR Workshop: Rights Management of Information Products on the Mobile Internet*, HIIT Publications, Helsinki, Finland, August 27-28 2003, pp. 47–52.

14

Predicting the Evolution of Digital Rights, Digital Objects, and Digital Rights Management Languages

Jonathan Schull

As a sometime biological psychologist and sometime DRM pioneer, I suggest that biological principles are at least as important as technological principles in anticipating future developments in the field of rights management, and requirements for digital rights languages. Among those possible developments are (1) increases in the virtuality and virality of rights-managed objects, of distribution systems, and of payment systems, (2) systems for tracking the copying and redistribution of digital documents, (3) application of digital rights to data derived from document tracking, (4) attribution of those rights to the individuals who do the re-distributing, (5) development of rights management systems for the aggregation, protection, anonymization, and monetization of personal information, (6) rights-managed digital objects whose content changes spontaneously as a function of normal use, and (7) digital objects that adapt through a natural selection-

like process of mutation, recombination and differential reproduction. Such ideas pose interesting challenges for rights management languages.

I. Introduction

Any rights management language that hopes to keep pace with "facts on the ground" must be extensible to rights management practices that are uncommon, but predictable, today. We can better design a digital rights language for the future if we can anticipate the changes and change processes we will have to accommodate.

As a sometime biological psychologist and sometime DRM pioneer [1,2,3], I believe that biological principles are at least as important as technological principles in anticipating future developments in the field of rights management.

Today's digital rights management situation represents the convergence of two historical trends: virtualization and biologization. Of the two, biologization is the least discussed, let alone well understood. But its implications are most fundamental for digital rights management and for the transformation of the information economy.

Here's what I mean. Traditional economies are based on the delivery of valuable "things" (products and services) in exchange for receipt of valuable "things" (including money). However, starting at the dawn of civilization, value came to be represented first by tokens, then by coin, then symbolically in money, and then virtually in disembodied bits. That is virtualization: symbolic representation with more and more impact with less and less mass and energy.

At the dawn of life, value was embodied first in analog form in the biological processes of single celled organisms, and then symbolically in digital form by RNA and DNA. That too is virtualization. But life also teaches us that when things are virtualized, reproduction becomes easier, and biological dynamics of reproduction and evolution arise. Virtualization is a step on the road to biologization. Today, information products are being virtualized. To fully understand alternative rights management options, it may be helpful to look closely at a spectacularly successful economy based not on state-sanctioned currencies, but upon unregulated reproduction, competition, and innovation. That economy is all around. It is the world of biology. My goal in this paper will be to provide a broad historical, if idiosyncratic perspective on the past and present evolution of digital objects and rights management systems. Needless to say, these ideas are offered as useful speculations, not confident predictions, about the future.

II. Behavioral Engineering and Digital Goods

In the early 1990s, I was a biological psychologist and amateur programmer interested in the co-evolution of biological, social and informational ecologies [4,5]. I studied animal behavior, and had created some useful software for analyzing my data. I wanted to distribute this software, to be compensated for my work, and to take advantage of the then-emerging virtualization of software products by distributing and selling my software over the Internet. I wanted my software to reproduce, like a positive virus, so that users would "infect" their friends by making and sending copies. In those days I was literally studying and observing paramecia as they swam around, reproduced, and proliferated; I had those images in my mind.

The shareware concept had been around for almost a decade, [6] but I knew that my customers, like me, were unlikely to assemble a check, an envelope, and a stamp if their only reward was the delivery, weeks later, of a now-redundant diskette or a postcard-of-thanks. As a behaviorist, I knew that contingencies of reinforcement dictate that meaningful and relevant rewards should be delivered within a fraction of a second of the behaviors they are intended to encourage.

The instant reward I could use was obvious – increased access to the most valuable features of my product. But it was less obvious how I could ensure that the product would be purchased again (and again) each time it was redistributed. Before we consider that puzzle, I would like to revisit the twin issues of virtualization and biologization. Because it turns out that my solution to this practical problem also led me to rethink my understanding of the information economy.

III. Virtualization and Economics

Even with shareware, money usually changes hands under the consensual delusion (or user-interface metaphor) that information products are things – "goods"–

and that publishing is a business in which manufactured things (like books) are traded for things (like gold doubloons) owned by the purchaser. The irony, of course, is that what consumers "hand" over these days typically cannot be "handled" – it is symbols (digitally encoded, perhaps in plastic credit), which give the "bearer" (who "bears" nothing) the right to control the disposition of other symbols in the future. And what consumers get back from publishers is less and less likely to be physical as well: software and music, books and movies are all moving into a realm in which delivery and consumption is the symbolically-controlled execution of virtual operations by virtual machines in virtual places "on the web" or "in the bank".

As these examples show, money was virtualized long before other forms of intellectual property. And as money became virtualized, it became more and more copy enabled. Today it takes the constant vigilance and full force of the most powerful political and military forces in the history of mankind – governments, businesses, and the police forces that back them – to prevent money from being copied by unauthorized parties. Thus, copy-prevention is a time-honored solution to the fact that virtual goods are copy enabled goods.

However, while copy prevention may well be necessary to preserve the integrity of our monetary system and civilization, as we know it, it may well be counter-productive when it comes to other virtual value-objects. The thing-based transaction-metaphor adopted by commercial publishing may have outlived its usefulness.

IV. Virtualization, Biologization and the Information Economy

"Publishing" actually has two very different meanings and histories. The "thing-based manufacturing metaphor" can be said to have started with Gutenberg: books are manufactured, and exchanged for "cash on the barrelhead". But there is also a much-older idea-based information dissemination activity called "publishing" that has been practiced non-commercially for millennia by authors, scholars, pamphleteers, theologians, by flowers (which disseminate vast amounts of genetic information and arrange to have it distributed, at little cost, on the wings of the wind.)

The essential "product" in this case, is information. And information is not a thing. It is a process by which patterns "in-form" – impress themselves upon things. Further, as we have noted, since these patterns are only loosely coupled to the media they inform, they reproduce, they spread, and they evolve. They do not just move from place to place like traditional "things".

To make a long story short, patterns that reproduce, spread and evolve originated in the primal soup 3-4 billion years ago, they spread into (and helped create) protocells, RNA, DNA, and organisms that make their living by informing their environment. Approximately 1 billion years ago, propagating patterns branched out to a new media animal nervous systems that allowed them to reproduce, first via learning, then via spoken patterns of sound, then via written patterns of ink on paper, and just in the last century as patterns of electrons in yet another culture-medium that is now known as the global internet. [7,8]

Thus, over the last century the remarkable dynamics and "technology" of biology have come to be understood. My claim is that digital rights practitioners need to recognize that those dynamics and emerging analogous technologies are an increasingly fundamental part of their own discipline.

V. Nature's Publishing Economy

The "economy of nature" depends relatively little on the principles of thing-based manufacturing economies. Plants and animals do sometimes organize reciprocal resource exchange relationships, but the resources that are exchanged are services (including reproductive services) as often than as they are things. Here is how this observation applied to my own work, and the concept of superdistribution.

You will recall that I wanted my users to copy and redistribute my software, and I wanted to be able to reward those who decided to purchase it by giving them instant access to the product's advanced features. I imagined a happy purchaser passing a copy on to a friend with a recommendation. When the friend executed the program, she would have limited access to the advanced features her friend had purchased, until she committed to a purchase. The moment she made a payment, the product would provide full access. However, she passed copies on to her friends, the copies needed to revert to "demo" mode. Thus, I needed a lock that would respond to a combination of code plus context.

I am sure there were other ways of getting to the right answer, but my inspiration was biology. Biological functions are embodied not in genes nor in the environment, but in the dynamic interaction of genes (code) and the environment. Change either genes or environment, and function (skin color, say) may change.

My code was not going to change; it was going to be copied perfectly (and, I hoped, often). But the environment of one user would be different from the environment of another user. So I could have my code behave differently when it detected that it had been moved from the environment of a purchaser to the environment of a non-purchaser.

(In most systems, including mine, the environment that the software responds to is the user's computers. But in the patent I eventually wrote, and in the future, the enabling environment should be the user herself. After all, it is she who purchases the service. Rights management languages are going to have to accommodate the vagaries and constraints of biometric systems. Can matters of biology and individuality be expressed in ODRL?)

So here is how I ended up vending my animal behavior software. When the program started up, it profiled the user's computer, made a list of relatively stable but idiosyncratic features, added up all the ASCII values of the characters in that list (literally!) to produce a large number, used that computer "fingerprint" as the seed to a random number generator, and generated a many-digit magic "password". The program then looked for that magic number in a "password file" on the users hard drive, and if the right number could be found in that password file, it functioned in "professional mode"; if not, it functioned in "demo mode" and encouraged the user to login by his own password. The nice thing about this arrangement was that even if the password file was copied and redistributed along with the software, the program would still come up in "demo mode" because the magic password for one user's machine was not valid for another user's machine.

Now, the only person who knew how to generate passwords was me. When a customer decided to purchase, she called a software vendor (by phone), he took payment (by credit card or purchase order) and wrote down the fingerprint, and he called me (by phone). I would get calls (sometimes while delivering lectures on cultural transmission and gene environment interaction) and speak the password to the vendor who would later speak it to the customer who would later type it into her password file.

After a year of this, I realized (1) this was working, (2) the idea was potentially more significant (even as biology!) than the animal behavior I was trying to analyze, (3) that it could be applied to software products other than mine, (4) that software was a service (even though I occasionally referred to my business as a random number manufacturing and vending facility) and (5) a password vending service was a good job for a computer – running from class to phone to computer to phone and back to class was silly. So the patent I wrote [1] and the business I started was (SoftLock Services aka DigitalGoods.com) was based on the idea of a software toolkit that could accommodate multiple authors, multiple products and multiple features, all coupling these product to a password vending system that took payments, delivered passwords, and distributed funds to software developers (and us).

VI. The History of "Superdistribution"

To my knowledge, this is the earliest example of software-only "superdistribution". The term itself was invented some years earlier by a Japanese computer scientist named Ryoichi Mori who defined it as an "approach to distributing software in which software is made available freely and without restriction but is protected from modifications and modes of usage not authorized by its vendor"[9]. But in fact, Mori's own system presumed the existence of special tamper-proof hardware, as did Brad Cox who popularized the concept and emphasized usage-metering in book and magazine publications around 1994[10, 11]. The concept was further popularized, and arguably co-opted, by Intertrust's founder Vincent Shear.[c.f. 12]

My impression is that most people think of "superdistribution" as a software-only process, like what I implemented. But in any case, a software-only process is certainly more virtual and more viral than one that requires the distribution of special hardware.

It is worth noting, however, that today's superdistribution concepts can be taken still further. Superdistribution could be more virtual. We do not have to assume an "earthbound" payment processing system run by a credit card processing system and linked to the banking network. With peer-to-peer architectures and web services, its possible to imagine a system in which software services or non-monetary information assets were the only "coin of the realm," with transactions being remunerated not with money but with scrip, redeemable for services or information assets. While some of these services would presumably have to be redeemable somewhere, somehow, for something of "nutritional" or "reproductive" value, our concept of payments as well as our products can and will go ever more virtual. It is not clear to me whether ODRL can currently accommodate non-financial remuneration.

A well-worked out example of non-monetary currency is "whuffie," as described in digital rights activist Cory Doctorow's science fiction novel, *Down and Out in the Magic Kingdom* [13] which depicts a world in which "whuffie" a constantly updated measure of reputation that motivates people to do useful and creative things. Anything is available to you if you have good whuffie, and those who make those goods available gain whuffie indirectly. But if you make a lot of enemies, your whuffie plummets. It is a good read, and except for the fact that the whuffie market is mediated by internet-connected brain implants, this futuristic scenario is actually hundreds of millions of years old: among many social mammals mating opportunities and access to environmental resources are often based upon hard-earned social status.

A less outlandish example of non-monetary currencies arises when we consider compensating users for virally superdistributing content. Consumers who recommend and distribute products to their friends are providing marketing, distribution, sales, and technical support services to their recipients. Why should they not be compensated? And if we are going to compensate them, why not compensate them with something that we can "manufacture" at no cost – the right to consume other digital products?

Rights management languages will, therefore, face new challenges as the virtuality and virality of superdistribution arrangements increases. Can ODRL specify compensation rights for people who redistribute but do not modify rights-managed content, and can it specify alternative currencies? (Incidentally during the "Great Ebook Boom of March, 2000", when Stephen King's published his ebook *Riding the Bullet* [14], I tried to determine how much redistribution was actually happening. To my surprise and dismay, there was relatively little. A survey suggested the reason – many of our customers told us they thought that that "wasn't allowed", even though our marketing materials explicitly encouraged them to pass copies to their friends. So one reason we were interested in compensating redistributors was to create some pro-copying propaganda to counter industry brainwashing that implies, with misleading simplicity, that copying violates copyrights.)

VII. Tracking Information Flows?

In order to compensate users for redistributing our products, we would need a good way of tracking redistribution. As a would-be "information ecologist" this was of great interest to me for other reasons as well.

First, I think that tracking the flow of digital objects and activities is a huge scientific opportunity. A field biologist once told me that hydrologists sometimes map Biscayne Bay in Florida by dropping thousands of oranges into the water, and taking aerial photos a day later. Because oranges float just beneath the surface and drift with the currents, the aerial photos capture a huge "map" marked out in orange-dotted lines. The lines trace water currents; interruptions in the lines show shipping lanes, deviations in the lines provide clues to submerged topographies, etc. The shapeless murk of Biscayne Bay is illuminated and articulated simply by tracking the flow of waterborne objects through the system. We live in a transparent, sea of cyberspace, and for the first time in history, the flow of information through that sea is trackable and accessible over a global, growing Internet. This is a major development in the multi-billion year history of life and mind, and it is happening in our lifetimes. It is a big story, and a big scientific opportunity.

Second, as a sometime entrepreneur, I think that tracking documents and information transactions will be a big business opportunity. When the information economy is as significant as the physical economy, "infonomic indicators" should be as important and as valuable to economists and market analysts as balance of trade statistics, the Dow Jones Industrial Index, etc. etc.

This raises further questions for rights-language developers.

Can ODRL allow content owners or superdistributors to claim ownership of valuable tracking data that are by-products of data-transactions, but not embodied in the rights-managed digital object itself?

VIII. Tracking Information Flows: How?

Not surprisingly, my ideas about how to track information flows came from biology [2]. By exploiting the fact that each individuals genetic code is unique yet similar to that of close relatives, biologists have recently learned to reconstruct amazingly precise lineages of descent (pedigrees) going back hundreds of generations. These techniques have produced profound advances in biology, ecology, medicine, pharmaceutics, forensics, etc. Similarly, significant advances would probably follow from a comparable system for reconstructing digital pedigrees of redistributed and evolving digital objects. After all, digital objects are increasingly the DNA of civilization.

One way to make digital objects trackable is record document transformations, reproductions, and the current context of use in a data field embedded within the object. Each time the object is accessed, we can check to see if the current context matches a previously stored fingerprint of the context, and if it does not, we can know that the object has been moved to a new context. In that case, we can append the new context fingerprint to the data field (thus preserving lineage information) and update our record of current context. In this way (and there are other ways) each digital object could have a family tree that would allow us to trace redistributed objects back, through all of its intermediary stages and users, to the original source. Then we can examine those data objects "in the field," or monitor their passage through mail servers, or have them periodically "phone home" to databases, and cross-reference with other data about purchases, purchasers, etc.

Does ODRL allow us to assert rights over, and prohibit tampering of, portions of a document that are intended to change, randomly or in a directed fashion, over time?

IX. Redistribution and the Privacy Problem

Document tracking also raises profound ethical issues. I suspect that a lot of redistribution tracking is already happening, but that it is unpublicized because document tracking invades the privacy of those who receive files as well as those who send them. It is a serious concern – suppose right-to-lifers used this methodology to identify and harass women to whom friends forward documents on abortion counseling? And recommended best practices are of little help: even if senders are informed about corporate privacy policies and allowed to specify the uses to which their personal data might be put, recipients of redistributed documents have no such choice or control.

I think digital rights management languages could be pressed into service here. Since the privacy problem has become a digital data problem, why not treat personal data as intellectual property owned by the people to whom it applies? If each of us owned our personal data, each of us could use rights languages, copyright laws, and rights management systems to protect our privacy, fatten our wallets, and/or heighten public awareness of intellectual property law, the masses would benefit from the growing power of intellectual property law, and we could encourage people to make valuable data available and marketable. (Does ODRL allow users to assert ownership of data generated by their handling of a given document?)

A number of organizations have envisioned an anonymizing infomediary service, a "Personal Information Trust" (PIT), which collects, protects, and optionally sells anonymized personal information data in such a way that marketers could communicate with specific individuals (with consent under specified conditions) without learning the individual's identities, and in such a way that each individual could discontinue that communication at any time. Essentially, the PIT would be a "go-between" or "Swiss bank account" that could increase the value, and decrease the liabilities, of personal information by pooling information from diverse sources and by making a market for information buyers and sellers. [15]

The economics and ecology of the PIT would be quite interesting, because isolated snippets of data become more informative and therefore, more valuable when they are commingled with other data in the PIT. This would allow the PIT to pay information deposits, and each information purchase would add still more value to the PIT because data the information purchases are themselves valuable. A healthy PIT, like a healthy ecology, could actually "clean" the personal information environment by creating a value-gradient that would cause personal information to aggregate in the value-enhancing, privacy protecting, database, where it would earn money for the PIT and for the people it represents, through the sale of data and permission to contact targeted consumers.

While one can imagine many models for the governance, economics, and regulation of the PIT, the initial questions for rights language developers are clear. Can ODRL be applied to data generated by information transactions between and among individuals, marketers? Does it allow individuals to specify the conditions under which they are willing to be contacted by marketers, or to let marketers or analysts make use their personal data (anonymized or otherwise) for other purposes?

X. Evolving Digital Life

As I said earlier, living things do not just move from place to place. They reproduce, they spread, and they evolve. So far I have argued that digital objects can reproduce, can spread, and can be profitably tracked much like living things. I now want to suggest that its just a matter of time before they are "genetically engineered" to evolve and adapt through a process very much like natural selection.

Consider the case of a computer program that runs in "demo mode" for a certain number of minutes before demanding that the user purchase a "professional license". What is the right number of minutes? This might be hard to predict, and might vary from one market niche to another. But (1) if the number of minutes is controlled by a mutatable data field, and if (2) the number of minutes influences the probability that users will copy and redistribute the product, then the number of minutes should evolve, through random mutation and differential reproduction, toward values that maximize the likelihood of redistribution.

Thus, by putting functional aspects of a digital object under the control of mutatable code embedded in a frequently copied object, the conditions for natural selection could be created. We would want to select functional aspects that might affect the utility or attractiveness of a product, and we would want to constrain the degree of functional variation so that mutations could not have unacceptably negative (or fatal) effects. But even within such constraints there are many ways we might do this.

Of course, natural selection maximizes reproduction and this may not maximize purchasing, which is what product creators probably care about. But there are ways in which we might select mutations for purchase-encouragement rather than for copy-encouragement per se (see [2], columns 11 and 12).

The point is that in the long run, the difference between software and biology may become vanishingly small. Differential reproduction of inheritable characteristics – may eventually become another tool in the toolbox of the software engineer and the information marketer. If and when that happens, a new chapter in the billion-year history of life and life-like evolution may have begun. Indeed, in retrospect, we may conclude that the new chapter has already begun.

The last few decades brought us several digital revolutions, the open source software movement, the spam explosion, the copyright and patenting of DNA sequences, genetic algorithms, the onslaught of computer viruses and worms, and the emergence of a global information network. All of these things are driven by the "out of control" replication and propagation and evolution of digital objects, many with significant commercial value and social significance. It is the presumptive function of rights management languages to describe and facilitate the regulation or husbandry of these phenomena.

In this sense, rights management languages are themselves among the most interesting recent developments in the primal soup that constitutes today's information ecology. It will be interesting to see how well rights management languages can be designed for adaptive evolution.

(Jonathan Schull received a Ph.D. in Biological Psychology from the University of Pennsylvania in 1980, taught at Haverford College until 1992, and then gave up tenure to found SoftLock Services, an early rights management company, that later changed its name to DigitalGoods.com. Schull now teaches Human Computer Interaction in the Interactive Media group, in the Information Technology Department of the Rochester Institute of Technology, and continues to pursue his long-standing interest in the dynamics of intelligent and adaptive networks).

References

1. Schull, J "Method for encouraging purchase of executable and non-executable software". US Patent 5509070, 1992.
2. Schull, J "Method for tracking software lineage". US Patent 6266654, 2001.
3. Open Ebook Forum, Framework for an E-publishing Ecology, v0.78, 2000. *www.openebook.org/doc_library/ecology/A%20Framework%20for%20the%20* Epublishing%20Ecology.pdf
4. Rozin, P, Schull, J "Adaptive-evolutionary perspectives and experimental psychology". In S.S. Stevens' *Handbook of Experimental Psychology*, R Atkinson, R, Hernstein, G Lindzey, & R.D. Luce (Eds.), New York: Wiley, 1988.
5. Schull, J, "The View from the Adaptive Landscape". In *Parallel Problem Solving from Nature*, H.P. Schwefel and R. Manner, eds. Springer Verlag, 1991.
6. Association of Shareware Professionals. *History of Shareware. http://www.asp-shareware.org/ users/history-of-shareware.asp 2000.*
7. Dawkins, R The *Selfish Gene*. Oxford: Oxford University Press, 1976. Chapter 11.
8. Kelly, K *Out of Control: The New Biology of Machines, Social Systems, and the Economic World*, 1994. Reading, Mass.: Addison-Wesley, 1994. *http://www.kk.org/outofcontrol/contents.php*
9. R Mori, and M Kawahara, "Superdistribution: The Concept and the Architecture". *The Transactions Of The Ieice; Vol.e 73, No.7 July l990 Special Issue on Cryptography* and Information Security. *http://www.virtualschool.edu/mon/ElectronicProperty/MoriSuperdist.ht ml#Mori*
10. Cox, B "Superdistribution". *Wired*, 2.09, Sept 1994. *http://www.wired.com/wired/archive/ 2.09/superdis.html*
11. Cox, B "Superdistribution". Reading, Mass.: Addison-Wesley, 1995
12. Weber, R The *Superdistribution Chronicles, Pt. 1. http://robertweber.typepad.com/ rightsmanagement/2005/02/the_superdis tri.html*
13. Doctorow, C *Down and Out in the Magic Kingdom*. New York: Tor, 2003. *http:// www.craphound.com/down/download.php*
14. King, S *Riding the Bullet. http://www.simonsays.com/content/content.cfm?sid =33&pid= 479688*
15. OpenPrivacy.org, *An Annotated OpenPrivacy Bibliography http://www.openprivacy.org/ bibliography.shtml*

DRM Vs Spyware

Digital Rights Management (DRM) is touted as a technology that prevents digital piracy in a big way. However, there is a debate about the acceptability of certain features of DRM, which is similar to a typical Spyware.

For example, Sony-BMG has used DRM technology in its CD to stop illegal copying of its music files, however, it turned out to cause serious security and privacy problems for users. The company used the XCP and MediaMax (these two are anti-copying technologies) to stop illegal copying of music files. These were designed in such a way that they get installed without user's consent, they resist deletion, and transport the users information back to the vendor; thus, it led to the public outcry and are considered as Spyware.

For vendors like Sony-BMG, DRM is anti-copying technology, but from consumer point of view it is spyware as it is invading the privacy of the consumer. This leads to legal quandary.

Can the future DRM systems overcome this legal quandary? The future is uncertain, nothing can be predicted.

The only thing we can say is that organizations must take enough care before implementing any DRM, as it may be possible that in an attempt to protect their intellectual property, they may intrude into others privacy.

INDEX

E

F

G

H

I

J

K

M

N

P

R

S